GABLE'S WOMEN

JANE ELLEN WAYNE

GABLE'S WOMEN

Prentice Hall Press • New York

To Jerry Perles,
my lawyer and friend,
for his faith and counseling

Copyright © 1987 by Jane Ellen Wayne
All rights reserved, including the right of reproduction
in whole or in part in any form.

Published by Prentice Hall Press
A Division of Simon & Schuster, Inc.
Gulf + Western Building
One Gulf + Western Plaza
New York, NY   10023

PRENTICE HALL PRESS is a trademark of Simon & Schuster, Inc.

Library of Congress Cataloging-in-Publication Data

Wayne, Jane Ellen.
  Gable's women.

  Includes index.
   1. Gable, Clark, 1901–1960—Relations with women.
2. Moving-picture actors and actresses—United States—
Biography.   3. Actresses—Biography.   I. Title.
PN2287.G3W39   1987   791.43′028′0924   [B]   86-25598
ISBN 0-13-346040-1

Designed by C. Linda Dingler

Manufactured in the United States of America

10 9 8 7 6 5 4 3 2 1

First Edition

ACKNOWLEDGMENTS

Clark Gable, who began his amazing career as a bit player, never forgot those years of struggling. After he became the "King of Hollywood," he preferred the company of the "little people," as he called them—the extras, supporting players, directors, writers, photographers, and technicians who knew him best.

These old-timers reminisced about Gable's marriages, romances, flings, and affairs—the broken hearts, frustrations, and indiscretions—and how he tried to live up to his reputation as the greatest lover of all time.

Sincere thanks to the late Joan Crawford and Robert Taylor and their friends, who walked the lonely path to stardom with Gable. I respect the anonymity of those who wished to contribute without credit or fanfare.

—THE AUTHOR

CONTENTS

PREFACE

Joan Crawford confessed to an affair with Clark Gable that lasted thirty years. "He was a dear friend who came to me whenever he needed advice," she said. "There will never be anyone like him again. He had more magnetism than any man on earth. But he wasn't a satisfying lover. I often tried to distract him from the bedroom."

Gable had four wives during his affair with Crawford, who was delighted that he married actress Carole Lombard. "They were so right for each other," Crawford said. "We could never have made a go of it."

Lombard, who did not mince words, told friends during her engagement to Gable, "He's a lousy lay, but I adore him!"

Though Gable made love to hundreds of women, he had his favorites, such as Joan Crawford and an ordinary-looking Hollywood writer who was his constant bed partner. "When Clark gets to the crest of his passion," the writer told a friend, "it's nothing, really. Never was. But when I opened my eyes and saw it was Clark Gable looking down at me, I got into the swing of things."

Crawford, who knew him best, had compassion for Gable. "It was impossible for him to live up to his reputation," she said. "He had no ego, but he knew his performance in the bedroom lacked fireworks. So he spent a lifetime trying to change that. Even when he was married to Carole, whom he loved more than his career, he was always in bed with someone else. Very few women got past him."

Gable was a quiet man who rarely bragged about his conquests, and caused quite a sensation when he was shown a photo of the MGM stable of gorgeous leading ladies and said smiling, "They're all beautiful and I've had every one of them!" In direct contrast, he was very blunt about rumors of his impotency. "Everyone says I'm a bad lay," he quipped. "I guess I'll just have to practice more."

To understand Clark Gable is to understand the many interesting women in his life. He had five wives, but one marriage never was consummated and one elopement occurred during a drunken binge. One wife taught him how to act before he walked out. Another gave him a taste of the finer things in life before he walked out. He was introduced to society by his fourth wife before he locked her out. His true love was Carole Lombard, whose untimely death set off in him a death wish. And there was the mother of his son, who was born after he suffered a fatal heart attack.

There never would have been a Clark Gable had it not been for his women on and off the screen. It was female influence that guided him to the throne of Hollywood and to the grave where he rests next to Carole Lombard. He was a man's man but could not attribute what he called "luck" to anyone or anything but the opposite sex.

He was not fond of Vivien Leigh, his co-star in *Gone With the Wind*, because Gable liked "dishy" dames. He considered playing Rhett in the first place only because he thought Carole Lombard would be cast as his Scarlett. And he was an all-American guy who objected to a British girl's getting the plum role that every Hollywood actress wanted so desperately. He worked harder on this award-winning movie than he did as a boy on the farm, but it was Vivien Leigh who won the Oscar. Losing to Robert Donat for *Good-Bye, Mr. Chips,* Gable was relieved to say, "Good-bye, Miss Leigh!"

Regardless, *Gone With the Wind* has kept the legend of Clark Gable very much alive today and undoubtedly will do so forever.

He was a humble, endearing gentleman—a bull and a beast on-screen, but a lamb off-camera.

The women who loved Gable were not after his money or the limelight. He was irresistible but never lied about his intentions. Maybe he was married or maybe he was single, but if anyone called the shots, it was Gable, not the other way around. "One dame is pretty much like another," he said. "They're all the same."

If Clark Gable wasn't the lover we assumed he was, he had a wonderful time trying to live up to his reputation. To have a deeper insight into his women is to know the man who was King of

Hollywood . . . a man to be admired and pitied. No one could change him. What you saw was what you got, and if that wasn't so great, why did they all come back for more?

Only Gable's women knew the answer.

*Our engagement is off, you
son of a bitch! Here's one
dame who isn't chasing you.*

—LOMBARD TO GABLE, 1936

I
THE
EARLY
YEARS

CHAPTER ONE

Gary Cooper was called "Studs" because he was a well-endowed lover. *In like Flynn* was a popular term after Errol Flynn went on trial for statutory rape. Tyrone Power loved men but married women. Robert Taylor was almost ruined by his "Pretty Boy" image. And the press referred to Rudolph Valentino as "The Pink Powder Puff."

They were legends on and off the silver screen, but there was only one King of Hollywood—Clark Gable.

"I don't believe it," he said, "but the public docs, and I know why. They want to believe it. They see me as an ordinary guy, like a construction worker or the guy who delivers your piano all by himself. And when I make love to a woman on the screen, I rough them up a bit before they beg for a kiss. I don't open doors for them. They open doors for me! Light my cigarettes, too. A dame won't admit she likes it, but men are getting away with a slap and a boot. It's reality. So I'm king for showing them how to treat a lady."

Clark Gable climbed to his throne in *A Free Soul*, his sixth movie. In 1931, Norma Shearer was an Oscar-winning star. Though she wasn't beautiful by Hollywood standards, she had the ability to convince millions that she was. And she was married to MGM's boy genius, Irving Thalberg. That didn't hurt. Despite her high-pitched voice, mediocre talent, and plain looks, Norma had determination, class, and a knack for stealing a scene without trying. Much like Gable, she possessed the "it" factor—that indescribable something that attracted moviegoers.

In *A Free Soul*, Shearer was rich, spoiled, cold, and sexy. Clark was a self-made racketeer who wore checkered suits and flashy ties. Void of a virile, socially acceptable bed partner, she finds him physically attractive, and Gable becomes her stud until she flaunts his lack of breeding and culture. She teases and plays with him, taunts and laughs, changes from ermine to chinchilla, and finally makes it obvious that he's good for one thing—a roll in the hay.

"Come on," she whispers. "Put your arms around me."

Gable smiles and picks her up in his arms, but instead of going to the bedroom, he dumps her on the living-room chair and growls, "You're a spoiled silly brat who needs a hairbrush every now and then."

When Norma tries to get up, he pushes her back in the chair and says, "Take it and like it!"

Moviegoers went wild. Women crouched in their seats with one thought: "My God, what a thrill to have that big handsome brute do that to me!" And the men said to themselves, "It's about time we showed these dames who's boss!"

Gable was a hit. He became a symbolic blend of man and beast. A good-looking, easygoing guy who could take just so much. This summed up the Great Depression the country was struggling through. It was "get tough" time with broads wearing ermine. After all, people were standing in bread lines. But moviegoers managed a few pennies for stamps and sent thousands of letters to MGM asking to see more of "the guy who slapped Norma Shearer."

The studio capitalized on what the public thought they saw in *A Free Soul* by rushing Gable into *Night Nurse*. This time he took a good swing and socked Barbara Stanwyck in the kisser. (He would do this to her again twenty years later.)

Though Gable proved that he was King of Hollywood, it is difficult to say whether he would have caused such a sensation had he had any competition. In the early thirties, there was a shortage of leading men in Hollywood. Not long after Valentino died, the talkies ruined matinee idol John Gilbert. Talent scouts invaded college campuses and legitimate theaters looking for handsome young men. Meanwhile, with a little help from Robert Montgomery, Gable was responsible for tempering Constance Bennett, Jean Harlow, Fay Wray, Greta Garbo, Marion Davies, Claudette Colbert, Myrna Loy, and Loretta Young almost singlehanded.

Then there was the matter of his looks, which left a lot to be desired. Ben Piazza, casting director for MGM, said, "With those ears, Gable's head looks like a giant sugar bowl!" Others said his ears stuck out like barn doors. He had rotten teeth that were badly capped, and huge apelike hands.

MGM publicity man Howard Strickling said, "Meeting Gable for the first time was quite an experience. He was the biggest man I had ever seen. His hands and feet were tremendous. His head was too big, and his ears... well, they were tremendous. He was a powerful man, and I worried that he might hurt somebody, but he never did. I said to myself, 'What a hell of a man!' Nothing actorish, but he had charm and knew how to handle people. I felt that he genuinely liked me at our first meeting."

Gable's straightforward, gentle manner and devilish grin endeared him to everyone on and off the screen. Joan Crawford described his aura: "I knew when this man walked on the set, and I didn't know which door he came in, but I knew he was there. That's how great he was. This magnetic man had more sheer animal magic than anyone in the world, and every woman knew it."

Claudette Colbert said, "Gable was divine. I jumped at the prospect of working with him every day and getting paid for it besides."

Jean Harlow never admitted to an affair with Gable, despite the fact that they could not keep their hands and lips off each other. Much like Greta Garbo and John Gilbert during their first love scene together, Harlow and Gable did not let go when the director yelled, "Cut!" It was hard to say whether their kisses were hotter off-camera or on.

Barbara Stanwyck and Joan Blondell had to sit down or faint when he arrived on the set for *Night Nurse*. Gable was a nobody then, so it wasn't the great sweat of anticipation. Blondell said, "Any woman who wasn't attracted to him was dead."

Gable's ego wasn't inflated by the enormous attention he was getting, but he rarely passed up an opportunity with women. "It's not a matter of 'if,'" he once said. "Only a matter of 'when.'" But the game of getting to the bedroom was more fun for Gable than closing the door behind him. He was, underneath a tough exterior, a romantic fellow. In his youth he wasn't aware of it, because there were no roses or champagne during the conquest. Was there time? There were no words of love, no lies, and no promise of a next time. Perhaps his attitude was misjudged occasionally. There was a famous story about the maid who walked into his hotel room while he was naked in bed. She apologized, but he asked her to join him.

"How much?" the maid asked.

Gable sat up in bed and laughed. "I would think, my dear, that being with me is payment enough!"

Apparently it wasn't, because she left.

MGM officials spent millions trying to avoid such situations.

Their stars were like precious jewels—priceless and irreplaceable. Male stars were vulnerable and easy prey for scandal and blackmail. In the thirties the only venereal diseases, syphilis and gonorrhea, were curable, but not so elopements and adulterous affairs. MGM had good reason to have a cat house near the studios. Many of the girls were former actresses and studio rejects; the rest were carefully chosen for their beauty and skill, and groomed and attired for passion. They were great company, apparently, because MGM's stable of gods spent many delightful evenings there.

After five years in Hollywood, Gable admitted he'd rather go to a whorehouse. "When it's over, it's over. No questions, no tears, no farewell kisses." And then he met actress Carole Lombard. She was blond, slim, witty, talented, beautiful, and the woman Gable had been waiting for and never thought he would find. No one will dispute the fact that Gable's first two marriages, to older women, were for convenience, giving him every excuse to play around, but the pattern did not stop after Carole Lombard became his wife. Yet he loved her more than life itself, and she knew it.

Maybe Clark Gable wasn't the lover fans thought he was, but he had a glorious time trying. Not that he cared what anyone thought, because he did what he wanted to do so long as no one got hurt. He was a devil, a man's man, a woman's Lancelot, a movie fan's dream, Scarlett's Rhett, a King of Kindness and integrity who just happened to like the bedroom more than applause—a guy who could love one woman even if he did not know how to be faithful. Gable could get away with more than most. It wasn't what he did, but how he did it. When the motherless boy came forth, all resentments melted.

Proof of this is his affair with Joan Crawford, who was blunt, revengeful, and possessive. She usually got what she wanted, one way or another. Her second husband, Franchot Tone, was forced to his knees when she demanded an apology. But Tone did not have the guts that Gable did; as Crawford put it, "Clark had balls." Their relationship defied everything written about her. She had a brief fling with Spencer Tracy, until he lashed out at her on the set one day when she forgot her lines: "For Christ's sake, Joan, I thought you were supposed to be a pro!" She stormed to her dressing room. End of affair.

With Gable, she learned to be a friend if that was what he wanted. Her shoulder was always available to him, and he took her advice. Otherwise, it's more than likely that he would have walked out of *Gone With the Wind*. He detested the movie and he disliked Vivien Leigh. But Crawford asked him to stick it out, which was unusual because she had fought for the part of Scarlett O'Hara, with her spite, her talent, and her body, and ultimately it was probably because of Gable that she wasn't chosen.

Crawford apparently made an exception in Gable's case throughout their affair. If a man cheats on his wife, it's considered normal, but if he cheats on his mistress he's a louse. Gable's attraction to Loretta Young in 1935 was common knowledge. How did Joan feel about this? She married Franchot Tone. "He's mature, considerate, and stimulating," she said. Ironic, because Gable was divorcing his second wife and on location in a mountaintop with Young, who may have had his child. She retired from the screen for a year and came home with an "adopted" daughter who looked just like her mother and who reportedly had big ears!

There were never any secrets in Hollywood, but the stars had mutual respect even though they would fight one another bitterly for a good role. Off the movie set, however, to avoid being ruined themselves, they protected their peers from scandal. The gossip today is that Gable has a daughter living in Los Angeles, born in 1936. Director William Wellman was blunt in his biography: "All I know is that Miss Young went away after making *Call of the Wild* with Gable and returned with an adopted daughter who had the biggest ears I ever saw with the exception of an elephant." At the time, it was illegal in California for a single person to adopt a child—a strict law that was not enforced in Loretta Young's case.

A year later Gable was involved in a paternity suit that resulted in a sensational court trial, but he had never met the girl who claimed she had met Gable in England. Gable won, and rightfully so.

He thought the worst was behind him when Carole Lombard came into his life. And he was selected for the part of Rhett Butler in the movie of the century, *Gone With the Wind*. Almost forty years old, he had finally found happiness, security, and contentment in a town that bred suicide and scandal and sin. Fame, however, had its price. Didn't Crawford find this out when she was blackmailed for having made pornographic films when she needed the money? Then there was Marilyn Monroe's nude calendar, Clara Bow's busy boudoir, Mary Astor's diary, Jean Harlow's impotent husband, and Robert Mitchum's marijuana bust.

Gable had a skeleton. As a struggling actor in the twenties, he admitted doing anything to become a star. His involvement with silent screen idol William Haines was an attempt at recognition. Haines was an admitted homosexual, and his film career was finally ruined. He became a successful Hollywood interior decorator and stayed friendly with director George Cukor, who was assigned to direct *Gone With the Wind*. Gable was powerful enough to have Cukor replaced by Victor Fleming. According to producer David Selznick, Cukor was showing a preference for Vivien Leigh, and Gable claimed that Cukor was a "woman's director." In every account of this switch in directors, there are lame excuses, none of which made sense. What did was Gable's intense hatred of Cukor, who preferred men to women off the set. *Photoplay* magazine had just damned the Gable-Lombard affair (among others) and Clark wanted to make sure his image was clean for *Gone With the Wind*. Any hint of scandal in 1938 would keep moviegoers away from the theater, and regardless of Gable's popularity, Selznick demanded purity from his cast.

Clark's fear of being exposed by Cukor was most likely exaggerated, but the ladder is shakiest at the top. That can be said for the perfect love, too, because after Lombard's death Gable cared about nothing, including himself. Most people have a drink before dinner. Gable had a fifth. He got into World War II hoping to get killed. Instead he got gray, and he refused to dye his hair. He was tired, but not old—fed up, but not through. Clark Gable was still a star, but he thought of himself as a widower and a war veteran.

Headline: GABLE'S BACK AND GARSON'S GOT HIM.

He hated *Adventure,* his first movie after the war, and wasn't fond of MGM's pet, Greer Garson. The slogan made him sick. At this time in his career, Gable wanted to retire from films. "I'm acting strictly for the money," he told a friend. "I don't want to be very rich, but I won't give up what I have."

He dated Lombard look-alikes. Reporters said that if they blinked, Gable was with another girl. He drank heavily, took Dexedrine to lose weight, almost killed himself in a car accident—and got laid.

He got too drunk and married again, sobered up and suffered through an endless hangover of booze, unhappiness, and divorce.

He and Grace Kelly almost tied the knot. They did nothing to hide their feelings. Each lays claim to the breakup. The consensus is that Gable wasn't in love, despite her startling resemblance to Carole.

His last marriage brought him happiness and a son born too late.

Who knows how long he would have lived if Marilyn Monroe's tardiness hadn't driven him mad during *The Misfits*. He drove himself too hard—too much liquor, too many cigarettes in heat that reached 115 degrees, and stunts that men half his age wouldn't attempt.

Joan Crawford claims that Gable called her when he was making *The Misfits*. "The title sums up this mess," he said. "Miller, Monroe, and Clift. They don't know what the hell they're doing. We don't belong in the same room together. It's a mess—a goddamn fucking disgrace!"

Marilyn Monroe's fantasy was Gable. She wanted him to make love to her. In one of their bedroom scenes the towel she was wearing slipped off and his hand touched her breast. "It was the most thrilling moment," she said. "When he kissed me, I wanted to go on and on and on. When he pinched my ass, I got goose bumps. I'd have followed him anywhere, done anything. It was a miracle just to be in his arms."

When he died, she was brokenhearted. Accusations that her tardiness had killed Gable drove Marilyn to another suicide attempt.

Robert Taylor, a close friend of Gable's, said it was tough being on his own after so many years under the protective wing of MGM. "Hell, we were told what to do and how to do it," he said. "If we weren't on time for work, the studio had the right to suspend us. They arranged our marriages and divorces. We were disciplined and controlled. We were brainwashed, but we made better movies, because there was organization. Clark was with MGM for twenty years, and I left five years later. Major studios weren't signing stars to long-term contracts anymore, and television took its toll of those of us who wanted to make good films. Decent scripts were hard to find. Clark did *The Misfits* for the money, simple as that, but he was too professional to sit around and wait for his co-star to show up. I might have done those dangerous stunts too. I don't know..."

Marilyn Monroe reminded Gable of Jean Harlow. Both actresses had fragile egos despite their blond sex-goddess images. They lacked self-confidence, and Gable knew it. He helped Harlow through her husband's suicide scandal and was co-starring with her when she

collapsed and died. Thirty years later he found himself with another
pathetic young girl who desperately needed his kind words and patience. Was Marilyn Monroe responsible for Gable's death? Or was it
the same lack of masculine ego that forced him to prove his virility in
bed? Was he trying to prove to the younger generation that he could
keep up—maybe outdo them? Would he have done his own stunts
anyway? Was he still on the self-destructive path he took after Lombard's sudden death?

It was a known fact that he had a heart condition. He wasn't able
to get insurance for *The Misfits* until he stayed in bed for a few days.
Gable was a risk, but, like Tracy in his final film, he managed to
finish before closing his eyes for the last time.

What's in a name?

Hollywood thought it should match the image of the star being
molded. Lucille LeSueur became Joan Crawford, Spangler Arlington
Brugh became Robert Taylor, Harlean Carpentier was Jean Harlow,
Marion Morrison was John Wayne's real name, Hedy Lamarr was
much more glamorous than Hedwig Kiesler, and Frederick Austerlitz
tap-danced as Fred Astaire. Edythe Marrener was known as Susan
Hayward, and Issur Danielovitch became Kirk Douglas. Doris Day
was born Doris von Kappelhoff, Claudette Colbert as Lily Chauchoin, and Mickey Rooney's birth certificate read "Joe Yule, Jr."

. . . And then there was William Clark Gable, who decided his
middle name suited him before MGM knew he existed. He preferred
not to be a junior anyway, since he wasn't in touch with his father,
who referred to actors as "sissies." Reliable sources claim that the
name Gable was derived from Goebels. It was true that Clark's an-
cestors came over from Germany and settled in Pennsylvania. Like so
many German immigrants, they referred to themselves as Pennsylvania Dutch. MGM did not deny the Goebel connection, but for obvious reasons made no mention of it.

Clark Gable was born in Cadiz, Ohio, at 5:30 A.M. on February
1, 1901, weighing in at almost eleven pounds. The doctor's fee was
ten dollars.

Giving birth to such a big baby was difficult for the frail and
sickly Adeline Gable, who had been warned by her doctor not to have
children. She died seven months later.

Her husband, William Gable, was a wildcatter. He owned his
own drilling rig and worked six days a week. Sunday was his only day

with the family. When his wife died, he left his son with Adeline's parents. William did not discover oil, but he did find another woman, Jennie Dunlap. When Clark was five years old, they settled in Hopedale, Ohio. He described his stepmother as gracious, slim, and well bred. "She was the best thing that ever happened to me when I was a kid," he said. "She treated me like her own."

"Clarkie," as she referred to him, had a birthday party every year and was the first kid in town to have his own bike. She dressed him like a gentleman, helped him with homework, and dedicated herself to his well-being. "She wanted me to be somebody," Gable said. "It wasn't easy, because my father was the kinda guy who believed in being born, working hard, and dying... if possible, all in the same town. Jennie encouraged me to play the piano, to sing, and to read. On the other hand, my father thought books were a waste of time and he resented paying for them." It was hard on Clark and Jennie to have William take over on Sundays, because his prime aim was to make sure his son was not a sissy. It became an obsession. One reason was the difference in the backgrounds of William and his second wife. He worked with his hands, and Jennie, whose parents were well-to-do, was educated and soft-spoken. It's doubtful that she had ever traveled, but reading brought her the outside world. She wanted Clark to be aware also, and to have a goal, not just dreams. Jennie was well aware that William would expect his son to follow in his footsteps. She didn't want that unless Clark did too. Even then she might have been disappointed.

She encouraged his friends to come to his home, and always had something in the oven. Hopedale was a town of only five hundred people, so it wasn't difficult later to find those who had known the future King of Hollywood.

Thelma Lewis, a pretty redhead, was Clark's first date. "He wasn't good-looking," she confessed. "His ears were too big. He wasn't interested in school, except for playing the alto horn in our band. Clark wasn't a good dancer, either. He was all feet."

Gable was six feet tall and weighed 155 pounds when he was only fourteen years old, but his school chums agreed he wasn't physical. He had the ability to talk fast and be convincing. His one bad habit was smoking, and he'd never give it up.

The turning point in Clark's life was his father's decision to settle down on a farm—another traumatic farewell to friends and familiar surroundings. As much as Jennie wanted William home, she was concerned for her stepson. Farming was not a job for one man. It required teamwork from sunrise to sunset. This move came at a time when Clark was sure he wanted to be a doctor. So Jennie went along with her husband's new venture with mixed emotions.

In later years, Gable described what happened. "Working on that farm meant getting up at four in the morning every day of the year, spring, summer, fall, and winter, and the winters sure were cold in Ohio. I fed the hogs, the rest of the stock, plowed in the morning until every muscle ached, and forked hay in the hot sun until I was sweating crops of calluses. I did what I was expected to do on the farm, but I just didn't have what it takes."

He missed Hopedale, too—the high-school plays, romping on second base when he wasn't hitting well, and the basketball team. "Nothing was the same," he said. "I towered over the other kids on the school bus, hated doing homework, and dreaded coming back to that farm. When I was sixteen, I made up my mind to go back to Hopedale and work for a while. For five dollars a day hauling water for the miners, I might be able to afford a Model T. A buddy of mine, Andy Means, said he was going to Akron because there were good-paying jobs there in the rubber industry."

William was furious. "You'll stay here and work on the farm!"

Clark remembers well the fighting and how Jennie sided with him. William never gave his permission and made it understood that he would not give his son a penny. "There wasn't a doubt in my mind that I'd go to Akron with Andy," Gable said, "but I respected my father and wanted his blessing. It was Jennie who convinced him to let me go in peace. If it hadn't been for her, I'd probably still be pitching hay in Ohio."

Jennie told him not to be proud. "You're not that far away from home," she said, "and if you don't like the big city, you can always come back."

She regretted his quitting school. Clark did too, but he felt he had no choice. He got a job as timekeeper at Miller Rubber Company for twenty-five dollars a week. "I'd never been to a movie," he said. "We didn't have theaters where I came from. I loved westerns, but it never entered my mind about becoming a movie star. It was the stage that thrilled me. The Music Hall on Exchange Street was featuring a play called *Bird of Paradise,* about the South Sea islands. I'd never seen anything so exciting in my life—but then, one has to realize where I came from."

All other thoughts and ambitions came to a halt—medicine, money, cars, and sports. He took a job as callboy for nothing but tips, slept in the theater, showered at the YMCA and did odd jobs for extra money and a decent meal. "I even sewed buttons on costumes," he said, "to get the actors on cue."

Gable was hungry and broke, but he was the happiest guy in the world when he was offered a walk-on part that called for three words: "Good evening, sir." It was the thrill of a lifetime, and despite the grand moments to follow, he would never forget how he felt on-stage the first time. Only a telegram from his father about Jennie's serious illness dampened his excitement. He was with her when she died. "I lost my best friend," he said.

After selling the farm, William asked his son to accompany him to the Oklahoma oil fields, but Clark returned to Akron. Unfortunately, the stock players had left town, and the new group did not give him a job, with or without pay. Depressed and broke, he joined his father as an apprentice near Bigheart, Oklahoma. For twelve dollars a day he chopped wood to fuel the boiler fires, swung a jackhammer, and cleaned the stills. He slept in a hot tent during the summer and a shack in the cold of winter. Only two things kept him there—his determination to be an actor and the three hundred dollars left to him in his grandfather's will. On his twenty-first birthday, Clark was waiting at the courthouse in Meadville, Pennsylvania. William expected him to return to Oklahoma after claiming the legacy, but Clark went to Kansas City, where, he had heard, a new repertory company was being organized.

William was shocked and disappointed. "I told the stubborn mule if he left me this time, he needn't ever come back. I was through with him!"

Gable had no roots after Jennie's death and felt no obligation to his father. Had William ever understood him? Had he ever had feelings for anyone else other than himself? Though unaware of it at the time, Clark had an uneasy trust in men. His friend Andy Means had run home when he lost his job, but through it all, Jennie had sent food and money until she was too weak to stand. During these hungry and frustrating weeks, he developed a hatred for his father that would exist forever. As for William, he had no respect for Clark even when his name blazed on the marquee. "Actors are sissies," he maintained.

•   •   •

When Gable arrived in Kansas City, he found himself with a traveling tent show. He convinced himself that they hired him for an occasional acting part, but the owners saw a big husky brute ideal for hoisting tents. "I did a little bit of everything for ten dollars a week," he said, ". . . played the French horn in the orchestra, hawked plays dressed as a clown on street corners, and occasionally had a chance to act. That's what they called it."

He mentioned an affair with an older woman who was a member of the tent show; he claimed she had only one eye. Those who knew Gable's sense of humor in later years assume he was kidding. And what about the whores who were sheltered in the oil-field shacks in Oklahoma? Was he bragging? Exaggerating? Telling tall tales? Maybe, but William was too anxious for Clark to become a real man, and one sure way to accomplish that was to put him in bed with a spirited woman who was desperate for a buck. The one-eyed actress in the tent show wasn't so farfetched, either. When Gable was every woman's passion on the screen, he often bedded down the ugliest. Why? "She was there," he said. During the heavy snowstorms in Butte, Montana, when the tent show went broke because customers were stranded in their homes, anything was possible. If there is anything of significance, it was Gable's attraction to older women.

When the tent show folded for good, he hopped a refrigerator train and got off in Bend, Oregon. "The first thing I saw was a lumber company near the tracks, so I went inside to get warm. They were hiring, so I stayed for three months. My hands were raw because I couldn't afford gloves. I toughened them with vinegar and lard. Never needed the gloves after all."

After he accumulated some money, he headed for Portland. "I figured I might find a theater there," he said. To avoid starving, he sold ties in a department store, where he met Earle Larimore, who was directing an amateur acting group, the Red Lantern Players. Gable hung around backstage every night until Earle was invited to join a stock company in nearby Astoria. "I tagged along," Clark said, "to try my luck."

This was a turning point in his life.

On July 23, 1922, Gable played the part of Eliza, a Negro cook, in *When Women Rule*. This was the only time he blackened his face for a role. In *The Villain Still Pursued Her*, he was dressed as a baby and seen on-stage in a huge crib. It didn't matter to him why the audience laughed so long as they reacted. Though it could hardly be considered the beginning of an acting career, anything was better than working with his hands. He liked the players, the scenery, the makeup and dusty costumes, the heart beating a little faster as the audience filed into their seats. The applause. For such a husky fellow from a farm in Ohio, who was all feet and hands, only dedication could have persuaded him to put on baby clothes and be wheeled on-stage in a baby carriage. He never said it was humiliating, never complained, and never was discouraged.

Maybe falling in love had something to do with his optimism...

Franz Dorfler was twenty-two years old, a petite five feet two inches tall, with light brown hair and soft dreamy eyes. She had given up schoolteaching to become an actress. Spunky and bright, Franz was serious about the theater and cared little for dating until she met Clark. They met when he auditioned for the Astoria Stock Company. "He was well dressed," she said, "but otherwise I wasn't impressed. He was big, but not healthy-looking. His complexion was yellowish and sallow. He was clumsy, too, and stumbled over his words with a high-pitched voice. However, he was well dressed, because he got his clothes at a discount where he was working."

Gable was having a root beer and flirting with another girl who was waiting to audition. When she left, he offered a sip to Franz, who ignored him. She was eager to get the part of the ingenue and resented being distracted. She got the job and was leaving the theater when Clark offered to walk her home. She said, "No, thank you," and continued on her way. He followed. "He came on too strong," she said. Franz had no idea where he came from or what he wanted, and she wasn't interested in finding out, but he refused to give up and complimented her all the way home. It was love at first sight, she was a fine actress, and so on. By the time they arrived at her house, he almost had her convinced he couldn't live without her.

If Franz and the stock company thought they were through with Gable, they didn't know him. He had nothing to lose by showing up at the tryouts every night. He hadn't been chosen for anything yet, but Franz was there and he continued his flirtation. "I found it difficult to ignore him," she said. "He wasn't good-looking or very mature, but he was lonely, undernourished, and sad. He had no one except Earle, who had a girl friend." When Clark wasn't studying his lines, he was turning on the charm or telling everyone in the theater how much he loved Franz. He'd known her only a few days and was jealous of every man who spoke to her. She didn't take kindly to the fact that newcomers to the theater thought he owned her. Over and over he declared his love. Franz said, "It was hard to believe that he was so possessive and jealous. We barely knew each other, but he wouldn't give up. It was impossible not to like him. Maybe I felt sorry for him, too."

Rex Jewell, director of the Astoria Stock Company, rejected Gable. "He had nothing, absolutely nothing, to offer the stage. He tried so hard, and I tried to find something in his readings or how he carried himself, but he was, in my opinion, hopeless. He barely got on and off stage without a great deal of difficulty."

Clark wasn't able to convince Jewell to take a chance on him, but in the love department, Franz was melting. She was getting used to his being around, beginning to enjoy his compliments, and missed his attention when he wasn't with her. He was always there, but how long does a drifter stay in one place? She was beginning to understand his restlessness and frustration, couldn't help but have compassion for his loneliness and determination to make something of himself. She shared his frustrations. He wanted to be on the stage as much as she did. They had a common goal that few people could fathom.

With all his drawbacks, Clark had something she couldn't identify, but whatever it was, he won her over in a few weeks. Somehow they would find a way to be together. They'd work it out. However, the stock tour was scheduled to leave very soon, and Franz with it. Clark still had his job selling ties, but in his own selfish way, he didn't want her to leave him. Franz was just as mesmerized by the stage as he was and would not consider giving up any part, for him or for anyone else.

If anything came out of those days in Astoria, it was Clark's ability to make friends. Earle offered to help, and with Franz's lovestruck eyes, they managed to convince Jewell that it might be a good idea to take Clark along on the tour. Could he fill in for the actors? He knew all the parts. He could help with the scenery and carry the trunks. What convinced Jewell was Clark's doing all this without pay.

It was a glorious day when the little theater group boarded a paddle-wheeler that would take them up the Columbia River. Franz coached Clark on his lines. They became very close in this romantic setting. Pathetically, he blurted out his aloneness. He had never had anybody. Never. He had never been loved or cared for . . . always ignored. That was why he was so happy with her. Love had overcome all obstacles and suffering—all his needs and wants. Despite his youth and lack of sophistication, he had developed a way with women and a clever line to get their attention and sympathy.

With Franz on this special boat trip, he poured it on and grabbed his first kiss. "I was shocked," she said years later. "But I liked what he did so impulsively. It was wonderful because we could share each other. He was my first beau and I was his first girl friend. We had been looking for each other."

They were young, optimistic, and in love. William had no way of knowing this, of course, because he had no idea where his son was living—whether he was alive or dead. But if the fool still wanted to be an actor, there was proof on the front pages of every newspaper that William was right about the acting profession.

While Clark waited for one of the stock players to get laryngitis or drown in the Columbia River, sin and evil were oozing out of Hollywood. Sad proof of this was beautiful stage and screen actress Olive Thomas, who married Mary Pickford's brother, Jack. Olive was labeled "The Ideal American Girl," and her marriage to Pickford afforded them the title of "The Ideal Couple." But in 1920, Olive's nude body was found in a Paris hotel room. Next to her was a bottle of toxic bichloride of mercury granules. Why would this gorgeous Ziegfeld Follies queen, star of Selznick Productions and sister-in-law of America's Sweetheart, want to kill herself? Jack had a nervous breakdown, for good reason. Poor Olive had been trying, unsuccessfully, to obtain cocaine and heroin for him (and her?). She had been seen in Paris dives the night before her death. A dope ring was exposed, along with the memory of the ideal girl, Olive Thomas—addict.

In 1921 comedy king Fatty Arbuckle was accused of raping and killing actress Virginia Rappe during a wild party in San Francisco. He went on trial three times. Hollywood was on trial, too, because testimonies exposed bootleg booze, orgies, bigamy, and dope. Fatty was acquitted, but his career was ruined. Virginia Rappe's numerous abortions were exposed. Not only had she been pregnant at the time of her death, she had had a bad case of gonorrhea, too. Virginia had been only twenty-five.

While Fatty sat in the courtroom sweating for his life, the press was working around the clock trying to keep up with slander in

Hollywood. On Clark's birthday, February 1, 1922, William Desmond Taylor, famed Paramount director, was shot to death in his bungalow apartment. His servant called Paramount mogul Adolph Zukor first, as is the custom in Hollywood. The police are called after any incriminating evidence has been removed—in Taylor's case, love letters, bootleg booze, photographs, and any signs of sexual misbehavior. Unfortunately, a neighbor called the police, who, during their thorough search for clues, revealed Taylor's affairs with Paramount's virginal beauty Mary Miles Minter and Mack Sennett's star and mistress, Mabel Normand. Their "autographed" panties were found, and again a link to cocaine. Taylor's murderer was never found, but Mary and Mabel were forced to retire.

The saddest Hollywood revelation in 1922 concerned Wally Reid, King of Paramount, the All-American Boy, who was admitted to a private sanitarium. Wally was a victim of overwork and leaned on morphine to keep him going. Happily married, humble, handsome, and talented, he was used by Hollywood—rushed from film to film without a chance to rest. He was a human robot. Morphine gave him the energy and desire to keep up the pace, but he became an addict, and died in a padded cell from the shock of withdrawal.

The loss of thirty-three-year-old Wally Reid—the refreshing chap every girl would be proud to take home to Mother, the guy one would meet at a church picnic or the ice-cream parlor on Main Street, U.S.A.—was a pawn of the camera that focused on him seven days a week, grinding out money that benefited everyone but the innocent Wally.

If William had had a chance to throw these scandals in his son's face, Clark's typical answer would have been "I have no desire to make movies, Father. The stage is beyond all that, a different world and a better one. Don't compare me to film actors."

But Gable didn't have to answer to anyone now. In fact, he wasn't the least bit concerned that he wasn't as talented as Franz, whose life was very organized. She knew precisely what she wanted, and had the patience to wait for it and some credits to prove her ability. Part of her well-thought-out plan was to share her career with a man she loved. Knowing that that would be difficult, she had never been one to date or go to parties. But on those beautiful nights sailing up the Columbia, Franz knew she had found the right man. She would have to wait until he mastered the art, got enough experience to earn a decent living, but that was all she wanted.

She was a well-educated girl who came from a prosperous family. It took a great deal of thought to give up a good teaching job for the sake of acting. No one, including Clark, would stand in her way. But he was willing to follow her, learn everyone's lines, and wait patiently for a walk-on part—all of this to watch her grace the stage each night while he stood in the wings. Franz tried to talk him out of his frequent depressions. He leaned on her for encouragement. "What I liked most about him," she said, "was the ability to always look immaculate. He had that scrubbed-clean look. I never saw him unkempt."

Clark's big chance finally came along when one of the actors in the company quit. Jewell cringed. "Gable fell down the first night. He hasn't fallen since. Now he only staggers, stumbles, and stammers all over the stage. It was a disaster." But Jewell was stuck with him. As it turned out, he was forced to close down for a while, and told his group he planned to reorganize. If they stayed in the area, he'd contact them as soon as possible. Franz was willing, and Clark felt that, despite his blunders, it was worth another try. Besides, Jewell needed him. "I wasn't making ten dollars a week," he said, "and sometimes not even that. All we were really guaranteed was a place to sleep, but it was a challenge. You're always scared the first time you find yourself broke. Later you just feel interested in what is going to lift you out of it this time."

Clark and Franz vacationed at a friend's small cottage in Seaside, with other members of Jewell's cast. They all took turns sleeping on the beach. These were happy times—breezy, romantic, and free. They built fires on the beach, sang songs, took long walks, and discussed their dreams. Clark and Franz became closer than ever as fall approached. He wanted to marry her, and she was willing. They would tour with Jewell's theater group, save money, and pursue the stage together.

In September 1922, they boarded a milk boat and began another river tour. Living conditions were terrible, but Clark was on-stage every night. Because of his high-pitched voice and his clumsiness, he was made for comedy; in drama, the audience laughed for the wrong reasons. But Clark was content knowing that he could snuggle up to Franz on deck and they could read to each other under the stars. Only youth and puppy love could withstand a wooden floor for a bed—often in the rain.

When Jewell closed down, Franz and Clark went to her parents' farm in the Willamette Valley, near Portland. He earned money picking hops and spent his spare time impressing the Dorflers.

When the hop season was over, he got a job with a lumber company for three dollars a day and settled down in a boardinghouse. Each weekend he stayed on the farm with Franz. Her family was his family. The Dorflers, however, began to question their daughter's relationship with this drifter. When Franz hinted at marriage, they tried to discourage her. It was all right for a girl to become an actress, but marrying an actor was asking for trouble. They liked Clark, but made it clear that they could not accept him as a son-in-law. It's possible they influenced Franz to live with her brother in Portland.

Gable was stunned. Why hadn't she discussed it with him first? One day they were happy together and the next she announced, "I want to be near the theater." He stayed behind to earn some money. The Dorflers welcomed him on the farm and tried to cheer him up over the lonely Christmas holidays. A month later he quit his job at the lumber company and went to Portland to be with Franz—who had left for Seattle. He found out later that the heavy snowstorms had delayed her letter to him explaining that she was offered a part in a good play.

Putting his own ambitions aside, Clark got a job as a telephone lineman to earn enough money to marry Franz. They exchanged letters. Hers were full of encouragement. "You have such a fine voice," she wrote. "Why don't you take singing lessons!"

He thought about it. Maybe she was right. If it made her happy, he'd be a singer. Clark felt his efforts were rewarded when Franz attended his recital in June. "He wasn't bad," she said. "Before I returned to Seattle, I promised to marry Clark by the end of the year."

Optimistic again and looking forward to a Christmas wedding, Clark worked hard at the telephone company and studied music. The Dorflers had changed their minds about him now that he was a respectable hard-working young man with a steady job. He spent weekends with them, and never forgot how they welcomed him whenever he knocked on their screen door.

During the summer Franz wrote to Clark about a good drama coach who had moved to Portland. She had heard only praise about this teacher, who had once appeared on the Broadway stage.

CHAPTER TWO

Josephine Dillon was born in Denver, Colorado, in 1888, graduated from Stanford University in 1908, and completed her education in New York and Paris. The Dillon family settled in Long Beach, California. Her father was a judge, and her mother, when she wasn't busy caring for her six children and their eighteen-room house, busied herself with the arts. Josephine's only brother became a lawyer, and her sisters studied opera, painting, and music composition.

She chose the theater and earned a starring role on Broadway. According to her, she did not have the personality for performing and preferred teaching others how to present themselves before an audience.

She settled in Portland after appearing there in a play with Edward Everett Horton, decided it might be an excellent city in which to open a drama school, and was successful during her first year in the Northwest. Though Clark would probably always have the acting bug, he was more intent on marrying Franz, who sent him to Dillon in hopes that he would learn how to act well enough to become the actor husband she wanted.

Gable enrolled in Dillon's evening classes. The young lady with him had no interest in the lessons. She sat restlessly reading a magazine in the back of the room. Josephine's subsequent casual remark about her not seeing this particular girl again—but she wasn't absolutely sure, because "he had so many"—indicates Clark's pattern with women even at this stage in his life, when he could hardly be considered good-looking. Nor did he have any degree of charm, but obviously the ability to attract women was part of his inborn charisma. He was a student of life. It takes a particular breed to be a street hawker and member of the carnival life of con artists. He had no other training, education, or experience. If, like the Pied Piper,

Clark could lure a crowd to the tent show, he had the power to entice women regardless of his awkwardness.

Josephine said, "He was young, sad, expressionless, but he was deep and thoughtful. Even though he was tired and undernourished, he had that winning smile and the eagerness so necessary for the theater. Desire often compensates for talent. I could tell he was absorbing every word I said."

She claims to have made up her mind that evening to concentrate on Clark's growth as an actor. Whether it was the challenge or because she was attracted to him subconsciously, no one will ever know. A sophisticated and learned woman, Josephine never hinted at any physical attraction. She was too professional for that. Rather, she emphasized her keen insight.

But it was Clark who approached her initially. When their first session ended, he waited until the other students had left. "May I speak to you?" he asked.

"It's very late," she said, studying him carefully.

"Tomorrow then?"

"All right."

He smiled. "I'll stop by after work."

Josephine was unable to get him out of her mind when she tried to sleep. In the morning she wondered what time he would arrive at the studio. She knew nothing about the young man—how old he was, where he came from, where he worked. Nothing, but she waited all afternoon and into the evening.

If Josephine was expecting a shy knock on the door, she was greatly surprised when he dashed through it enthusiastically with a brief greeting before bursting forth with his deepest desires and ambitions. Josephine sat and listened.

"It was great reading last night," he said. "I want to act. I have to act, but not the kind I've been doing. I know I can be a good actor if someone will give me the chance. My goal is Hollywood. I'm not sure if you want to hear that, but it's what I want. The stage is fun, but if you goof, well . . . that's it, you know? In Hollywood, if I make a mistake, I can do it again until I get it right. I like westerns . . . Tom Mix, mostly. I could fit in, don't you think so? I do. If I learn the techniques . . . that is, and you can teach me. I'm willing to study, but I want to know all the tricks, too. I think I could do it. How does a guy break into the movies? How do I go about it? Where do I start?"

Josephine watched him pace the floor, and listened until he ran out of words. "He was talking so fast," she said, "there was no way I could say anything. I felt he had to spit it out—everything that was locked up inside. He wanted me to know his silly ambitions. It was a showdown, of sorts. I could take it or leave it. He was very, very determined. I could see an abundance of strength in his eyes and could hear it in his voice. He was going to do whatever it was he wanted, with or without me, but there was a plea for my guidance. My desire to help him intensified. We were in tune. He was in a rush, but Clark was a sincere listener despite his dream world that I would be forced to invade. He wasn't the least bit discouraged by my summation of Hollywood. Fan magazines did not describe the majority of hopefuls who, by the thousands, arrived with his enthusiasm and left broke and defeated. Nor did they tell of the disappointments and the tears and false beliefs that, if one had the strength, could be overcome."

He said, "All I need are the tools to get in the door. Will you give them to me?"

"It might take a long time."

"How long?" he asked.

"That remains to be seen. You must be patient and willing to make sacrifices with no guarantees."

"What do I do first?"

"Learn," she said. "And then the key—practice."

"I'll do all those things," he said anxiously.

"And more practice," she emphasized.

"No one has really taken an interest in me before," he said quietly. "They all pretended, I guess, and then laughed behind my back. I make the audience laugh instead of cry... know what I mean? I bump into props when I should be picking them up. I take other actors' cues and..."

"That's nervousness," she said, "and perhaps being overly enthusiastic."

"Is that all?"

"What else could it be? The true essence of acting is being in control, and that takes timing. Practice and timing..."

"Is that hard to learn?"

"Learning is only half the battle," she said. "The rest is..."

"Practice." He laughed.

"You might get tired of my lecturing."

"No, I won't."

"It's getting late. We'll talk more tomorrow."

He was wide awake and not anxious to leave the little studio. He wanted to get started. He wanted to read or recite or talk about himself, but Josephine showed him to the door. Clark stood on the threshold for a moment and said, "You're a fine-looking girl!" She was taken aback, because she wasn't the least bit attractive and couldn't remember any man's having said that to her before. This compliment was overwhelming to Josephine. She soon realized it was the giver, not the meaning.

With the new day, she thought of very little other than her new student. The others were unimportant, though they were better actors than he was. Clark was terrible. What the audience did not recognize, Josephine most assuredly did. What the other players complained about, she strove to change. As the days and weeks passed, he became her life. Her classes became smaller. If she was aware that he possessed her thoughts, Josephine never said so. He was her favorite, yes, but her purpose in life was to prepare those who came to her for the stage . . . those, who at the time, had far more potential than Clark did.

If his acting left a great deal to be desired, that indefinable magnetism was there. Women pursued him. He was attracted to the wealthier ones, relished their attention and extravagant gifts, but was able to separate playtime from the productive hours with his teacher. Clark was very taken with Josephine. He had never met a brilliant woman before. Thirteen years older than he, Dillon was a Broadway actress, an artist, and his savior. She represented the outside world Jennie had talked so much about. He wondered how she could leave the stage to devote time to others so they might experience the magic of facing an audience with pride. How could she turn her back on Broadway, give it all up for a drama school in Portland? Clark's admiration overflowed.

Josephine Dillon had short dark hair, a low forehead, a broad nose with exaggerated nostrils, and thin lips. She was a small woman who carried herself well. She never married, but claimed that the man who was the love of her life (until Gable) died shortly before their wedding. Those who remember Josephine on the stage describe her as mature. She resembled someone's mother or aunt, had a pleasant, quiet personality, and could discuss any subject. Well read and well traveled, she was an asset in a cultured group. Her piercing eyes were narrow but sympathetic. At first glance she had a hard face, because it was square and too defined. She was not a woman who warranted a second glance.

Clark was attracted to her knowledge. He was impressed that her entire life had revolved around the theater, and so grateful that she thought he had possibilities. After five years of pitching tents, whistling in freight cars, and stumbling across the stage like a wild horse, he was finally seated on a piano bench next to Josephine Dillon, searching for the proper key to his voice. It was boring and tedious, but he believed in her because she believed in him.

Breathing exercises are a mystery to the novice, but more important than anything else in basic acting principles. She told him to forget everything he had learned in the past. She would teach him how to walk, talk, and breathe all over again.

It was a rebirth.

Josephine described Gable as a "gorgeous skeleton" who had a straight-lipped set mouth of the do-it-or-die character—the man who has to fight things through alone and who tells nothing. She was concerned about his health—the yellowish complexion and bad teeth, his muscles melting away to the bone. When she noticed some progress in his speech and breathing, Josephine insisted that he quit his job at the telephone company, and arranged for him to work on a farm where he could eat properly and get fresh air and plenty of sun to regain his health. In the fall, she got him a singing job at the Portland Hotel, where society gathered for dinner on Saturday nights.

There is no doubt that Josephine played the role of Clark's mother. She allowed him his freedom, took telephone messages from women, watched him disappear into the sunset with a wealthy lady in an expensive car, did not ask where he had been or with whom, and observed patience as she prepared his lessons for the next day. She had turned his life around in only a few months, but he was young and needed time with girls his own age who were interested in long drives, laughter, dancing, and petting in the moonlight. Above all, she did not want a frustrated student who might turn his back on her. Through it all, he had put himself in her hands completely. If she was concerned about other women, she never said so. There was too much energy and drive in Clark for any serious thoughts of marriage, especially to the type of woman he dated. Whether they were rich or poor, he was playing around.

What interested Josephine was his preparedness. Had he read the latest book she gave him? Yes; they discussed it at length. Was he taking his singing lessons regularly? Yes; the music teacher said he was always prompt. Was he practicing his breathing exercises? Yes, because she was seeing positive results. Every second they were together, he leaned on her every word.

Franz received letters from him regularly and was delighted with his progress. She told him, "I've been offered a play in Portland and will be back soon. We can be married as planned."

Clark's letters were filled with hope and accomplishments. He was finally on the right road. Every day meant something to him. He thanked her for recommending Josephine Dillon, "because she's changed my whole life."

If Franz had any doubts about her fiancé's future as an actor, she changed her mind when she laid eyes on Dillon's creation. He was all that she could hope for and had never thought possible. His eyes were radiant, the pale yellow skin was brown from the sun, and his six-foot frame had filled out. He had so much to tell her. Maybe she could pick up some pointers too. After all, his teacher was a Broadway star!

Franz listened for hours on end about this plain goddess who worked miracles with his health, his career, and his mental being. He said Dillon gave him the courage to earn a living with a talent he hadn't known he had—singing. He wasn't afraid any longer, and above all, he had faith in himself. "But," he said, "I have a lot more to learn. This is only the beginning."

Clark showed Franz his work sheets, books, and plays, encouraged her to breathe properly and to walk with the knees slightly bent, but not once did he mention their getting married. She waited a few days before asking him. "Mother would like to begin making plans for the wedding," she said.

"I think we should wait," he exclaimed.

"But you were so anxious only a few months ago."

"One thing at a time."

"I'm afraid I don't understand."

"I've decided to study for a few years."

"A few years?"

"At least . . ."

"I want the same thing," Franz said. "We planned to do that together, remember?"

"Things have changed. We thought it would be easy working on the stage, but it's not that simple. There are some things you have to do alone."

"Is it the big wedding that's upsetting you?" she asked. "Because if it is, we can go to the justice of the peace."

"It wouldn't be fair to you, Franz."

"Why? We both want the same thing. We can help each other."

"It wouldn't be fair to you," he repeated.

"You keep saying that. What do you mean?"

"Well," he stammered, "a doctor told me once I should never get married."

"Why?"

"I'd rather not discuss it, but that's what he said."

Clark's excuse was so farfetched, she was speechless.

Until she could find out the real reason for his hesitation, Franz dated him only occasionally. He loved to visit her parents on the farm. This was a glimmer of hope, but there was an invisible wall between them. The boyishness was disappearing. He had higher aspirations and a balanced outlook. Puppy love was a thing of the past. He no longer followed.

Franz was anxious to meet the phenomenal Miss Dillon, and Clark was proud to oblige. The two women were introduced at the little theater. Whether Josephine was aware at the time that Franz was not just another girl isn't certain. She took charge of her protégé, and the rehearsals began. According to Franz, Clark was "upstaging" the other actors skillfully. These were the tricks of the trade, he said, and there was nothing unprofessional about it.

Franz said, "I felt upstaged that night, too. I was given the impression that I was not a part of Clark's life any longer . . . that I wasn't wanted. I could accept that in time, but he wasn't sure what he wanted. He told me he didn't love me anymore. A few weeks later he took it all back."

Gable wasn't sure how to put these two women in proper perspective. He was still jealous of any man who paid attention to Franz, and became possessive if she showed interest in anyone else. When there was competition, he was in love with her. If she was warm to him, he felt crowded. Franz's ambitions for the theater put her in direct conflict with his teacher. If there was a balance, Gable couldn't find it. He wanted Franz on his terms—when and if he needed her at all. She had made her choice many months ago, however, by leaving him alone in Portland and putting the theater first in her life instead of Clark, who had wanted so desperately to marry her then. When she asked him if there was another woman, he said, "No." There were many women.

As for Josephine, she was Jennie's replacement—the mother he had never known. Dillon was educated, well bred, soft-spoken, patient, and understanding. Jennie had said he deserved the very best, and so did Josephine. Both women were anxious to guide, counsel, and serve him.

Need was more important to Clark than want. He had all the women he wanted, all the money he wanted, and all the attention he wanted. He needed a mother and teacher. This was where the main highway in his life came to a crossroads.

Josephine considered Franz a threat; in particular, Clark's visits to the Dorfler farm. He spoke of their hospitality and warmth. It was a close family attachment, he said, that could never be severed. Though he had hated farming as a child, it would always be a part of his life. It was clean, relaxing, and a refreshing break from the impersonal city climate. So long as Clark looked forward to his visits with the Dorflers, there was a chance that Franz could work her way back into his heart.

Josephine decided to close her school in Portland. "I was concentrating on Clark totally," she said. "Gradually the other students dropped out, and I wasn't recruiting new ones." She told friends there were more than a hundred thousand actors registered in Hollywood—what better place to open up a new drama school?

She told Clark yet another reason. "It's time for you to break away," she said. "To begin getting some valuable experience on the stage and meet people in the theater. As soon as I'm settled, I'll send for you. In the meantime, I've made arrangements for you to work for a stock company here in Portland."

Josephine was a very clever and well-organized woman who knew precisely what she was doing. Otherwise, it is doubtful that she would have placed Clark in the same theater with Franz, who was sorry she had broken her engagement to him now that Dillon was moving away. She was not aware that the man she loved had an arrangement to join his teacher.

When Josephine's school was shut down and its mistress had left Portland, Franz waited for Clark to approach her for a date, but he managed to stay away from her—though not out of any loyalty to

Dillon, because he was seeing other women. There were no more visits to the Dorfler farm, either. This was a difficult time for Franz, who did not know how to entice him back. Was she being punished for leaving him when he needed her so much? Did he want her to beg? It had gotten to the stage where she was willing to do that and more. Her intuition was to wait until he made the first move, and several months later he did.

"I'm going to Hollywood," he said.

Franz was heartbroken. "I threw his love letters into the fireplace," she said, "and cried every night for years because I never heard from him."

In August 1924, Josephine sent Clark the fifty-dollar fare from Portland to Los Angeles. He arrived with spirit and enthusiasm, babbled and bubbled like a kid at the circus. The excitement and glitter of Hollywood were everywhere, including the back streets and the dingy hotel where Josephine arranged for him to stay.

They talked all through dinner at an eatery, and into the wee hours of the night in the tiny room she had reserved for him. It was a breathless and exhilarating reunion. Josephine said she was reading and typing scripts for Paramount Studios, until her drama school was established. Her rented bungalow was twenty dollars a month, but she wanted to finish painting the interior before he saw it.

"I'll get a job as a mechanic," he said enthusiastically.

"That will be only temporary," she stressed. "Lessons, conscientious studying, and practice come first. You won't have the time to work."

Josephine, who was approaching her fortieth birthday, thrived on her hectic schedule of working at the studio and hurrying home to make dinner and tutor Clark. He had, by now, won her heart, but she would never admit to an intimate relationship. They were a team, not lovers, she insisted. Her only admission was to falling in love, never to making love. Odd that she would be adamant about this when he was King of Hollywood, but she indicated that to go to bed with him was to lose his respect. Gable was her ultimate goal. She would gain recognition through his success.

The relationship between Dillon and Gable has always been puzzling, fascinating, beautiful, and unbelievable. Those who knew him in later years found it hard to accept the tale that he did not give himself to Josephine as payment for her efforts. If a woman was available, that was reason enough to turn off the lights. "One woman is just like another" was the theory not only of the star but of the man as well. There was no way, he said, to make it without her.

Josephine emphasizes their togetherness as work—day and night. Study—day and night. Learn—day and night. More work, reading, breathing, walking, sitting, standing, talking, breathing, memorizing, smiling, turning, singing, dancing, climbing stairs, walking downstairs, diction, more breathing, Shakespeare and Coward. Repeat and repeat. A pound of criticism and an ounce of praise. A mile of practice and an inch of results.

She showed him common courtesies, social graces, and the tongue of the upper class—how to hold his own under any circumstances, anywhere. Gable had an instinct for good grooming and a smart wardrobe. "He knew all about fine clothes," Franz said. "He always wore French cuffs to detract from his large hands. If he had one suit, somehow it was neat and pressed."

After four months in Hollywood, Josephine bought Clark an old car for sixty dollars. "It's time for you to make the rounds of theatrical producers," she said. "I'll help when I can." They did not discuss motion pictures, because she wanted him to learn from the stage and get the feel and reaction of a live audience. But all their efforts were fruitless. It took Clark less than a month to miss his weekly income as a mechanic and to feel the sting of rejection.

Josephine had little money left, but she was not nearly so discouraged as he was. "If you have to lower yourself to get work as an extra in movies," she said, "that will afford you some dignity. You might meet someone who's connected with a theater group."

Gable would never forget the thousands of people waiting in line at the studios for bit parts. Day after day he made the rounds, but either he was too late or not the type or there was no work. There were times he couldn't afford gas for the car. On such drab occasions, Josephine managed to stay home too, but there were no days off. No wasted minutes. Study, practice, and read. Walk, sing, and recite.

Josephine could not afford two tickets to the movies, so Clark went alone when their budget permitted. She has to be admired for taking on such a burdensome responsibility of working, teaching, cleaning, washing and ironing, cooking, and trying to organize a drama school, and never complaining.

But Clark's dream was crumbling. He had nothing left. She controlled the money, and without it, he was caged. He was a gigolo without the rewards, a frustrated philanderer, and a lost child clinging to his mother for survival.

As strange as it seems, he decided that marriage was the only way to gain his freedom. "I was thinking," he told Josephine, "if I didn't have to live in the hotel, that would sure help out the finances, wouldn't it?"

"Yes, but I haven't room for you in the bungalow, and besides, it wouldn't look right."

"Suppose we got married?" he said.

"We're not in love."

"We can't go on this way."

"And we can't live together," she exclaimed. "Maybe it would work."

"It has to if we're going to succeed."

"All right, I'll do it."

"You're very special," he said. "I'll never forget you."

Josephine maintained that they took this drastic step because she could no longer afford two residences. It had nothing to do with love or physical attraction. "Our marriage was in name only," she said.

They were married by the Reverend Meadows in his rectory on December 18, 1924. Clark gave his age as twenty-four, she hers as thirty-four, a span of only ten years instead of thirteen. Clark moved into her tiny bungalow. There was no honeymoon and, according to Dillon, no wedding night. But there was only one bedroom . . .

Clark was devoted to Josephine, but no more than before they were married. He never doubted her true value but was depressed driving off every morning knowing he would have to stand in line— if he could find the end of it—for a mere three dollars a day just for a walk-on part in films. He made the rounds of the studios faithfully each morning before dawn until he realized that hundreds of people slept near the gates at night. Josephine refused to let him do it. "Our evenings are devoted to your lessons, and it's vital you look well rested."

After weeks of waiting and standing and hoping, Clark decided he was struggling for something he didn't want. The more he saw of the movie business, the more he hated it. He told Josephine she was right about Hollywood. "It's depressing, dull, and humiliating," he complained.

"Are you terribly disappointed?"

"I've been observin', you know . . . watching what goes on. It's
who you know around here. The same people get work. I see it every
day! It makes me sick. Hollywood doesn't interest me anymore."

Josephine smiled knowingly. "So you know what you want?" she
asked.

"The stage."

"Broadway."

"Yes."

"That's the ultimate, honey. The big time."

He grinned. "I feel better. Now that I know what I'm aiming for,
it won't bother me to stand in those long lines, because it's only for
the money. It's different when you don't care, isn't it?"

Yes, Josephine said to herself, it is. When I didn't care about
him, I was better off. He's become my life, my whole world, my
reason for working eighteen hours a day. He makes me breathe, he
makes me young, he makes my heart sing in the morning and dance
when I sleep. If he only knew the wonderment of it and how much
joy came into my life when he walked into my studio. But he mustn't
know. I can't frighten him away, though I find that he needs me and
will for a long time.

Josephine chose their friends carefully. Socially, she surrounded
Clark with struggling artists, painters, and composers who were talented and cultured. Sometimes the upper crust would slum at these
parties for their own amusement. Clark was attracted to wealth.
When he walked into a roomful of people, his eyes roamed for
women wearing expensive jewelry. Within the hour he was dancing
cheek-to-cheek with one of them. These ladies found him shy, sincere, flattering, and very persistent. The first time Josephine found
Clark whispering into a diamond-studded ear, she was crushed. If
money was the sole reason for the existence of her marriage, a
younger and wealthier woman could easily take Clark away from her.
This was her greatest fear. How long could he hold out in a city of
lavish mansions and rich movie stars who flaunted themselves in
polished McFarlans, Rolls-Royces, Packards, and Lancias?

Though the marriage was "in name only," the relationship deter-
iorated quickly after they took their vows. He was too confined being
with Josephine day and night, without privacy or freedom. His later-
day friends are sure that he married to further his ambitions and that
he would have fulfilled his obligations in bed as payment due. He
refused to discuss this period of his life, but a close acquaintance

said, "I don't think the Clark Gable in 1925 was any different from the one who signed a contract with MGM. It meant nothing for him to hop in bed, get it over with, turn over, and go to sleep. I've seen him with women who made Josephine look like Miss America. She was a means to an end, and he was the kind of guy who paid. In my opinion, Josephine stuck to her story to protect him."

Gable's stick-to-itiveness finally paid off when he got a bit part in the silent film *White Man*, for fifteen dollars a day, but it's doubtful whether Josephine saw any of this money. He came home with a set of secondhand golf clubs. One can only imagine how she felt knowing that he was playing on the links with a few unemployed actors while she read and typed all day. She asked no questions, however. That was the deal. She kept quiet about the times when he didn't come home at all, without any explanation. When they were together, he was oblivious. When they went for a walk, he had a roving eye. The only way Josephine could keep him at home was to work him unmercifully. Often he felt pressured going over the same recitations again and again—standing, sitting, walking, breathing, and listening to her criticisms until he was compelled to run out into the night and slam the door behind him.

Many years later they both complained about the other's compulsion for acting. "I don't know what he thought about other than the theater," she said. "He never discussed anything else with me. I haven't any idea what went on in his head."

Gable, in turn, grumbled, "I'd come home and she'd start teaching. I wasn't walking right, I wasn't breathing deeply, or I entered the kitchen all wrong. My voice was too high. She never did anything but teach, teach, teach!"

But he managed to work as an extra for five dollars a day in several films. Finally, he got his name on the credits as an extra in *The Merry Widow*, starring Mae Murray and John Gilbert. Gable would dethrone Gilbert within ten years, but in 1925 Clark's worth in this film was a mere seven dollars and fifty cents.

Having money in his pocket made him tolerant toward Josephine, who said Clark bought her only two gifts during their five-year marriage—a pair of shoes and an alarm clock. "He wanted to make sure I was able to walk to the studio on time."

Gable's exposure to the glamorous movie sets did not impress him. As an extra, he was snubbed in the unusually huge cast of the elaborate production of *The Merry Widow*. Being one of the crowd made Clark yearn for the stage. He asked Josephine to use whatever contacts she had in the theater. "I'll do anything," he said, "to work with a select few and be somebody instead of getting shoved around, pushed off-camera, and treated like dirt."

It was this intense hatred for motion pictures that gave him the desire for one last attempt at smoothing over the rough edges that Josephine had been harping on for months.

"There will be several good plays opening here soon," she said, "and you will audition, but don't expect to get a lead part. The stage is just as competitive as moving pictures. If you want to be outstanding, you must be worthy."

"I don't care," he said. "In the meantime, I'll take whatever jobs the studios have to offer for a few bucks. The movies aren't for me and never will be. We wait around for hours until the big shots show up, fight over the script, complain about their costumes and makeup while the rest of us bow and smile. That's no life for me, and I sure wouldn't keep all those people waiting just because I'm a star!"

He never tired of Josephine's stories about her rewarding life in New York—what a thrill it was to perform with the great artists and to hear the applause. "The world is at your feet," she sighed. "Those few minutes were worth years of sacrifice and doubt. You'll see."

She was enthusiastic about Jane Cowl's opening in the L.A. stage production of *Romeo and Juliet*. Josephine made sure that Clark was the first to audition. He got the part of a spear carrier for thirty dollars a week. He was on the stage! Nothing else mattered.

Jane Cowl, who was featured as the teenage Juliet, was pushing forty, but she had the talent, youthful face, and figure to prevail. She watched the auditions intently, pointed to Clark, and exclaimed, "I want him!" He stepped forward, drooling with appreciation and ambition, which were surpassed only by his shy sincerity.

During rehearsals, he was Cowl's obedient servant, picking up after her, fetching a glass of water, a footstool, taking messages, opening doors, fawning over her when she was upset and massaging her shoulders when she was tired. Cowl was so impressed by his gallantry that she offered to give him her private and personal opinion on how he should effectively hold a spear on-stage! Lessons were conducted in her dressing room over dinner. Clark was such a good student that Cowl promoted him to "leader of the extras." This gave them an added excuse to be alone.

Carrying a spear did not take much practice, but handling a leading lady did. In less than a week, Cowl asked him to appear with the group in Vancouver, Seattle, and Portland, and she raised his salary to forty dollars a week.

Josephine was overjoyed that her husband was touring in Shakespeare. Clark had many reasons to rejoice, too. It was a relief to be free of his teacher-wife, grand to see the Northwest, where he had, not too long ago, suffered from starvation, humiliation, depression, and a severe case of puppy love. Franz seemed so long ago as he enjoyed the familiar sights with Cowl. He had once again used his magical charm and gained ground with limited talent, if any.

When the tour was over, producer-director Lillian Albertson MacLoon, who had not been impressed with Clark when he auditioned for *Romeo and Juliet,* changed her mind and offered him a minor role in *What Price Glory.* Shortly after production began, the leading man in the part of Sergeant Quirk left the play, and Clark was chosen to replace him. Josephine, who had remained in the background until now, took over. She went with him to work every day and coached him during rehearsals. Her sudden invasion disrupted the cast's timing and gave Clark a severe case of nerves. MacLoon decided that one director was enough and banned Josephine from the theater. This would not be the last time Gable was embarrassed by his wife's overbearing interference.

Lullaby took Clark to San Francisco, where he ran into Franz, who was a dance instructor in a studio near the playhouse. Though she had followed his recent career, it was a shock to meet him again face-to-face. A friendly handshake in passing might have disturbed her and set her back, but Clark made every effort to see her and took their reunion in stride. Franz accepted his invitations but was sorry she did. He wasn't cocky, but Clark was very sure of himself. He had updated and polished his charm, smoothed his gift of gab, and perfected his lines. She gave in to her happiness and hoped that his desire to make the most of this miraculous reconciliation was genuine. He was truthful about his marriage of convenience and gave Franz the impression he wasn't living with Josephine any longer. Franz believed him and made herself available for dates whenever he asked. His kisses were long and passionate. He was jealous of other men in her life and displayed a possessive, often obnoxious, attitude.

"I regretted seeing him again," she confessed, "because I realized how much I still loved Clark. Our relationship ended abruptly when he stood me up."

Clark wasn't sending money home to Josephine. His letters were filled with backstage gossip and how many curtain calls he had. She knew when he was coming home because his laundry always arrived first with a note—"Will need clean shirts for theater, etc." On such occasions, her old fears mounted. Clinging to the hope that she and Clark would make a real marriage of their treaty, she had no doubt that he was seeing women who could provide him with expensive clothes. Josephine had not been able to afford anything for herself in many months, but this was not the time to think about that! After all, he was the one who faced the public. Not her. It was only right that he look his best. She tried to convince herself he wasn't sending her money because he needed every dollar for fine clothes.

She watched every one of his performances in Los Angeles, and, regardless of his good fortune, he was not a good actor. Clark was awkward and clumsy on stage, and had yet to master the art of lowering his voice. Josephine knew he had a long way to go before he was ready for New York.

When she told him the truth, Clark was annoyed. He came home just long enough to pick up his clean clothes. His letters changed from theater talk to sarcastic remarks about how other women enjoyed his performance without finding fault. Maybe it was time she treated him more like a man and not a little boy. How about some encouragement once in a while? What about his accomplishments?

Josephine didn't think there were any. He was too impressed by his leading ladies and by praise from people who knew nothing about acting. She wanted to know if he was practicing his diction and breathing exercises regularly. Was he conscious of how he walked on-stage, how he made his entrances? Was he reading the books she gave him? Did he take the time to get into character? Was he that other being instead of Clark Gable, ". . . because you seem to enjoy being yourself and that is not acting. Nor is it what the audience paid to see. If you are taken with the admiration of a few flighty girls who are stagestruck, I fear for your future as an actor."

Clark avoided her company for any length of time. Rather than give him some credit and encouragement, Josephine pounced on him "for his own good" and to balance the compliments with constructive criticism. These brief, but heavy, confrontations drove him further away. Her mistake was trying to cram his lessons into these infrequent and short encounters. In his defense, Clark warned his wife that if she could not be comforting and complimentary, there were other women waiting at the stage door to cheer him on. Had Josephine been sympathetic and proud of his achievements, insignificant as they were, she might have seen him more often. What she saw coming through the front door was an actor, not a husband. What she felt in her heart was the reverse.

While he played, she forged ahead and convinced Clark that his teeth detracted from his winning smile. "The front ones should be capped," she said.

He scowled. "I can't afford it."

"I can't either, but we'll make a deal with the dentist and pay him off."

Josephine accepted this financial burden alone and was still in debt long after Clark was out of her life for good. It was her obsession to see him through the awkward years of apprenticeship.

Gable's affairs during these lean years were numerous. In 1926 he appeared with film and screen actress Pauline Frederick in *Madame X,* his fourth play. She was forty-four years old, famous, rich, and divorced three times. She was a femme fatale in and out of costume. Just as Jane Cowl looked Clark over carefully and liked what she saw, Pauline made it easy for him. An irresistible, full-figured, dark-haired, energetic, multitalented lady, she left behind a string of brokenhearted lovers still pining for her. One of them, a young man, committed suicide when she discarded him. He left behind a note expressing his unrequited love. Pauline was the other woman in many divorce cases, and did not deny her overwhelming appetite for sex. She was exquisite, witty, and dramatic, and lived life to the ultimate. Gable was not only getting better roles, he was moving up in class when he had an affair with this elegant actress.

Whatever unfavorable publicity she received during her lifetime, the public adored her and they filled the theater wherever she performed. By the time she met Clark, Frederick had made nine Hollywood films. Critics loved her unique ability to project emotion with the eyes and hands. She was one of the first to use her shoulders effectively—one up and the other down or one thrown back and the other forward. She knew more about lighting and camera angles than the experts, but had a gentle, professional approach. Those who knew her well are amazed that she never aged. "Pauline went from one phase of youth to another," they said.

On the opening night of *Madame X* in San Francisco, she received more than thirty curtain calls. No one counted, because they were crying with joy—all but Clark, who watched this fascinating star take her bows, each different from the others because it wasn't the applause necessarily, but how one received the honor. Frederick knew a hundred ways to show her appreciation—each more glamorous than the last.

While Josephine struggled with her drama school, and read and typed scripts to pay her husband's dental bills, Frederick insisted that Clark have his teeth capped "properly"—a little gesture of thanks for his nightly company at her fabulous mansion on Sunset Boulevard.

Gable described Pauline as "a woman who acts as if she's never going to go to bed with another man." He complained of stomach trouble "because Pauline insists I eat lots of oysters to get me through those exhausting nights." This electrifying affair gave Clark the courage to move out of Josephine's humble little bungalow and into his own apartment, with his new wardrobe, beautifully capped teeth, and gifts of gold from Pauline. If he was so inclined, convincing her to get him into films would have been easy, but Gable hadn't changed his mind about New York.

When *Madame X* closed, the lovers said good-bye cheerfully. Frederick went on to conquer Europe, and Clark accepted a small part in *The Copperhead* with Lionel Barrymore, who was amused and flattered that the young actor followed him around the theater. Clark wanted to impress Barrymore, who was his childhood idol. "But not on opening night." He cringed. "I stumbled over a stage prop and my hat fell in a well. I was embarrassed, and to make things worse, I tried to dig out my hat! I didn't know how to minimize a mistake and go on as if nothing happened. Barrymore chewed my ass off that night. I was sure he was going to fire me, but after he cooled off we got along well and he helped me over the rough spots."

Gable needed that faux pas despite the humiliation. He had yet to realize much of his success so far was attributed to his warm and gentle personality, his eagerness to learn, and his puppylike shadow, which followed those he admired, the same way he pursued Franz Dorfler and won her over. He was always there, deaf to rejections and happy with whatever crumbs were thrown his way. He knew how to show his appreciation, was a pro with compliments, and possessed a dimpled smile that was hard to resist.

Regardless of his failures and triumphs, there was always Josephine to remind him of his mistakes and how to correct them. He tried to stay away from her as much as possible. "She rattled my nerves and I couldn't think," he said. Forging ahead, he got the part of a reporter in *Chicago* with Nancy Carroll, who had just signed a $5,000 weekly contract with Paramount. The only significance in his role as Jake, the loudmouth newspaperman, was Clark's own adaptation of what the character should be—and that was Gable, hat tilted back on his head, coat collar up, the cocky grin and lumberman's stride. It was also his first chance to use Josephine's trick of upstaging. When he wasn't stage center, Clark managed to get attention by standing still with a smirk on his face and the devil in his eyes. *Chicago* got good reviews, and Clark was given special mention. He enjoyed the role of Jake, which gave him a chance to be himself. He said, "Reporters don't have time to stand up straight, walk like a gigolo, and talk like a prince."

He would eventually play the part of a newspaperman in nine films, but in 1927 Gable wanted nothing to do with movies. He was offered a screen test and turned it down.

The popular male stars were John Gilbert and Rudolph Valentino —smooth-talking, hand-kissing, slick, suave, and dashing. Clark never minded any competition, but he wasn't the type to pick up a lady's hanky or kiss her temples. Aside from bit parts in films, he had no other offers. There was a lull in his love life, too. Suddenly the frantic activity and hectic traveling and applause came to a halt. He had little, if any, money. Disappointed and confused, he turned to Josephine.

"Maybe I should make the damn screen test," he groaned.

"That would defeat our purpose," she said.

"What the hell am I going to do?"

"Give me a little time. We'll work things out."

Now that Clark needed her again, it was difficult for Josephine to admit that he needed more training with a good stock company. He had gotten this far. If he gave in to films, he'd never make Broadway. She had seen it happen too often. How much did he want that dream that brought them together in Portland? Very much, he said.

Within a few weeks she accepted an offer for him to join a Houston stock company. The Gene Lewis Players put on a different play every week. "But I don't learn that fast," he said. "It'll never work out!" Josephine convinced him to go to Texas because he was promised lead roles. "The experience will be invaluable," she said. "The money is good, too." Gable couldn't argue with that. He had made a total of $1,000 in the past two years.

He went to Texas reluctantly, and within one month he had the lead role of Matt Burke in Eugene O'Neill's *Anna Christie* and was earning $200 a week. When Clark called Josephine with the good news, she rushed to Houston and took over. She interrupted rehearsals with her suggestions and coaching. Clark was furious, and so was the director, who told her to go home. Josephine stayed in Texas long enough to notice the crowds of teenage fans waiting at the stage door for their heartthrob to appear. Gifts from admirers arrived daily. Young girls begged for his autograph. Society matrons were more subtle. They sent engraved invitations to the elite parties that only Houston could offer. He was flattered, and didn't mind at all when dowagers rubbed their silk gowns against his magnificent body. At twenty-six, Clark Gable was taking form. The sallow complexion had disappeared permanently, and his crooked teeth were straight. His apelike hands were partially concealed with French cuffs held together with solid gold links. His ears were still prominent, but what shone between them was sensuously handsome. The dimples were deeper, and his lips were dangerously curved into perfection.

Is it any wonder Josephine was interfering? He didn't need or want her coaching, now or ever. She was in his way socially by referring to herself as Mrs. Gable. It meant nothing. Never did. Their marriage and their partnership were over, but Josephine did not go along with that. "I'll consent to a divorce," she said, "but we made a deal and I'm going to see it through to the end. I won't give up until you appear on Broadway. That's the way it's going to be."

Josephine said in later years that she was certain Clark was seriously involved with another woman in Houston. He was too sure of himself and wanted nothing more to do with her. "Clark never forgave me for sending him to Texas," she said. This is a direct quote, but does not make sense, since it was Josephine who should have never forgiven herself for making that choice. Just as Franz Dorfler was responsible for Gable's meeting Dillon, Josephine was responsible for making her worst fear a reality.

CHAPTER THREE

As the legend of Clark Gable unfolds into a series of romances, no one will deny that Franz Dorfler and Josephine Dillon had the greatest impact. One of them was mentioned in his will. The other came to his rescue when his Hollywood career was almost ruined by scandal. Franz never married, and Josephine wished to be called "Mrs. Gable" until she died. Both women outlived him.

Clark wanted to forget his past. His success in Houston was a boost to his ego, and he liked the sweet taste of recognition. He nurtured his lucrative social connections and took advantage of every opportunity.

Meanwhile, Josephine was in New York, making the rounds for him. Though Gable's name was not recognized on Broadway in 1928, he arrived with excellent letters of recommendation from the Houston company.

Producer Arthur Hopkins was casting for *Machinal*, a new play by Sophie Treadwell. Clark read for the lead opposite Zita Johann, who wanted a big name. "After all," she said later, "I turned down a contract with Universal to do this show and wasn't taking chances on a nobody." Hopkins, a soft-spoken, persuasive man, changed her mind.

When Gable arrived in New York, he said, "All my life I had been waiting for the chance just to plant my feet on the sidewalks that all actors have walked at some time. I came with money in my pockets and some good clothes. I didn't feel like a beggar. My Houston engagement had given me a barrel of confidence. A little money and wardrobe did the rest."

Josephine, who had paved the way for him in New York, assumed he would need her coaching during the four weeks of rehearsal, but Clark told her to stay out of his life. "He signed the contract with Hopkins," she explained, "got himself a good agent, and phoned to

say he was through with me. I said I was going to California and that
he had better become the best actor he could, as he could never be a
man."

She went home before Gable made his debut on Broadway.

Gable was on his own, but it's doubtful that Josephine could have
helped him through the hectic days that followed. "We had a three-
day tryout in New Haven," he said, "and I lost my nerve . . . got a
horrible case of the jitters. I mumbled my lines and floundered
around and lost all semblance of character. I tried too hard. The next
day I told Hopkins to replace me, but he was an easygoing guy and
told me to relax."

On September 7, 1928, *Machinal* opened at the Plymouth
Theatre. "I panicked," Gable said, "but dear old Hopkins told me to
forget the house was full of people and to play it the way we rehearsed it. He was quiet and relaxed . . . last thing he said was that
he'd be sitting in the back where he always did. I felt better."

Gable walked on stage with confidence, and he gave a superb
performance. "I heard a lot and read a lot about the New York
critics," he said, "and how they could make or break an actor. I sure
wanted to meet them, from the other side of the footlights—scared
to death, you understand, but anxious just the same. I wanted to see
exactly what they would do to me."

The *Telegraph* said, "Gable is young, vigorous and brutally masculine."

The *Times* reported, "Gable is an engaging adventurer who
played the casual good-humored lover without a hackneyed gesture."

And *The New Yorker* referred to him as an "excellent lover."

His leading lady, Zita Johann, complimented him also. Despite
her reluctance in the beginning, she said he was very good in the
part and gave her complete support. "I wasn't attracted to him at all,"
she said. "We got along well and I liked him. He insisted on walking
me home, but only as far as the door. I wouldn't let him go any
farther. He invited me to supper, but I wasn't interested. He had
impact on the stage, but no impact for me."

During the three-month run of *Machinal*, Gable lived the gay life
after the curtain went down. A cast member recalled, "Clark was
always out with women. I don't know when he slept. Maybe with
them, because he was never in his own bed."

By now Gable had a pattern with women—running around until
he found a golden nest—and, as usual, he didn't have to do the

searching. *She* came to him without invitation or coaxing . . .

"We noticed that there were several players from Houston in the cast of *Machinal*," Ria Langham explained. "My brother, who was also an actor, knew them and suggested we go backstage after the play to chat. I had seen Clark in stock in Houston, but never met him. After the show we were introduced and he went to supper with us."

Her daughter, Jana, had been one of Clark's biggest fans in Houston. "It was a thrill to meet him at last," she said. "A month after opening night I paid a visit to Mother in New York and she asked, 'Guess who I've been seeing a lot of—Clark Gable!' I was very happy for her."

He was twenty-seven years old. Ria was forty-five.

When *Machinal* closed in January 1929, Clark concentrated on his relationship with the aristocratic, wealthy Mrs. Langham, who was trying to shed her third husband. Clark blended in nicely at her formal dinner parties and intimate cocktail gatherings at her elegant apartment on Eighty-first Street and Park Avenue. Though New York City was enveloped in a snowy winter, if the country roads were passable, it was pleasant sitting around the fireplace at a friend's mansion on Long Island. Society has always been lenient toward its own kind. Divorce is such a bore, but a common trip for the very rich. Wasn't it a damn shame that Ria and Clark were both so anxious to be free of their spouses, the elite whispered.

There was, of course, gossip on the elite East Side of New York:

"Do you suppose that Gable chap is after Ria's money?"

"So what? She's madly in love with him."

"Everyone knows that, but it's common knowledge his agent can't get him a job."

"Ria can afford him, darling. He's devastatingly handsome, isn't he?"

"Breathlessly so . . . except for his gold teeth!"

Ria Langham had auburn hair worn in a fashionable wavy bob, ivory skin, and soft dark eyes. She was a tiny five-foot-two and resembled Franz Dorfler. Ria, however, wore matching hat, gloves, and shoes, tweed or wool suits, an heirloom pin holding a silk scarf in place, and was always groomed to perfection. She was stately, proper, and plain —a woman who might have been more attractive had she not been so conservative. Her pictures did not do her justice. She was a poised, graceful, handsome, stylish woman, a gracious hostess and devoted mother.

Born Maria Franklin on January 17, 1884, in Kentucky, she was raised in Macomb, Illinois, where she married William Prentiss at the age of seventeen. Four years and one son later, Ria moved in with her aunt and uncle in Houston. She thrived on the single life until millionaire contractor Alfred Thomas Lucas, twenty-two years older than Ria, proposed to her. It was an ideal marriage. She had two children by Alfred, lived in a palatial home, and became the belle of Houston society. After ten years of wedded happiness, Lucas died, leaving his fortune to Ria. In 1925 she married Denzil Langham, and she left him two years later.

Though Ria was an active and admired lady in Houston's closely knit association of the very rich, she was a homemaker, mother, and wife above all else. Her style was unique. She had a regal stance that placed her in the upper class with little or no effort. Ria was not one to rough it or lower her standards to suit the occasion. She wasn't outgoing, because it wasn't necessary. Her friendliness was sincere and appreciated. Most important, the social status she had attained as Mrs. Lucas was ingrained in her. Like Josephine, Ria was very bright and well read, interested in the arts and culture, nibbled elegant food, and surrounded herself with people of refinement. Her children attended the best private schools and spoke with a Texas drawl.

Clark wanted to fit into Ria's gracious living, and she was anxious to show him how it was done. Though he was famished after her delicate meals, he would learn to like the smaller portions of poached sole and filet of steak with small round potatoes and tiny green peas that were impossible to manage. Who needed apple pie à la mode when he could finish a petit four with one bite? He might have taken a long walk from Ria's swank apartment across town to the West Side automat for a solid meal, but . . .

Gable was broke again.

Had he reached the end of the rainbow? Was Broadway the end of the beginning? He was living in luxury, wearing a derby, carrying a gold-headed cane and sporting a thin mustache, but he missed performing. As he sipped a martini before dinner and gazed out over Central Park, he was honest with Ria. Should he give up acting and go into business? He was twenty-seven and going nowhere. Was he washed up?

THE EARLY YEARS 57

Ria was willing to do anything for him—say anything that would make him feel better. He was a fine actor, she said. By now he should know the rewards of patience. There was, however, a matter more important than his career right now.

What was that, he wanted to know.

Josephine. For a hundred dollars he could get a quickie Mexican divorce.

Papers in hand, Clark kissed Ria good-bye and boarded the Twentieth Century Limited for Los Angeles. Josephine knew all about Langham and was sure Clark had been involved with her in Houston. He'd never convince her otherwise. "In Texas he had met people who are now in his life and I was asked to step aside," Josephine said. She considered his reasons for wanting to marry Ria no different than his proposal to her five years ago. Both women had what he needed and wanted—Josephine the knowledge to make an actor out of him, and Ria the money to afford him the luxury of this dream.

"Clark had one of those Mexican divorce papers that he wanted me to sign," Josephine related. "I refused to enter into any such affair, knowing that the next woman he married would find herself in a legal mess if she trusted herself to Mexican marriages and divorces. I filed for divorce in March 1929, on grounds of desertion. I could have added all the other things, but I was protecting Clark. I asked for nothing, no settlement and no alimony. But he would have to wait a year before the divorce was final."

Clark returned to New York and Ria. At least, he said, Josephine had agreed to a divorce and wanted nothing from him, but the best news was an offer to play the lead in George M. Cohan's *Gambling,* which opened in Philadelphia. Gable's performance was terrible. He was fired when the curtain went down. His only consolation was that Cohan replaced him in the lead.

Gable went right into *Hawk Island* and despite its short run, the *Tribune* said, "Gable was the most competent in the cast."

A producer who remembers Clark in *Hawk Island* said, "I don't know if it was fear or determination, but on matinee days he made the rounds in costume and makeup. He wanted to line something else up before he was out of work. My memory of him is vivid because he used white paint on his gold teeth and sometimes the paint streaked."

After *Blind Windows* flopped, Gable was out of work again. "At least I could go to the theater," he said, "and see other actors at work. I studied their techniques, and remember Katharine Cornell in *Dishonored Lady*, Constance Collier in *The Matriarch*, and Francine Larrimore's *Let Us Be Gay*."

Without Ria, Clark could not have afforded this lull. His financial slump began after *Machinal* closed, and by now he might have been living with Josephine in her tiny Los Angeles bungalow. What choice did he have? Fortunately, it didn't come to that. Watching him stroll down Fifth Avenue with Langham and stop for lunch at the Plaza after an exhausting shopping binge, no one could possibly know he was in debt.

Though Gable didn't know it at the time, his last appearance on the Broadway stage was in *Love, Honor and Obey* with George Brent and Glenda Farrell in the lead roles.

In April 1930, his divorce was final. When and where Clark and Ria were married remains a mystery, because they did not admit they were man and wife. Why they kept it a secret might have had something to do with his strained relationship with Josephine, who swore that Clark and Ria staged their "first" meeting in New York when in fact they had been having an affair in Houston. It's possible that Ria was having her own problems with ex-husband Langham. Or that she felt her children might be upset. There was also a rumor that her influential friends liked Clark but felt the seventeen-year age difference was disgraceful. There was too much gossip already revolving around his very sad financial status and that Ria was keeping him.

In his biographical sketches, Gable gives the year of his marriage to Ria as 1930. The one that was publicized occurred in 1931, when MGM found out his New York marriage to Ria was not valid in California. They were rushed into a second ceremony that, for publicity purposes, was considered Gable's official marriage to his second wife.

With the exception of his Broadway credits, no information was given about where or how he lived in New York. This is highly unusual, since MGM's publicity staff took great pride in retracing the lives of their major stars and describing, fiction or fact, where and how they suffered during the bad times. Carefully, his two years in New York were skimmed, emphasizing his stage appearances.

We will never know if Josephine threatened Clark. She reappeared in his life when he became a star, demanding money from

MGM to compensate for her investment in Gable.

Gable was, without a doubt, happy in New York and had no intention of leaving. His life with Ria was divine. As for his career, he wasn't about to give up his ambitions to be a great actor on the Broadway stage. But Lillian Albertson MacLoon, who had chosen him for the Shakespeare stock plays in California, had other plans for Clark. She thought he would be perfect for the role of Killer Mears in *The Last Mile*. "Spencer Tracy is playing the part on Broadway," she told Gable on the phone. "I suggest you take in the performance and let me know if you'd be interested in doing it out here in Los Angeles."

Clark saw the play and was in awe of Tracy—one reason he decided *not* to accept the offer. "How can I follow a guy like that!" he told Lillian.

She laughed. "You won't have to be that good out here."

"I'll have to call you back," he said.

Ria wanted him to accept. "I'll join you when the children are out of school."

Gable laughed. "Don't bother. The play opens in June, and I'll be back in New York a few weeks later."

He fought to the very end. It took a good deal of convincing by Lillian and Ria to change his mind. "I hate California," he said, "but the only thing that'll keep me going out there is knowing my agents here in New York will be working like hell to find me a good play."

Reluctantly, he headed west with only four weeks to rehearse for *The Last Mile*, a powerful story about prisoners on Death Row and their desperate attempt to escape. Clark played the role of a heartless, vicious killer who spits venom—his huge hands grasping the cell's bars and his sunken eyes screaming for freedom and revenge. Gable was in command of his audience at the Majestic Theatre on June 7, 1930—his greatest triumph to date.

He couldn't ignore his success, or the three hundred dollars coming in every week. Trying to forget that the only genuine legitimate theater was on Broadway, he needed to restore some faith in himself as a wage earner after six years of begging and taking.

Though Hollywood was bustling with the birth of sound, Gable wanted no part of films, despite the many talent scouts knocking on his dressing-room door. He wanted nothing to do with agents, either, until he met Minna Wallis, sister of producer Hal Wallis. She didn't try to fill his head with big ideas, never mentioned a screen test, and admitted that she was just starting out also. Gable liked her refreshing approach. For the money they were paying extras these days, he'd be a fool not to give her a chance.

Minna took him to Pathé, where William Boyd was filming *Painted Desert*. She did all the talking. The casting director said Gable fit the part very well and added, "I assume you can ride a horse." Clark's mouth dropped open, but Minna said, "He certainly can!" The deal was set for $750 a week. She took his arm and got him out of the studio before he fainted, because Gable was ashen. "I can't ride a damn horse!" he bellowed.

"So what?" she said casually. "You can learn."

He went to the Griffith Park Riding Academy and told Art Wilson, the instructor, his problem. The lessons began. "I don't think the guy believed me," Clark said, "'cause I mentioned I lived on a farm, but it just wasn't my thing to ride. He took the small horse and me to the top of a hill and said, 'Get on and meet me at the bottom where we came from.' I hung on, and that little horse didn't know how to do anything but run. I made it, though. Every day I took lessons, and by the end of two weeks I could ride fairly well."

Gable had a few dollars in his pocket, and he had faith in Minna, who was not only his agent, but a dear friend. "She and her mother invited me for dinner almost every night before I left for Arizona to make *Painted Desert*."

He was still stiff and sore from learning how to ride a horse, and wasn't thrilled about doing a B western in the desert. "Something went wrong with the mine I was supposed to blow up and it exploded just as we were chargin' in. One man got killed and several others were injured. I got hit by falling rocks, but wasn't hurt. The whole thing was a mess. Depressing and very discouraging."

When he got back to Hollywood, Minna told him Pathé was almost bankrupt. "We can't rely on them for a contract," she said.

"I almost got killed out there!" he said. "And not by a horse."

Minna was optimistic. "I'm negotiating with Warner Brothers to test you for *Little Caesar*," she said. "I think a scene from *The Last Mile* would work out just fine."

But Jack Warner took one look at the screen test and howled with laughter. "What the hell am I going to do with a guy who has ears like that?"

Gable didn't know why he was turned down until years later, when Warner saw one of his better films. "That's the guy with the big ears! I don't believe it!" He remarked that Gable obviously had had them fixed.

Clark brooded over his bad luck with Pathé and Warner's. He felt like taking the next train back to New York, but Ria had settled down for the winter with her two youngest children in Los Angeles. Seventeen-year-old Jana and eleven-year-old Alfred liked Clark, who preferred being a friend to them rather than a stepfather. With nothing better to do, he became a family man on picnics, at ball games, and on country drives.

Gable was a loner, however, and his thoughts revolved around the sound boom, which was making movies bigger than ever. He worried about his high voice, which Josephine had attempted to lower time and time again. "When I thought I was a good movie actor," he said, "the director would ask me to lower my voice."

The gossip columns were full of John Gilbert's shrill "I love you," which wasn't all that bad, but one giggle led to another in the theaters, and the highest-paid lover in the twenties was ruined. Old-timers claim that L. B. Mayer, head of MGM, tampered with the sound to prevent Gilbert from marrying Greta Garbo—what better way than to destroy his career? Garbo demanded he play opposite her in *Queen Christina* two years later, but the public would never accept Gilbert again, despite his fine performance.

Gable had good reason to worry. If the highest-paid actor in the late twenties was ruined by his high voice, how would moviegoers accept a newcomer with the same problem? Gilbert wasn't the only victim. Francis X. Bushman, Conrad Nagel, Charles Farrell, Buddy Rogers, and Ramon Novarro failed the transition. Douglas Fairbanks was one of the few male stars who survived.

Meanwhile, Minna was not wasting any time. She had met several influential people at RKO and MGM. They might be interested. After all, the studios were losing their matinee idols every day.

Clark said Hollywood wasn't his town. "I haven't made one friend here except you," he told her. "No one paid any attention to me while I was making *Painted Desert*—like I was an outsider and shouldn't have been there. In the theater, people are friendly. We all knew each other. Isn't that the way it's supposed to be? Ha! Not beyond the studio gates, apparently. I dreaded coming out here, and it turned out like I thought it would. This is not my racket. It stinks."

Ria was content anywhere so long as she had Clark, and willing to see him through another slump. He had her loving and financial

support. She left her close friends in New York and Houston to be
with him. In Los Angeles, Ria Franklin Prentiss Lucas Langham
Gable was just another wife and mother. Her social connections
meant nothing in a city of movie celebrities. She was nudging fifty
and wanted roots. She forgot her own problems and focused on her
husband. Without Ria and Minna, Gable said, he was lost and defeated. He missed the smell of the theater, the audience stirring in
their seats, the quick costume changes, the lost props, the precious
minutes between curtains, the late suppers, and the variety of sensuous roommates who woke him up in time for brunch. Life is downhill
all the way, just as it was with the small horse at the riding academy.
Hang on with fear in your heart and end up where you started, with
nothing and nowhere.

"RKO is interested in you," Minna said, "and MGM officials
want to discuss a contract."

Ria threw her arms around Clark. "I knew it!" she rejoiced.
"Minna and I never gave up hope."

If Gable couldn't have the theater, he'd make damn sure he
signed with the best movie studio in the world—MGM. Their boy
genius, Irving Thalberg, made the decision to hire him. Louis B.
Mayer had nothing to do with it, but took the credit when "bat ears"
became his number one box-office attraction.

On December 4, 1930, Clark Gable signed a one-year contract
for $650 a week.

Afraid of close-ups, he had his teeth capped properly, compliments of Ria, who was as thrilled as he was about the future. Their
life changed overnight. MGM was a family studio. There were many
people who would be responsible for Clark, and one was publicity
man Howard Strickling, who said he was amazed when he set eyes
on Gable for the first time. "The man was tremendous. I was afraid
of his strength, frankly—that he'd hurt someone. He never did."

Gable liked Strickling at first handshake. They would become
very close friends. This was a good start for the thirty-year-old actor,
who hadn't had a permanent job since he worked in the lumberyard.
Odd that he should meet a best friend so soon in his career, especially a man who worked with Valentino, Barrymore, Garbo, Wallace
Beery, Joan Crawford, and Norma Shearer, to mention a few. Strickling was a master at handling temperamental stars. He understood
them as unique individuals with their own fears, quirks, desires,
secrets, habits, and limits. He often accompanied stars on their

honeymoons, was called upon at all hours of the night to go to the scene of an accident, fight, suicide, or murder if an MGM star was in trouble. Very simply, Howard Strickling made sure there was no scandal connected with MGM's family. He was a man to be trusted, and the man responsible for so many legends. Gable said, "If it hadn't been for Howard, I never would have lasted."

His first film was *The Easiest Way* with Constance Bennett, Adolphe Menjou, and Robert Montgomery. Clark was the laundryman husband of Anita Page. He appeared to be much younger on the screen, almost pretty, but portrayed the type of fellow who would not be pushed around. MGM didn't particularly care if he was noticed, because they had yet to mold him into an image—a distinctive personality like no other. Six days a week, he reported to what is commonly known as the "studio system"—posing for pictures, choosing a new wardrobe with Minna and Howard, working out in the gym regularly, and learning how to fire a gun, control an expensive fishing rod, and perfect his stance on a horse. Howard said, "We were showing him how, but Clark was a natural. He loved to fish and hunt whenever he could for the rest of his life. I don't think he was at ease posing for pictures or being interviewed in the beginning, but he had many things going for him. Clark wanted to learn. He wanted to be a star. He wanted to be a success. So he cooperated and always had a smile. The guy had charm. He really did. I saw it the first time we met."

He accepted criticism. Did he have a choice? Those who remember him in 1931 think that the Clark Gable who was perfected by MGM did not think of himself as handsome. He was concerned with his ears and how to face the camera at the right angle. He was self-conscious about his big hands, too. There was little anyone could do about his ears until he mastered the dimpled grin that became Gable's trademark. There was a saying in Hollywood: "When Clark looks straight at the camera, his head resembles a sugar bowl."

Cameramen who worked with him in the early stages of his career said he learned how to deemphasize his shortcomings with ease. He was willing to make mistakes if it meant improving himself. Strickling said, "Clark was very much like Robert Taylor. Neither had an ego during their remarkable careers."

If Josephine taught an undernourished gawky kid to walk and talk properly, and Ria showed him how to be a gentleman, it was MGM's team of experts who put the raw pieces together into one hunk of dynamite. They were methodical and patient. Gable's past and present life was thoroughly scrutinized, screened, and glorified. There was nothing MGM officials could do about Ria, who would not be the people's concept of Mrs. Clark Gable. Her social status was an asset when and if she was mentioned at all. Fan magazines said she was a "bit" older than he and, if pressed for how much, only ten instead of seventeen years. Occasionally they were photographed together. Ria looked more like his mother, but the camera never did her justice.

MGM preferred their male stars to remain single and available for the millions of women who thought they had a chance—enough reason to buy a ticket at the box office to dream of what could be.

In later years Ria would be referred to as Gable's "sponsor" in much the same way that Josephine was his "teacher," with no emphasis on marriage. In 1931, however, MGM had plans to co-star their new potential star with their sexiest leading ladies.

But the past caught up to Clark again when he found out that Franz Dorfler was in Los Angeles. She was aware of his MGM contract and little else. Gable turned on the usual charm and then sighed how lonely he was. "You're my only friend here," he said. Franz, who knew nothing about Ria, wanted to know why his marriage to Josephine ended. "She did a lot for me," he said, "but she was forever preaching and too domineering. She was always right. Oh, well, I can't be around any woman for too long . . ."

He gave her the impression Hollywood had not accepted him. "I'm a very lonely guy," he said. She asked about beautiful Constance Bennett, who worked with him in *The Easiest Way.* "She didn't know I was alive," he complained.

Franz was caught in Gable's web once again. He wanted her to be the first to take a drive with him in his new car. They saw each other frequently, until he dropped her as suddenly as he had back in San Francisco. Franz found out about Ria in an article about Gable and was devastated for the fourth time. Clark didn't lie, exactly. He just eliminated the facts.

Whether Joan Crawford asked for Gable to appear with her in *Dance, Fools, Dance* or MGM assigned him hasn't been established, since she was known for glamorous fibs. Though she had influence at the studio, it's unlikely that it was her choice and not theirs. "I was terrified the first time we met," Crawford said, "because he was

a stage actor and that gave him an edge. Their training is far superior
to the studio's drama school. He'll make me look bad without trying,
and I know he'll laugh behind my back."

Gable was the one who was petrified. "My God, she's a major
star! She knows everything there is to know about making movies.
I'll feel like a jerk, and probably look like one, too." And he prayed
she wouldn't laugh in his face. Clark had more to be concerned
about, too. Crawford was married to Douglas Fairbanks, Jr., and her
mother-in-law was Mary Pickford. My God, Ria would sell her soul
for an invitation to Pickfair, Hollywood's Buckingham Palace, and an
"audience" with America's Sweetheart and her husband, Douglas
Fairbanks, Sr.! The star on Joan Crawford's dressing-room door was
impressive enough, but as one of the royal family, she attended the
very exclusive dinner parties at Pickfair. That Crawford woman had
guts and took it all in her stride. She was one of the few contract
players who fought for the roles she wanted and didn't stop until she
had the script in her hands.

"Every experience I had and every mistake I made during my
nightclub career has helped, if only to show me the things which I
should avoid," she said. "I learned to know men pretty well, but very
few of them could keep a secret. I didn't dare trust anyone. I was
snubbed in Hollywood, so I snubbed back, but only after I tried to be
a friend. I'm still learning how to differentiate between being used
and being needed. Yes, I learned a lot about men, but if a woman
knows nothing about men, how can she consider herself capable of
judging for herself and choosing the one man she can trust—the
man that could satisfy a woman's heart and soul?"

Joan Crawford's favorite actress was none other than Pauline
Frederick . . .

II
HOLLYWOOD

CHAPTER FOUR

Lucille Fay LeSueur was born March 23, 1905, in San Antonio, Texas. Her stepfather owned "The Opera House," where she learned to dance. "I didn't know my real father," she said. "He abandoned us when I was a baby. My mother succeeded in driving away my stepfather, too, and I never forgave her. When she got married again, her husband didn't want me around, so I was sent to boarding school. Sounds fancy, but it was hell. I had to clean all the rooms, do the cooking, and take care of the younger children. When I didn't do something right, I was beaten with a broomstick."

When she was sixteen, Lucille left school and worked in a department store wrapping packages until she had saved forty-six dollars—enough to get her to Chicago, where she got a job as a dancer in the stage production *Innocent Eyes*. Spotting her in a chorus line, an MGM talent scout gave her a screen test in 1924, and she was sent to Hollywood. Following her fourth movie, a fan magazine used her for their "Pick-a-name" contest, and Joan Crawford was born.

In 1928 she read *Our Dancing Daughters* and "I stole the script, went to producer Hunt Stromberg, begged for it, and got it! This was a Clara Bow part—a flapper, wild on the surface, a girl who shakes her wind-blown bob . . . and dances herself into a frenzy while the saxes shriek and the trombones wail, a girl drunk on her youth and vitality."

MGM doubled her salary. "I rode around town with a small box camera taking pictures of 'Joan Crawford' blazing on the marquees," she said.

She was twenty-one when she met the charming and brilliant Douglas Fairbanks, Jr., who introduced her to good books, the theater, and proper manners. The elder Fairbanks and his wife, Mary Pickford, did not approve of the hoofer-star. Joan was shunned at Pickfair, forcing her to elope with Doug on June 3, 1929. The marriage did not change how his parents felt about her, however. "They treated me like trash," she said.

Crawford lost twenty pounds in Hollywood to accentuate her cheekbones, and in spite of her athletic shoulders, she was the first movie actress to wear shoulder pads on the screen. Her bust was firm and abundant, her hips were slim, and her legs and thighs described as fantastic. She had big blue eyes, full lips, and a classic nose that blended better with her other features as she matured.

In later years she admitted to having an insatiable appetite for sex. This was no secret in the late twenties. Crawford exposed her deep cleavage and long legs, laughed like a sailor, and was brassy with the brass. Irving Thalberg, married to Norma Shearer, liked Joan and tried to help her at MGM, but he never forgot her gutsy "Why do you save all the good roles for Norma? Don't you think I deserve some consideration?"

"You wouldn't want people to laugh at you, would you, Joan?" he asked.

Punishment for such insubordination was a step backward in *The Law of the Range* with Tim McCoy. "I'm going to like it if it kills me!" she said. And Thalberg, who was a fair gentleman, proved he did not hold a grudge by giving her John Gilbert in the silent film *Four Walls*.

Her marriage to Fairbanks changed Joan's style considerably. She dressed modestly, toned down her makeup off the screen, spoke in a low, affected voice, and emulated Mother Pickford Fairbanks when she entertained only "intimate friends." "The others can go fuck themselves," she said laughing.

Though Crawford was one of MGM's greatest creations and held on to her popularity at the box office, she was never accepted by her peers as elegantly proper. Like Gable, she could not give up her roots and forget what she had suffered in her childhood and during her rough-and-tumble days as a hoofer in nightclubs. Crawford was manufactured and Mary Pickford, for one, wasn't fooled by expensive clothes (usually virgin white) or Paris hats (usually the garden type) or her well-timed innocence (sadly, she never knew what that was). She was treated like a man by producers and directors. Otherwise, she might have buried them.

While she reveled in her heavenly marriage to Doug Fairbanks, Crawford met Clark Gable on the set of *Dance, Fools, Dance*. As the rich girl who suffers poverty during the Depression, she becomes involved with a racketeer, played by Gable. "In the scene where he grabs me and threatens to kill my brother," Joan said, "I felt such a sensation, my knees buckled. He was holding me by the shoulders and I said to myself, 'If he lets go, I'll fall down.' He had more animal magnetism than any man in the world and, goddamn it, every woman knew it!"

In 1931 Gable was featured in twelve films — three with Joan Crawford. "We were attracted to each other instantly," she said. "Instantly. I had what he wanted and he had what I wanted. Call it chemistry, call it love at first sight or physical attraction. What's the difference? The electricity between us sparked on the screen, too. It wasn't just acting. We meant every damn kiss and embrace. God, we both had balls in those days!"

Their passion during the filming of *Dance, Fools, Dance* was limited to the set. Clark was a peon at MGM. Crawford was a major star. He wasn't sure of himself yet, and besides, it's only natural to get excited at the start. She gave her all as the pro she was, and he reacted like a man. It wasn't easy going home to Ria after romancing Joan. It wasn't easy at all . . .

MGM kept him so busy, Gable had no time to think. He still had Crawford's perfume in his blood when Harlow's flowed through his nostrils on the set of *The Secret Six*. If he had any ideas about the Blond Bombshell, they were forgotten when he was rushed into *The Finger Points* with Richard Barthelmess. When Gable had the time to have a quiet dinner with Ria, he was learning lines in a new script.

"Got another one coming up with Crawford," he told her, "called *Laughing Sinners*. Johnny Mack Brown played the part of the Salvation Army captain who saves a cabaret dancer—that's Joan—from suicide. They finished the damn film and decided to replace Brown with me."

"I thought it was Norma Shearer," Ria said.

"No, no, no! I work with her in *A Free Soul*. Aren't you interested in my career?"

"More than ever, darling, but why Miss Crawford so soon again?"

"She asked for me."

"How very odd, darling. She's famous and you're a novice."

". . . Trying to give me a break, I guess."

"In that case, perhaps we should show our appreciation by taking Miss Crawford and her charming husband, Mr. Fairbanks, out to dinner."

Clark scowled. "I don't think so."

"But, darling, I should love to meet the family."

"That, my dear, doesn't appeal to me."

"Pickfair appeals to anyone who has an ounce of class," Ria said.

"That's why it doesn't appeal to me. Now, my dear, if you don't mind, I have two scripts to study. If you're tired, toddle on to bed without me."

Crawford was waiting for the man she said had presence. "I knew when Clark walked on the set, and I didn't know which door he came through, but I knew he was there," she said. "I knew I was falling into a trap that I warned young girls about—not to fall in love with leading men or take romantic scenes to heart. Leave the set and forget about it, because that marvelous feeling would pass. Boy, I had to eat those words, but they tasted very sweet."

Joan made her desires known to Clark Gable during *Laughing Sinners,* a title describing its stars, who possessed each other totally and without interference or suspicion. Fairbanks was busy making movies, and Ria understood her husband's working late.

Joan described Gable as her soul mate. "Yes, our relationship was very physical," she said, "but we came from similar backgrounds— crap! We were unhappy kids and had to bum around for food and friends. Our families meant nothing to us and we meant nothing to them. We were nobodies transformed into somebodies by Hollywood and married to people who also tried to change our images. We asked for it, bought it, and had to live with it, and we were scared shitless. He was so relieved to know I felt the same even though I was famous and he wasn't. God, how we talked and sometimes cried. Could we hold on to what we already had? Would they see through us? Clark was the first damn one I could talk to in Hollywood. He never—and I mean never—talked about me to anyone. It took me a long time after he died to open up and tell the beautiful truth. In the beginning, he told me it wasn't his thing to get involved with a married woman. I was the exception, but we both were in and out of affairs, marriages, and divorces all the time. We outlasted them all."

Gable was more confident in his next film, *A Free Soul,* despite his making love to Norma Shearer Thalberg, the boss's wife. Clark was a tough racketeer again, and Norma a spoiled rich girl who likes rough sex and gets it from him. Eventually, she makes fun of his bad manners and flashy clothes. Outside the bedroom, he is far beneath her, she jabs. He knows that, but when she says it once too often, he sweeps her up in his arms. Norma coos, and Clark throws her into a chair and makes sure she stays there until he tells her what a rotten brat she is. Norma stands up to protest and is pushed back "where you belong!"

Gable wasn't a beast, you see. He was getting even. Audiences loved it. Here was a poor guy trying to make a crooked buck (who cared during the Depression?) and here was a rich dame who changed her furs as often as she changed her stockings. She wanted a good time and he gave it to her. That was fair enough, but her tearing apart his position in life (Americans were standing in bread lines) gave him every right to shove her around. Bored with the passionate dancing and gentle kisses of Valentino, typical of the leading men who dominated the screen in the twenties, Gable balanced the tipped scale of the sexes. It was the beginning of the rough-diamond image—a man who was raw, crude, and hardened, but had a heart of gold. If Gable couldn't get his woman, he either booted her in the fanny or carried her over his shoulder to the cave she'd never leave. Why? Because she didn't want to.

Men cheered and women swooned, and MGM raised Clark's salary to $850 a week. He wasn't a star yet, but he was the most talked-about movie actor in the country. Thousands of letters were addressed to MGM about "the guy who slapped Norma Shearer." People always exaggerate when they're enthusiastic about something. They thought he slapped her in the scuffle, and that bit of misinformation follows him to this day. It did, however, give MGM an idea. They released *Night Nurse,* and what a bombshell when Gable socked Barbara Stanwyck in the kisser, for real this time!

If Crawford sensed something in Gable, she wasn't the only one in 1931. Joan Blondell, co-starring in *Night Nurse,* said, "When he showed up the first day, Barbara and I had to sit down. There was something about him that was overpowering."

Irving Thalberg described Gable better than anyone else. "Gable was the man every woman wanted and every man wanted to be."

Minna Wallis wasn't satisfied with Gable's raise in salary. She knew how many letters were flooding into MGM about her client and how proud Thalberg was of his discovery. He refused more money. Minna indicated that there were other studios that wanted Gable. He could ride out the next five months. L. B. Mayer blew his stack, but he knew a potential box-office draw. Thalberg agreed wholeheartedly. Gable had that indescribable "it" worth possible millions. "All right," he told Minna, "we'll give him $500 more a week that will be put in trust." "Deal," she said, knowing that Ria was paying the bills anyway and MGM was being fair and tough at the same time.

In keeping with his image, he portrayed a crooked gambler in *Sporting Blood* with Madge Evans. The movie had one asset and that was Clark Gable, but this time his name flashed on the screen STARRING CLARK GABLE. No more "with" or "and." He would share top billing from now on. In less than one year, he had attained more than most actors did in years.

One should remember that Gable's films were not good ones in terms of quality. They were all run-of-the-mill, but chosen for him carefully as a buildup. Though he was almost thirty-one and had been around a long time, his sudden rise to stardom was remarkable. Some say he had no competition; they were all eliminated by the microphone. The practical ones knew there was only one of a kind, however, because Gable was Gable on the street or on the screen. If Valentino had lived, and Gilbert's voice been deeper, they could not have interfered with the rugged dimpled grin of a fellow who expected dames to light his cigarettes. In the early thirties it was the man who chased the girl. In Gable's case it was the other way around, and though he was mean, everyone wanted him to get the girl at the end. When he didn't, MGM had to kill him off, as they did in *A Free Soul,* to prevent a revolution. It is hard for us today to realize the popularity of movies in the thirties and forties, when there were no television sets and video tapes. Everyone went to see a film at least once a week. Movie magazines were sold out when they hit the stands, surpassing modern offerings. Actresses set the pace in clothes, hairdos, and makeup. Actors set the trends in hats, suits, sweaters, and shoes. During the Depression and World War II, movies gave Americans hope, made them laugh, got them out of their homes on Saturday night, and created another world apart from this one of sadness, death, and hunger.

Gable was a part of all this. His voice was one of the first heard coming out of the silver screen, too. The timing was right and Josephine was wrong. He never had a serious problem with the pitch of his voice unless he got lazy.

Ria never bothered with such tutoring, of course. She was still hoping for an invitation to Pickfair, Mayer's home, or possibly dinner with Norma and Irving Thalberg. She spent most of her time (and she had a lot of that) looking for a house in Hollywood. They had been living in two apartments (one for the children), but this was hardly appropriate for a great star.

She wasn't pleased that her name was rarely mentioned in the many publicity releases. MGM said nothing about his marital status. Before anyone could make a decision about what to do, MGM found out that Clark was not legally married to Ria. Howard knew this could erupt into a scandal and that the press was digging for information. Quickly and privately, Ria and Clark were married a second time on June 19, 1931, by a judge.

As they were leaving the courthouse, the "newlyweds" were attacked by reporters who had already done their homework. Did Clark meet his bride in Houston? Or was it New York? Why did they get married again? Had they been divorced in the meantime and decided to try again? Was Ria *the* Mrs. Langham of Houston and New York society? Why did they elope? Were they going on a honeymoon? How long? Where?

Ria broke down completely. She pleaded with reporters not to print anything about this. She had three children. "What about your children?" they asked. She began to cry hysterically, and mumbled her pleas while MGM officials helped Clark get her into the car. Ria was mortified over losing control with the press. What a dreadful introduction! She never forgave herself, and rarely permitted an interview after that. Clark was expressionless and composed.

It was decided to include Ria briefly in press releases, but only when absolutely necessary. There were not the usual "at home" pictures for the fan magazines. Ria was not glamorous enough to be Gable's wife. If the studio played her down, Clark's fans might forget she existed. MGM hoped so, anyway. Ria was seen with her husband only on very special occasions. This gave him the freedom he wanted.

MGM planned Gable's publicity campaign very carefully—feeding reporters just enough to get rid of them, but not enough to satisfy them. When the news leaked out that Greta Garbo wanted Clark for her next film, *Susan Lennox,* the press dug deep into his past to find out for themselves who and what he was. They didn't have far to look.

Josephine Dillon Gable, a nobody six months ago, was besieged by callers at her shabby front door and on the telephone. She was cooperative and sincere, but very innocent before realizing that the newshounds wanted to know about more than the acting techniques that had worked magic on Hollywood's newest star. They wanted the most intimate details. Josephine was appalled by their questions, but what echoed in her ears haunted her day and night: "Why are you so poor when your ex-husband is so rich? He has everything and you have nothing."

She tried to interest the press in the bony kid she sent to a farm for his health, the hours of Shakespeare and deep breathing and her determination to make him a success. Newsmen listened and yawned. "Did you live together in Portland?" they asked. "What about Los Angeles? Was he a good lover? Are you still in love with him? Do you feel used? Cheated? Deserted?"

The press brought the hurtful truth to the surface for Josephine. She had tried to bury her feelings and leave Clark alone, which would be impossible now that she was being labeled the fool for all the world to see. This was only the beginning.

Two months after Clark's official marriage to Ria Langham, L. B. Mayer received a letter from Josephine Dillon Gable, who, in a polite and dignified manner, stated her plan to sell her story about her life with Gable. Since he had never made any effort to repay her and she desperately needed money, there was no alternative. It was not a pretty sketch of Gable and might endanger his career. What was she to do? The press was making it impossible for her to live a normal life. She was trying to operate a school, but the publicity was preventing this.

MGM wasted no time settling this matter. If Ria was a disappointing image of Mrs. Clark Gable, Josephine was far below expectation. Mayer was used to all kinds of demands. This matter was annoying but not serious. He acted as go-between because Clark refused to negotiate with Josephine, who, he felt, had humiliated him by writing to MGM. Clark offered two hundred dollars a month, provided she did not talk about him to the press. She signed the agreement. Clark, who was close with his money, quietly fumed. Would he never be rid of her? Would she never stop using his name to bind them together?

Gable had other stresses at this time, and one was working with Greta Garbo in *Susan Lennox*. A film with Garbo was a Garbo film. Anyone else in the cast was chosen to complement her on the screen and in the plot. This was not to be one of Gable's best performances. He went after the girl in this one, but his five o'clock shadow, soiled

suit, and dirty hands pressing against Garbo's half-clad white body
gave his fans what they wanted. He was glad when *Susan Lennox* was
completed and said, "Every actor should work with Garbo. She gets
what she wants—in fact, she walked off the set six times because
she didn't like the script. And she went home every day at five,
regardless of what was going on. It was in her contract. I filed that
away until the time came when I could have the same clause in my
agreement." He was impressed with the power that Garbo wielded.
"But she could back it up," he said. "I was more at ease in our love
scenes than at arm's length. She had very deep concentration."

After finishing his tenth movie to be released in 1931, Gable and Ria
rented a house on San Ysidro in Beverly Hills. Their next-door
neighbor was Fredric March, and around the corner was Pickfair.
Ria was delighted to entertain at last, despite Clark's working six
days a week. He resented having to dress up and make small talk.
His passion for hunting and fishing far exceeded his desire to stay
home. Dining with the Thalbergs or bowing at Pickfair didn't interest him. Then there were evenings with the Goldwyns and the Selz-
nicks and weekends at San Simeon castle with William Randolph
Hearst and his mistress, actress Marion Davies. Joan and Douglas
Fairbanks were usually included on everyone's guest list. Joan and
Clark would settle for any occasion to see each other. She was falling
in love with him and he with her. They were earthy and restless,
hungry for romance and passion, desirous of each other and willing
to pay the price. Well, almost, anyway. . .

Gable, meanwhile, got rid of his frustrations on hunting and fishing jaunts between films. Ria tagged along painfully once in a while,
just to be alone with him. She would have preferred him to take
more of an interest in the arts, but those days were over. "One of the
reasons I wanted a house," he said, "was to have room for my sporting equipment after living in apartments most of my life. I'd forgotten what it was like to have a house."

Though MGM did not allow Gable to be interviewed as yet, he
admired and trusted Adela Rogers St. Johns, Hearst reporter, writer,
and author of *A Free Soul*. When this sophisticated lady met Gable in
1930, he was developing saddle sores for *Painted Desert*. They became instant friends. A brilliant journalist, St. Johns was touched by
his humility and transfixed by his handsome virility. He could always
count on her as a friend and loyal supporter.

When Josephine tried to take credit for her ex-husband's talent, Adela wrote to the contrary and described Dillon as what one might expect a teacher to look like. Their feud continued because Josephine refused to see St. Johns, who tried her best to protect Clark. As with virtually every woman who knew Clark well, there would always be rumors about his relationship with Adela. Fifteen years after his death, she was asked in a TV interview if she had loved him. "There's a difference between loving someone and being in love with someone," she replied. Reference was made to her having his baby in the thirties. Adela smiled. "What woman would deny Clark Gable was the father of her child?"

Crawford said St. Johns was a dear friend of Clark's who coached him in *A Free Soul*. "If it hadn't been for her, he wouldn't have been the actor he became. He was ever grateful. You wouldn't know it to look at her, but Adela had more men than I did, if that's possible. She used to cover up for Clark and me so often. That's the kind of friend she was."

Though 1931 was the beginning of a long career for Gable, he wasn't happy. Ria said he was quiet and moody. Grateful to be a member of the MGM family, he did not appreciate coming home to more obligations and schedules. Ria was a strong and understanding woman, and she gracefully tolerated his sullen looks and crankiness. Like Josephine, she had no idea what Clark was thinking except for his bluntness over budgeting. "I'd feel better," he groaned, "if I had twenty thousand dollars in the bank." Ria was thrifty, but she had supported him for three years and wasn't about to pinch too many pennies. Nor did she intend to use her own money.

Gable was beginning to feel like a freak. He had no idea how long his popularity would last. He was typecast as a leading man, a dangerous position to be in, he said. The public was fickle. One day they'll stand in line to see a star and the next they won't come at all. "I worked three months straight without a day off," he said. "If this is what it's like to be a success, when will I have a chance to enjoy it?"

The answer to that was *Possessed* with Joan Crawford, who was cast as the poor factory worker who falls in love with an influential lawyer-politician, Gable. The excitement on the set when the cameras were not rolling was far more intriguing and romantic than the plot of *Possessed*. Several weeks into production, Hollywood was buzzing about the Gable-Crawford affair. "We were madly in love," she said. "Everyone working with us could see it, because when the scenes ended, the emotion didn't." They lunched alone in her dressing room, sat close enough to hold hands on the set, stared at each other with longing, and did their love scenes with sizzling passion, as if no one else were around.

Except for an infrequent drive along the ocean, their alone time was limited to the studio. One observer said, "They were discreet, but it was impossible for them to hide their feelings. He was glowing and she was radiant. They were like two kids. I hadn't seen anything like this since Garbo and Gilbert in *Flesh and the Devil*. When their director said, 'Cut!' during their kisses, they didn't stop. It was like peeking into someone's bedroom. This is how we felt about Gable and Crawford, but would she leave Fairbanks? Everyone knew they were going their separate ways. First marriages rarely last in Hollywood anyway. As for Gable, he was known for his one-nighters to make his marriage bearable. There were those who felt he was using Joan the same way he used his wives, but I never believed that."

Crawford said they discussed marriage. "I suggested it jokingly, but Clark was quite serious. He thought we should both start divorce proceedings right away. I have no idea how it would have turned out. Maybe dreaming about it left me with fonder memories. I don't know..."

The Trocadero and Brown Derby were buzzing with speculation.

"Gable's a far cry from Douglas. I thought Joan was a social climber," said one actress to another.

"She is," was the snotty reply, "but she's horny as hell, too. Gable can give her what she wants."

"How do you know?"

"Meaning he's not the gentle type like Doug."

"How do you know that?"

"Where have you been? I'm surprised he and Clark haven't bumped into each other getting in and out of bed."

"Not mine, unfortunately. Do you think this affair will lead to anything?"

"Joan doesn't give up until she gets what she wants."

"Her career comes first."

"She's a flapper!" was the snide remark.

"Was, my dear, was. She's going in for dramatic acting, and does her best performing in Mr. Mayer's office. She complains about her parts, he cries, she cries, they embrace and compromise. They're both full of shit."

"We should be so lucky, darling. He's the most powerful man in Hollywood and she's a star."

"Where does that leave Gable?"

"Home with mother, I suppose. She understands him."

Guffaw. "If he starts making big bucks, Gable won't need her anymore. I never did go for that older-woman crap. If he finds what he wants—and Joan appears to be it—the very proper and matronly Ria Gable will be back in Houston."

"Which leaves the debonair Douglas Fairbanks, Jr., a free man."

"Have you ever been to Pickfair?"

Ria was accustomed to gossip about her husband but the rumors about his affair with Crawford were too intense, and the clues added up to truth. She kept her mouth shut and her eyes open. Clark had certainly changed during the filming of *Possessed*. For a guy who was completely exhausted from working so hard, Clark was leaving for the studio earlier than usual, with a smile on his face, and coming home later, in good humor. He was getting less sleep, but had a different attitude toward being overworked.

Ria did not attempt to discuss the obvious with her husband. He'd deny it or keep quiet. Either way, she would be playing into Joan's hands. Above all, Ria did not want to drive him away. They lived in a society of extramarital affairs that ended as quickly as they started. Making movies meant temporarily falling in love with one's co-star. The motto in Hollywood was "Don't marry your leading lady until you've made at least one more film."

Knowing the peculiar rules, Ria decided to take her children to New York for a while, and asked MGM to make the arrangements. In essence, she was officially traveling as Mrs. Clark Gable—"Hear ye, hear ye!" Though she had been catered to in the past, it was nothing compared to the attention she received as a movie star's wife. And she took advantage of every opportunity. On the train ride east, Ria signed autographs and was available for interviews. She was divinely happy living in Hollywood, but had business in New York. Clark was so busy making one film on top of another, you know. She missed him terribly, but the children had friends in the East. Then there were the new plays on Broadway. She would see them all because Clark was so very interested in what had happened in the theater since he gave up the stage to make films.

Ria made up for her bad performance at the courthouse in June. She was cooperative, smiling, cheerful, optimistic, and gracious. By the time she arrived in Chicago, the whole country knew exactly who Mrs. Clark Gable was.

She had a marvelous time basking in her husband's fame, and used his name at restaurants, department stores, box offices, and hotels. If Ria worried over leaving her husband alone with the woman he loved, no one would ever know it.

Clark considered her trip a separation, regardless of Ria's interviews to the contrary. He saw Joan day and night. Fairbanks was too busy making movies to pay any attention. He didn't have to rely on Joan for his social life.

Everyone involved was doing nicely until L. B. Mayer decided it was time he put out the fire on the set of *Possessed*. He summoned Clark to his office.

"You're doing a fine job in the picture. How do you feel about it?"

Gable shrugged. "What difference does it make?"

"The role's a serious one . . . that's what I was referring to . . ."

"Are you insinuating it's not for me . . . that I stink?"

"No, no . . . I'm quite satisfied with your performance."

"Is that all?"

Mayer scowled as he motioned for Clark to remain seated. "I haven't finished."

"What is it then?"

"I'm disturbed about your performance off-camera. The whole town's talking about it. Hedda and Louella are ready to break the news in their columns. They each want the scoop, and we can't let that happen, can we?"

"If you mean my divorce . . . well, it has to come out in the open sometime."

"Does it?" Mayer asked harshly.

"Doesn't it?"

"Have you any idea what we had to contend with when your first wife made herself known publicly? What I had to go through personally to shut her up?"

"I'm paying for it," Clark explained.

"If you think two hundred dollars a month is payment due, my friend, you're all wrong. You're getting away with murder. If she had been a smart woman, Josephine would have gotten herself a lawyer, put you on the front pages of every newspaper in the country, and be living in a decent neighborhood. Fortunately, I was able to reason with the lady. However, I don't think the present Mrs. Gable is going to be that innocent and stupid."

"That's my problem."

"As long as you work for MGM, it's my problem. I want you to get that through your head!"

"I'm not going to live with a woman I don't love."

"Why?"

"That's fairly obvious, isn't it?"

"Where you're concerned, nothing is certain. Suppose you spell it out so I'll understand."

"I'm in love for the first time in my life. Ria knows it, too."

"Who's the lucky lady?"

"Joan."

"I have more than one Joan on the payroll."

"Joan Crawford is the lady I'm in love with."

"She's no lady!" Mayer pounced.

"That's a terrible thing to say!"

"I know her better than you do, Clark, and she's good for only one thing."

"For your information, I intend to marry her."

Mayer smiled. "What about the others you've been sleeping with?"

Gable ignored the question. "Joanie and I are in love and we intend to get married."

"I'll extend my congratulations now, because when *Possessed* is finished, you and Joan are fired."

Clark smiled. "I don't think we'll have a problem."

"Neither of you will work for any studio in Hollywood. I'll see to that. I can make 'em and I can break 'em. It's as simple as that. Don't put me to the test."

"I don't understand you . . ."

"When you were a kid, did you understand your father?"

"No, and I still don't!"

"That's all in the past, my boy. MGM is your family now, and I'm your father. If you can't abide by the rules, you're welcome to leave."

"Where does love fit into this mess?"

"There is no such thing in this town," Mayer emphasized. "I

won't waste your time with the exceptions because you're not one of them. You like dames and none of them can keep you in one bed for very long, and that includes Joan. The wife you have now is superior to anyone in Hollywood. She's been very understanding. She hasn't caused us any trouble despite your indiscretions. Think about it."

"I don't have to. The marriage is over."

"Not yet."

"What?"

"You'll get on the goddamn telephone and ask your dear wife lovingly to come back. You miss her."

Clark scowled. "She won't buy it."

"Whether she buys it isn't important. That's what she wants to hear, and her heart will take over from there."

"Then what?"

"You'll take her out in public. She'll take your arm and you'll smile. The happily married couple will face reporters calmly, pose for pictures, and have a good time."

"Then what?"

"It will convince everyone that your affair with Crawford meant nothing. Maybe it never existed at all."

"But it did and it does."

"Not after you leave this office. Is that understood?"

"How can I tell her? We're in love."

"You don't have to say anything. I'll do the talking for you. Joan and I speak the same language. Now get on that phone and call your wife in New York!"

"Before I do, haven't you the decency to tell me what it is you have against Joan?"

"I have great admiration for her as an actress, but she's a slut. Maybe she sets a table better than Mary Pickford, but it's all an act, my boy. Her whole life is an act. She is what she is—a cheap flapper who likes to get laid. That's why she's not for you. Maybe you're not much better, but together you'll destroy each other—and me. I'm warning you not to see her again. I'd never do anything to hurt you, Clark. This is for your own good. Do what I ask and you'll have everything any man could ask for. I won't let you down if you don't let me down. But if you don't abide by my wishes, you'll pay. Believe me, you'll pay a high price."

"All right, but you can't stop me from loving Joan."

"You'll forget all about her. In the meantime, take your wife out dining and dancing. Let the world see what a happy couple you are."

"Suppose she won't come back?" Clark asked.

"Beg that charming woman to return because, more than any-thing, you want her here with you. Tell her marriage is sacred and all that crap. You're better at that sort of thing than I am."

End of conversation. Clark made the call, and Ria began packing.

"You certainly are the star of *Possessed,* Joanie. It's your picture!"

"How sweet, L.B., but Clark and I are always good together."

"I couldn't agree more." Mayer smiled. "It would be a shame to break up the combination, wouldn't it?"

"Of course," she sighed. "We're a team!"

"You're forcing me to break it up . . ."

"Why on earth would you do a thing like that, L.B.? Is something wrong? Are you feeling all right?"

"Joanie, you're headed for disaster. I've tried to protect you every way possible. Who knows that better than you? How could you be-tray me?"

"What have I done, L.B.?"

"You've been fucking around with Gable behind my back."

"I was going to tell you about it after the picture was finished." Joan smiled sweetly. "You see, L.B., Clark and I love each other. We plan to be married."

"He can't be true to any woman. He's not even faithful to you now! Would you like a list of the girls he's been sleeping with?"

"If we were married, that would change."

"I know different, and so do you. I'm not so sure you know what it is to sleep in only one bed, either. Frankly, it doesn't interest me much who the hell either of you plays with as long as it isn't with each other."

"Are you saying that . . ."

"I don't want you and Clark to see each other again."

Joan began to cry. "How can you do this to me, L.B.?"

"Because I have wonderful plans for you," he said, sitting down beside her. "Don't force me to change my mind."

"But I've finally found love," she wept.

"Not with that big oversexed lug. Listen to me, Joanie. Life hasn't been easy for you, but now that's all changing. You're a star, but more important, you're a great actress. How important is this to you?"

"It's my life!"

"I'd hate to take it all away. . ."

Joan wept on his shoulder. "What do you want me to do?" she asked.

"It's what I *don't* want you to do, my dear, and that is never to see Gable again."

Joan sobbed and sobbed. Mayer held her hand and said softly, "I'm doing this for your own good because, above all else, I don't want to see you get hurt. I want to see your name up in lights and to sit home by the fireplace and read your fan mail. Did I ever tell you that was a favorite pastime of mine?"

"No." She sniffed.

"So I'm giving you a choice—your career or Gable. Make it now, Joanie. . ."

"Do you have any idea how hard this is for me?"

"Sure I do. You're like a daughter to me."

"I'll do whatever you ask, L.B."

"Gable's off-limits after working hours."

"All right," she sobbed. "All right. You have my word, but I have a favor."

"Anything, Joanie, you know that."

"Bless you, L.B. I'm starting *Letty Lynton* soon."

"Fine movie, but better ones are coming your way."

"Then you admit it won't be one of my best."

"It's important to keep your face on the screen even though the script isn't the best."

"There's one way to make *Lynton* better."

"Anything you say, Joanie."

"Good, because Clark would be perfect for my leading man."

"Absolutely not!" Mayer raged. "How can you ask me such a thing?"

"But it's such a tiny favor."

"You'll do *Letty Lynton* with Robert Montgomery and like it!"

"My heart is broken," she wept.

"You don't know what suffering is, but you will if you go out with Gable again."

Joan and Clark agreed they would have to be very careful for a while, but it wasn't the end of their plans for a future together. Without Mayer's blessing, neither had a future. It was a mutual and deep understanding that kept them together for thirty years. Crawford said, "What Mayer would never believe is that Clark and I gave each other the courage to go on and . . . laugh at our mistakes. I cried through *Letty Lynton* and everyone was so sympathetic. The next few months were very hard for us. Very tough. Nothing went right."

Mayer kept his promise by rewarding Joan with the Academy Award–winning *Grand Hotel* with Greta Garbo, John and Lionel Barrymore, and Wallace Beery. Joan had to fight for recognition in this film and was determined to hold her own with this superb cast. Though Crawford was not one to admit her great admiration for another actress, she was in awe of Garbo. "We weren't supposed to go anywhere near her when we weren't filming," Joan recalled. "I accidentally bumped into her in the stairwell. We came face to face, noses almost touching, and my knees got weak. She was breathtaking. If I ever thought of becoming a lesbian, this was it."

Crawford was on edge, lonely, and feisty these days. When the MGM publicity department sent a reporter to interview her on the set of *Grand Hotel,* she snapped, "Why do you always have to ask me about my marriage? That's old hat! Can't you see I have more important things on my mind?"

Crawford climbed one more rung on the ladder when *Grand Hotel* won the award for best picture of the year. She had one especially fine scene, and Mayer was proud of her.

"You stole that scene, Joanie."

She winked. "I did my best."

"There are rewards when one concentrates on her work. I put you to the test and you came out with flying colors. When I watch *Grand Hotel,* I always have it set to that one great scene that you did."

"Are you serious, L.B.? Do you really?"

"I had to be convinced that you could handle the role of Sadie Thompson."

"Sadie Thompson!" Joan cried, dabbing her eyes with a linen hanky. "Sadie Thompson?"

"Yes. I'm loaning you out to United Artists."

"United Artists? Why?"

"Because they're producing *Rain.*"

"I don't know anyone at United Artists. I'd be lost! I don't know the lighting men, the cameramen, the makeup people—no one!"

"They know who Joan Crawford is. You'll get the star treatment over there too."

"I won't do it! MGM is home. I'm comfortable here. I'd be lost at United Artists!"

"Playing Sadie Thompson in *Rain* will make you one of the biggest stars in Hollywood. Maybe the best. That's what you've always wanted, Joan. It's what I want, too."

"Do you want the truth, L.B.?"

"If that's possible, yes."

"I'm terrified."

"There's nothing to fear. If you're dissatisfied with your dressing room or your wardrobe, just pick up the telephone and call me. I'll make everything all right again."

"Must I go over there?" she asked with tears in her eyes.

"You'll be working on beautiful Catalina Island. It will be a glorious vacation. Let me see a smile before you leave."

Forcing a whimpering grin, Joan sighed. "I'm better than Gloria Swanson, aren't I, L.B.?"

"She was a marvelous Sadie, but you do it your way, my dear."

Crawford went through hell filming *Rain* on Catalina Island. Her performance was so bad, she hoped they would destroy the film. Shattered by this flop and her broken romance with Gable, she went into seclusion in Hollywood, and Doug dashed off to Mexico for some fun.

Gable hated every minute of *Hell Divers*. His nerves were frayed, his moods were black, and his outlook was very sour. He found solace in straight gin and long talks with Minna. "I can't take it anymore," he said. "I'm tired and have nothing to show for it. Nothing different than working on the farm—up before dawn and home after dark, but MGM's making hay, not me!"

Ria was back, and just in time to see him through this crisis. Clark had lost almost twenty pounds. He was nervous, depressed, and ready to crack. "I'll go along with anything you decide," she told him, but before he had time to think it over, MGM assigned him to co-star with Marion Davies in *Polly of the Circus*. Mayer spoke to Clark personally. "We're doing this as a favor to my dear friend William Randolph Hearst, who will do anything for Marion."

Clark glanced at the script. "I'm not playing a goddamn priest!"

"Hearst will give you a bonus." Mayer smiled confidently. "He's a very generous man."

"I won't play the part."

"How about a minister?"

Clark grimaced. "The story is terrible."

Mayer spoke to Hearst, who spoke to his writers, who tried to oblige Gable, who walked off the set and hid out in Palm Springs while Minna tried to make peace. She told Mayer it wasn't only Hearst's picture. "Clark wants more money," she said.

"You tell him if he's not on the set tomorrow morning, he's suspended without pay and he'll never work again at this studio or any other in Hollywood!" Mayer roared.

Minna reported back to Clark. "L.B. means it," she said. "Maybe you'd better come home."

"The hell I will!" was the reply.

Gable would surely have been fired had it not been for another woman who was responsible for his survival—Marion Davies, who, with her famous stutter, cried to Hearst, "I'm v-v-very h-h-h-hurt. Please d-d-do something!"

W.R. convinced L.B. that C.G. deserved a raise, and on January 22, 1932, Gable signed a two-year contract with MGM for $2,000 a week, thanks to Davies, who was "s-s-so h-happy to have C-C-Clarkie back." *Polly of the Circus* was terrible, but everyone connected with its production was satisfied, especially Mayer, who needed the power and influence of the Hearst newspapers.

Thirty-five-year-old Marion was "off-limits" to her leading men because she was Hearst's mistress, but the fun-loving blond ex-Ziegfeld girl was discreetly naughty occasionally. She lived in Santa Monica and he preferred his castle, San Simeon, with its sixty guest rooms, on top of La Cuesta Encantada, the enchanted hill several hundred miles north of Los Angeles.

Hearst, worth $300 million, was forty years older than Davies, but their famous affair lasted more than three decades. He worshipped her and she sincerely loved him, but Marion found it hard to resist dallying with men like Gable. There was never any gossip about her, with the exception of the ill-fated cruise aboard Hearst's 280-foot yacht, *Oneida*. The cause of the sudden death of producer-director Thomas Ince has never been established. He was cremated before an autopsy could be performed. Newspapers controlled by Hearst attribute his fatal illness to "acute indigestion," but a reliable witness claimed he was shot in the head. Did Hearst find Marion with him, or was he mistaken for Charlie Chaplin, whom the old man suspected of making love to his mistress?

Louella Parsons managed to get off the yacht without being noticed and denied being on board. Hearst gave her a lifetime contract with his newspapers shortly after the tragic incident.

Mrs. Ince claimed she was at her husband's bedside when he passed away. Why did Hearst set up a sizable trust fund for her?

Hollywood insiders accept the theory that he shot Ince in front of witnesses. This was enough to scare off any actor trying to touch Marion off-camera, but Clark Gable was not just any actor. He frequently accepted her dinner invitations at the beach house after work on *Polly of the Circus*. They strolled arm-and-arm down Ocean Front Walk to the Venice Amusement Park to ride the roller coaster.

Marion, a very heavy drinker, found a devoted companion in Clark, who found solace in sharing the bottle with a genuinely friendly and radiant woman. Exactly when she gave him a piece of very valuable property in Palm Desert to lure him into one of her neighborhoods isn't recorded. Money bought the silence surrounding the Davies-Hearst unofficial alliance (their names were never linked in his newspapers) and to whisper about Marion was to defy a man more powerful than the President of the United States.

Clark's cozy dinners at the beach house with Marion were romantic, warm, and racy. Neither would ever have confidence, and their search for peace was infinite . . . she with her stutter and he with his big ears. But on those balmy nights under the moon and stars, the roller coaster made them forget that tomorrow never promises anything but ups and downs. And plenty of dangerous curves . . .

CHAPTER FIVE

"What kind of a woman do you think an actor should marry?" the reporter asked Clark Gable.

"The kind of woman I'm married to—my wife. I am the 'star' and Ria is my wife. She is a self-sufficient woman, has her own interests, her own friends, bridge clubs and parties, the children and our home. I could not and would not be married to an actress because one professional ego is enough in my house. Neither would I want to marry some sweet young thing many years my junior. A younger girl wouldn't know what it's all about. She'd be jealous and suspicious and resentful. She would be an easy victim of all the gossip. Things like that happen, you know. It did to Ria and me during our first year of marriage. Any number of people came to her with little tales to prove I was stepping high, wide, and handsome with this one or that one . . . that I was having an affair with a star. Did she know about it? What did she intend to do? But Ria is a wise, sane, and balanced woman. She survived all that.

"Ria knows I always tell her the truth. If she asks me about a certain so-and-so I was supposed to be playing around with, I tell her it's just not so and to forget it. Ria is a woman who has been about, who knows the world and life and how to handle men. She has never been on the set with me once. How about that for a good wife?

"Marriage is a seesaw. Our marriage balances evenly and one side is equally as important as the other."

Such was an article in a fan magazine complete with pictures of Ria and Clark Gable having a cozy drink at an exclusive nightclub. He wore a tuxedo with a gardenia in his lapel. Ria was decked out in low-cut satin with flowers bunched at the cleavage and a white fur draped over her shoulders. One hand on her hip, she was a lady of confidence. On the same page was a small photo of Clark and Joan embracing. Underneath it read, "Mrs. Gable never visits the set to check up on Clark's big clinches such as this one with Joan Crawford. Mrs. Gable is neither jealous nor suspicious and is content to remain in the background of his public life, serene in the knowledge that she is first in his private one."

The MGM publicity department was responsible for this lengthy interview, which went on and on and on to prove to one and all that Gable was loyal to his wife. And, if there were any questions, we dare to print a loving photo of his suspected girl friend, Joan Crawford, enfolded in his arms.

Gable wasn't the only supposedly happy husband in Hollywood. Another article by Douglas Fairbanks, Jr., entitled "Four Rules of Married Love," was a shocker in the early thirties.

"I don't think that married people ought to be conscious of the fact that they are married," he said. "They ought to live in sin, so to speak... I mean that after marriage you should keep up the same relationship that existed before marriage—to keep on courting your wife. Why take your wife for granted?"

And what were the four rules for a happy marriage?

"Be honest with yourself. Preserve the essence of comradeship. Never hurt the person you love. Never take anything for granted."

The article labeled Joan and Doug Hollywood's perpetual honeymooners.

But Clark, despite his new contract, and Joan, who was having a nervous breakdown over *Rain,* resumed their affair. He had gotten what he wanted, but was angry that Mayer hadn't offered more money instead of Hearst, who was under the influence of Marion Davies. All of his movies had made money, yet he had to fight for every dollar. Joan could only blame herself for her sad performance as Sadie Thompson—even more reason to hide behind locked doors and brood over Clark, who came to her when she called. They refrained from any discussion of marriage. It was too good just being together, and that was all that mattered. They talked endlessly, made love, tore Mayer to shreds, and made love again. Their careers were a mess, their marriages were falling apart, and they had no personal happiness. Clark felt the sting more than Joan. He wanted more freedom. Ria had attached herself to MGM, or was it the other way around? He was surrounded on all sides. Mayer controlled his days and Ria controlled his weekends. She had her children, whom he liked and wanted to help, but his time and patience were limited. Ria was in the web of Hollywood society and loving it. He tried and was hopelessly bored.

Fairbanks also preferred the tastes of the *jeunesse dorée,* who made Joan uncomfortable. She never quite fit in, and learned from her few visits to Pickfair that the nouveaux riches are what they were—nothing.

She poured out her heart to Gable, who leaned on her broad shoulder for comfort, too. Maybe they could make it—if, that is, there was a way to be together without rocking the boat.

There wasn't.

"Joanie, dear. Why did you do it?" Mayer asked sweetly.

"We're friends," she said casually.

"Then make new ones. Meanwhile, you've been under a great deal of pressure and I forgive you. How would you like a nice long vacation?"

"Well..."

"A second honeymoon with Douglas."

"Who?"

"Your husband."

"Where?"

"New York and Europe. Compliments of MGM."

"Why?"

"Gable's not for you. He never left the barnyard, Joanie. I know what you want, if you don't. Give old Doug a chance. He's got style. Now don't get me wrong. I like Clark, but he's wild, Joanie. He's a bull. A cocksman."

"You're exaggerating, L.B."

"How about that trip?"

"Oh, all right, but I want to say good-bye to Clark."

"You should get home and pack," Mayer said, walking her to the door. "Besides, Clark is having a script meeting with Jean Harlow."

"Harlow?"

"Very sad thing happened. Gilbert was going to star with her in *Red Dust,* but he's back on the booze. I'm replacing him with Clark. What a pair—Harlow and Gable!"

"You son of a bitch!"

Mayer smiled. "She's a bride, Joanie. Just got married to Thalberg's friend, Paul Bern."

"I know the little weasel, and he's not man enough to stop that harlot from massaging her tits in public."

"Wait until I'm through arranging this trip for you, Joan! Your fans will make you feel like a million. Leave it to me. And when they're not kneeling at your feet, you and Doug will be sipping the finest champagne and nibbling on caviar in the very best hotel suites in the world."

Joan's vacation with Doug was, as it turned out, a series of public appearances—too many fans and too little time alone. They appeared happy on board ship, and she loved Paris. Mayer might have accomplished something, because Gable fell in love with Harlow, but plans to strengthen the Fairbanks marriage failed.

Jean Harlow, known affectionately at MGM as "The Baby," was twenty-one years old. Born Harlean Carpentier in Kansas City, she was educated in private schools and at sixteen eloped with a wealthy Chicagoan. When the marriage was dissolved, she moved with her Christian Scientist mother and stepfather Bello to Los Angeles, where she worked as an extra in movies using her mother's maiden name, Jean Harlow.

Howard Hughes took a chance on her in 1930 in his $3 million film, *Hell's Angels*. Jean was terrible as the British girl who seduces the Royal Flying Corps, but her blatant sexuality as she purred to Ben Lyon, "Pardon me while I slip into something more comfortable," was so potent, moviegoers were aghast. MGM bought her contract from Hughes for $60,000 two years later.

Jean hated to wear underwear, but gave in to panties. "I'll never wear a bra," she told the press. "They're too uncomfortable." She rubbed ice cubes on her breasts and nipples to make them stand out. She walked, talked, and dressed like a sexy dish but wasn't seen in public with men very often. "All they care about," she said, "is getting their hands underneath my dress." Mayer offered Jean a full-length mink coat if she'd go to bed with him. She turned him down with a barrage of curses.

She was at the peak of her career in 1932, and her choice of husband shocked MGM, but Jean had made up her mind to marry a man twenty years older—MGM executive Paul Bern, who was short and balding, with a Hitler mustache. Known as "father confessor," Bern was a gentle, brilliant producer and Irving Thalberg's assistant.

He began the courtship of Jean Harlow by asking her to lunch. Harmless enough. Then dinner, but no passes in the back seat of the limousine. "My God, he wants to take me to the opera!" she exclaimed. When Paul invited her to his apartment, Jean suspected the worst. But Paul introduced her to good books, played classical music, and took her home without insisting on a good-night kiss. When he proposed, Jean accepted. "At last I've found a man who isn't interested in my body," she sighed.

Paul, however, was in desperate need of this sex goddess. His sanity was at stake. On their wedding night, the impotent Bern, who had the genitals of a young boy, expected a miracle to happen. When he failed as a husband, he got drunk and beat Jean across the back with his cane. To avoid scandal, they remained together until MGM felt it was the appropriate time for divorce.

It was Bern who recommended Gable for the part in *Red Dust*, but he soon regretted it. When he found out that Jean refused to wear a bathing suit during her bath in the rain barrel, he stayed away from the studio. He knew Gable's reputation with women, and now his wife was flaunting her nude body in front of the notorious lover.

Red Dust was a wonderful lift for Jean and Clark. Rumors sizzled once again. "Did you see them clinging together all day?" "He can't keep his hands off her." "She was all over him." They were usually huddled together, whispering and giggling. Too easy for Gable? He'd already seen it all, but the gossip continued. "He's nuts about her." "I heard they get their kicks in his dressing room." "Gable wouldn't dare touch Bern's wife . . . would he?" "Something's going on. Clark's hotter with the Baby than he was with Crawford!"

Gable entered Harlow's life during one of the most shocking scandals in Hollywood history. He did not try to hide his attraction to Jean, who was destined for tragedy. What he found was a product of Hollywood—a little girl who loved her body and found pleasure in sharing its beauty. She liked to tease men she could trust, and, most assuredly, she could trust Gable. His relationship with Jean was more dangerous than the affair with Crawford. At this time, no one knew about Bern's sexual problem, with the exception of a select few.

Did Harlow and Gable have a fling? Most likely. The many witnesses to their closeness on the set of *Red Dust* were rooting for it. "They wrestled," one of the cast said. "I don't know how else to describe it. Every time I saw them, they were entwined. Then they made love for the camera, and it was like they were made for each other. This beautiful couple blended together perfectly."

Jean's girl friend claims she wasn't interested in sex. "She was married at sixteen and described her wedding night as 'messy.' Jean was practically a virgin. She had a tough life. She supported her mother and stepfather, who was rumored to have dabbled incestuously with Jean. She hated him. Sex was not Jean's thing unless it was right. I don't think any man had her unless Gable succeeded. She adored him. More important, she needed him. He was a devil, but a harmless one with her . . . harmless in the sense that he'd never hurt Jean. I think they found a way to be together and share an intimacy that meant something worthwhile. Neither of them wanted to go home at the end of the day. Jean hated Paul, but she wasn't on the rebound. They were living under the same roof, waiting it out. I think Gable was doing the same thing. We were all rooting for a love affair, but no one would admit to it because nobody would hurt the Baby."

Three months after Jean's wedding, Paul danced into her bedroom wearing a dildo strapped around his waist. As crude as it was, she broke into gales of laughter and they frolicked together, but not in the bed. After their ritual dance of fun, they tried to flush the contraption down the toilet.

Sometime during the night, Bern shot himself in the head with a .38 pistol and left Jean a farewell note:

Dearest Dear,
Unfortunately this is the only way to make good the frightful wrong I have done you, and to wipe out my abject humiliation.
I love you.

Paul

You understand that last night was only a comedy.

The Berns' butler called L. B. Mayer, who wanted to destroy the note. Howard Strickling convinced him not to conceal any evidence of suicide. Otherwise, Jean might be suspected of killing her impotent husband. The note was on the front page of every newspaper, but no explanation was given.

Clark and Jean's stepfather, Bello, were on a fishing trip the day Paul's body was found. They didn't find out what had happened until that evening. Gable went home and waited for word while Bello forced Jean into a fake suicide attempt to demonstrate her grief.

Clark was appalled at the funeral, when, as the mourners were about to leave, they were asked to pay their last respects to Paul Bern. The coffin was put on an electrical contraption that swung around and tilted up, and the coffin opened! It was a dreadful moment as the Bern corpse appeared to sit up for a last look at his friends. Gable got blind drunk that night.

Harlow returned to the set of *Red Dust* and Clark's consolation. He made her smile again, helped her through each day, and was with her when the news broke that Bern's common-law wife had committed suicide, too. MGM hated bigamy almost as much as suicide, but there was more. It seemed Paul had been seeing this woman every week and supporting her with Jean's money.

With Gable's help, Jean was able to complete *Red Dust*, which was one of the biggest profit-making films in 1932. Audiences loved the nude Jean in a rain barrel telling Gable, "Scrub my back." She was considered a star now. *Time* magazine criticized the film's brazen moral values, and the lines at the box office got longer. *Red Dust* was labeled the epitome of sexual daring.

Gable had taken it upon himself to discontinue his monthly payments of $200 to Josephine because she had violated their agreement by granting interviews that appeared in print. She was very upset, but Clark was livid. To get even, Josephine talked to any reporter who would listen. She chose her words carefully, but the message was there. Without her, Gable would not exist.

In essence, Josephine was getting more press coverage than her ex-husband. MGM decided to give Clark an opportunity to speak for himself—to offset Josephine's cool wrath. Reporters were asked not to ask questions of a personal nature, however. It should, by now, be quite a scoop to talk with Gable—the man and the star.

"It isn't looks," he began, "and it isn't experience. It isn't ability, because everyone knows there are stars who can't act worth a damn. The public makes the stars, but they don't know what they want. You can't explain a damn thing in this business.

"It's a chain of accidents. When you get to Hollywood, you find yourself in lots of chains of accidents. If it turns out all right, you're a star. If you're enough of a gambler or a jackass to figure everything will turn out just fine, move to Hollywood. You want to be a movie star? Maybe you'd like it and maybe you wouldn't like it. You might not be happy at all."

That was the last interview! MGM made sure the press did not get near Gable, and he was told to keep his mouth shut.

Naturally, there were times one of his quotes got through to the press. "It's my business to work," he said, "not to think." Or, when asked about his new house, "Yeah, it's a hell of a lot better than the dump I lived in before out here!"

Mayer told him, "Your fans don't want to hear those things, my boy. You've got to give them the impression you love working for MGM. There are more stars here than there are in heaven. The public would give up everything to be in your shoes. Why else do you think they pay to see you?"

Clark scowled. "Damned if I know."

Gable was so down-to-earth he said the wrong things. Mayer asked him not to talk to reporters. Howard would handle his publicity from now on. That was fine with Clark. "It's all bullshit anyway," he mumbled.

With his new raise in pay, and no longer obligated to pay Josephine, Clark felt he might save the $20,000 that represented security. Ria, however, was on a spending spree and more intent on entertaining than ever. She had come back after his affair with Joan because MGM asked her to. That was not an easy thing to do. It was common knowledge in Hollywood that Mayer was responsible for keeping their marriage together, and Ria was trying to prove that everything was the way it used to be. She was anxious to redecorate and buy new clothes and have servants and invite the right people for dinner. It was important that he live like a star. After all, look what Marion Davies did for him! And dear Mr. Hearst, whose San Simeon was the most elegant estate (or was it a castle?) in the country. Maybe the world. It was wrong to refuse an invitation to spend a weekend there.

"But Hearst doesn't allow booze," Clark said.

"Don't be silly. Marion always has some hidden away."

"I'm not a closet drinker."

"Well, I suppose you could pack a bottle."

"That's the quickest way to get your name crossed off his guest
list. I like Will too much for that."

"It's only three days, darling."

That was a long time between gins for Clark, who had little else
to keep him going these days. He and Ria were growing farther and
farther apart . . . one reason she planned so many social gatherings
despite his obvious lack of enthusiasm. If he couldn't fish or hunt, he
much preferred relaxing with his friends at the studio—not his co-
stars necessarily. He enjoyed the stagehands and extras. Gable never
forgot the days when he groveled for a part—the humiliation of
being snubbed, the heartbreak of begging, and the feeling of being a
nobody. He'd never allow anyone working with him to go through
that if he could be a friend.

How many mini-affairs he had isn't important. There were more
than he could count, but he stayed away from the ones who talked.

When asked why he turned down an offer to spend an evening
with an exciting actress, he said, "She has a big mouth."

Was he afraid of getting caught?

"Hell no," he replied. "I know I'm not great in the sack, and she'd
blab it all over town!"

He saw Joan very discreetly, always had time for Adela Rogers St.
Johns and Jean Harlow. Howard Strickling was his closest confidant.
But Gable was depressed and lonely again. He wasn't anxious to start
Strange Interlude with Norma Shearer and to have her husband, Irving Thalberg, directing, but anything was better than sitting around
home and helping Ria with seating arrangements for their next dinner party.

The only significance about *Strange Interlude* is the mustache
Gable had to grow—the one that became a trademark because he
never shaved it off.

Gable's last movie in 1932 was *No Man of Her Own* at Paramount. His co-star was Carole Lombard, who was happily married to
actor William Powell at the time. It was an easy film and completed
quickly. Gable liked Carole, who loved to pull gags on everyone.
With her energy and ambition, she was difficult to catch, but Clark
wasn't chasing. She presented him with a ham (his name was on it!),
which he accepted with a broad grin for the photographer she had
hired for the occasion. "I'm one leading lady he didn't seduce," she
said.

• • •

Joan Crawford returned from her European trip with renewed self-confidence. She also had made up her mind that a divorce from Fairbanks was inevitable but kept it to herself. Even Doug didn't know. They made the rounds socially, including dinner with the Gables. Maybe not all was forgotten or forgiven, but the key word in Hollywood was "survival," and to survive, one had to dine with the right people regardless of the circumstances. Ria was known for her elegant friends—Gloria Swanson, Marlene Dietrich, and European royalty. Joan Crawford was MGM royalty and therefore entitled to attend Ria's exclusive get-togethers. Besides, they liked each other in their own fashion.

Joan had made up her mind to be a good girl by charming Ria and Mayer. Wouldn't it be wonderful if everyone could be friends again for the sake of better movies? Of course it would! Ria was thrilled with life in general. No one could dampen her enthusiasm when Clark agreed to move into a bigger house in Brentwood (around the corner from Joan). "And," Ria told the ladies of the bridge club, "Clark is going to do a movie with Helen Hayes. I couldn't be more thrilled!"

Ria was the only one.

The White Sister was terrible.

With Thalberg ailing in Europe, Gable was at the mercy of Mayer's son-in-law, David Selznick. Ria consoled her husband as usual. "Helen is such a gracious lady," she bubbled. "She's agreed to come to dinner. Isn't it marvelous?"

"She's a saint," Clark said. "That's the problem. I don't make good movies with madonnas. Thalberg knows that."

"Irving's ill, darling."

"He's still a genius."

"L.B.'s in your corner, darling."

"Or backing me into one."

If Gable had a few too many gins when his father appeared at the smart colonial house in 1933, he would need more in the coming months. Ria was anxious for this reconciliation after ten years. Retired and broke, William hadn't changed his mind about actors and rarely had a compliment for his son. Clark had no choice but to offer him a home with all the fringe benefits—cook, maid, butler, flashy cars, and expensive clothes discarded every day by his famous son.

Nineteen thirty-three was to be another difficult year for Gable. He had no way of knowing he was just around the corner from glory, but it would be uphill all the bumpy way.

Without Thalberg's keen perception and understanding ways, Mayer took over ruthlessly. He would learn from his mistakes, but Gable was one of many MGM players who were battered about like a tennis ball.

Yes, 1933 was a year of William Gable, Ria's lavish parties, the wrath of Mayer, and the return of Josephine. Before the storm, however, Jean Harlow was able to break through the gloomy clouds by asking for Clark in *Hold Your Man. Film Daily* described the film and its stars very well: "They're at it again. A sure-fire hit!" There was less wrestling and giggling on the set. Within such a short span of time, they had both become bitter and pessimistic about life and about Hollywood. Jean said her mother and stepfather were spending money faster than she could earn it. Bern's estate was nil. She was suffering from back pains, "Thanks to that little bastard!", and Gable was trying to kill the excruciating pain in his mouth and stomach with too much gin. He and Jean were close. They discussed their burdens and were grateful for each other. "I want to get out of this business," he said.

"So would I," Jean sighed, pinching one of her nipples.

"You know we haven't a chance to save a buck, don't you?"

"Save? I'm always in debt!"

"How the hell did we get into this mess?" he asked, glancing over her see-through gown.

"Because we're two dopes!"

"Suckers, baby. Suckers!"

Crawford disliked Harlow intensely. They were not invited to the same parties, nor did they have the same friends. Joan felt that Jean was a threat to her, with Clark and with MGM. She made it very clear to her friends, "It's either Harlow or me, and if you choose her, don't ever speak to me again!" Of course, she resented Norma Shearer, Constance Bennett, and Jeanette MacDonald, but Harlow, the humorous platinum blond vamp with loose-hanging "cow tits" underneath cut-to-the-waist gowns, infuriated Crawford, who knew as day turns into night and the moon comes out that Gable was bedding down that "frustrated tart." To add insult to injury, Jean's reviews were superior to Joan's. It didn't matter that one was a comedienne and the other a dramatic actress. If there was only one

MGM, there was only one queen. (Garbo was eliminated from the competition. She was in a class by herself.)

Harlow had what Crawford only preached—humility. Harlow had attended the best schools as a youngster. Crawford had too, but she cooked and scrubbed floors. Harlow had an accent that was almost British, but it was her own and unaffected. Crawford's was practiced on and off the movie set. Jean had no questionable past. Joan did. Harlow didn't care what anyone thought about her. Crawford dedicated every breath to being admired and loved. Harlow won without trying.

By this time Gable wasn't interested in Joan's opinion or willing to be dictated to by her. While Crawford brought Ria hostess gifts chosen very thoughtfully, Clark nourished the freshness of Jean, who, despite rumors to the contrary, did not share his fondness for alcohol.

When Mayer decided to put Gable and Crawford together in a movie, Clark had mixed emotions. He wasn't pleased with his silly role, inferior to Franchot Tone's, in *Dancing Lady*. While Crawford danced with Fred Astaire and Nelson Eddy sang, Gable contributed nothing. These were valid reasons, but the one he kept to himself was Joan's pending divorce. Working together in *Dancing Lady* would give her too many chances to put pressure on him. Moviegoers might have had eyes only for Crawford and Astaire in their famous dance sequence, but Hollywood concentrated on Joan and Clark during production. Her testimony on the stand when she filed for an interlocutory decree of divorce was public knowledge. "Douglas would sulk for days at a time and refuse to talk to me. I was unable to sleep because of it. When I spent the day working at the studio, he would ask where I was, where I had lunch, and what I had done. He was very jealous and unreasonable."

The judge awarded her a divorce.

Gable had second thoughts about marrying Joan. He wasn't happy at home, but Ria was so wrapped up with her society and movie friends, she didn't have time to check on him anymore. If she suspected he was playing around, Ria had learned to live with it. Joan would never accept his dalliances.

"We'll never have a better opportunity," Joan said to him. "L.B. can't say a damn thing if we're both unattached. I'll be free in a year, so why don't you get off your ass."

"Ria would destroy me."

"Nonsense. She's loaded. What would she want with your money?"

"Ria's been very good to me. I don't want to hurt her."

"Hurt her? What about me, for Christ's sake!"

"I have children to think about."

"*Her* children!"

"I've grown very fond of them and they depend on me. I can't hurt kids."

"Are you telling me that a couple of brats are standing in the way of our getting married?"

"The time isn't right."

"Make up your mind, damn it!"

"Ria will take me for everything I've got. I'll be broke again, and I couldn't take that."

"It's only a matter of time, right?"

"Right," he said.

"Oh well, I've waited this long...'."

Gable's strange behavior was partially a result of his ill-health and his heavy drinking. When he finished *Dancing Lady,* he was hospitalized for an appendectomy, according to MGM. During his two-month absence from work, his rotten teeth were removed. While he waited for his gums to settle before being fitted for false teeth, he joined the Masons. In later years stories circulated that he would not go to bed with a girl if anyone in her family was a Mason. Several of his close friends swear to this.

While he studied for his apprenticeship, he came across several articles written by Josephine that appeared in fan magazines in the form of "open letters" to the great Gable regarding his ability as an actor.

In the first letter she criticized his voice:

Dear Clark,

The other day a very pretty woman remarked to me that you should never try to play the polished gentleman parts, only "the rough-guy" things; for although you could look the gentleman, you hadn't the voice.

So, when I had time, I found the picture and watched it to see why she had said that. I watched it carefully, through all those reels of silly story, beautiful photography, handsome people, and unconvincing dialogue; and as I watched, I thought many things.

I am afraid that what the pretty lady said is true. I am afraid you have less variety of tone quality in your later pictures than you were using when the public discovered you and demanded you. And you are using a hard, brittle quality.

Don't let the microphone and its demands fool you. Don't let that machine's need for a front resonance fool you into getting careless in your study of the characters you play. Don't forget what you learned so well about voice. Make that man you are playing talk the way that man would in real life. You can. You used to.

Josephine

The second letter referred to his acting ability:

Dear Clark,

Are you on that screen to make a show of yourself, merely letting the girls look you over, or are you there to make an entertaining show of the story? You remember, don't you, that fine old definition of action?—"To act is to arouse in your audience the same emotions you are supposed to be feeling in the part you are playing." If people in the audience are not included in the varying emotions of the story, they don't get their money's worth, and they soon cool off. Just sitting in silent admiration doesn't last. I haven't seen The White Sister *yet, but I've been told that although you have one or two very fine scenes, you are still doing those funny things with your mouth to make your dimples show, and that the audience is distracted away from the story in watching your mannerisms.*

Aside from these growing mannerisms, your technique is excellent. You have never forgotten that technique, have you? You can still make a better entrance than anyone on the screen, and you make every move count, because your moves are right.

Will you ever forget all those thousands of times you went in and out, and in and out, and in and out, until the right habit was established? And the foot positions and the walks, and the turns, and the sitting, and the standing, and kneeling, and rising, and the exercises in holding attention and in reproducing emotion? And the hand studies? Those were hard for you. But no one would guess it now.

Personally, I think you should go back to the simple, straightforward, fine acting of your earlier pictures. I think you should go back to a keen interest in presenting the man in the story instead of presenting

Gable. I think you should avoid acquiring facial mannerisms and that you should "give a show" instead of "being the show."

I remember so well how furious you used to be when I criticized you. And you would slam out of the tiny house and go off in the old car (I never knew where).

So, if you should come across this letter, and should slam out of your lovely home and race off in your beautiful car to wherever you go— perhaps later, you will really think carefully over your recent pictures and realize that perhaps you may be on the wrong road, and will think deeply of your next roles and of what sort of men they are and will give us truly fine work you are well able to do.

Josephine

Gable returned to work in September 1933 and faced an angry Mayer about a raise and better pictures.

"Don't you have anything nice to say?" Mayer asked sarcastically.

"Give me a reason. You put me in that cruddy *Dancing Lady,* and gave Franchot Tone first billing. Why did you need me at all?"

"We've gone through all that, Clark, and I'm tired of your complaints."

"Do you hate Irving so much you'd jeopardize common sense? Seems to me you're blackballing every one of his projects."

"If you're so faithful to Thalberg, perhaps you'd like to work on one of them."

"It has to be better than the shit I've been shoveling."

Mayer had to punish Gable and knew how to do it. He owed Columbia Pictures a favor. They were working on a silly script called *It Happened One Night.* Mayer agreed to loan them Robert Montgomery, but changed his mind. He called Harry Cohn, head of Columbia, and said, "Gable's been a bad boy. I'd like to show him who's boss around here. You can have him."

It Happened One Night was originally entitled *Night Bus*—a low-budget total disaster. Gable knew that almost every good actor had turned down the part of the newpaperman. Finding out that he was the chosen one, he blew his stack. Ria said he stormed into the house and threatened to quit MGM—to walk out of his contract. "I told him if that would make him happy to go ahead and do it, but I thought he would be smarter to make the picture, do the best he could, and see what happened."

Claudette Colbert did it for the money, because Columbia doubled her salary. "I went into it deliberately," she said. "I had never met Clark and, like every other woman in the country, thought he was divine. I jumped at the chance of working with him every day and getting paid for it."

Gable, who had switched to bourbon for this flop, realized he had no choice. First on the agenda was meeting director Frank Capra. "He was plastered!" Capra said. "Loaded! He slurred his words and belched repeatedly and loudly. He said, 'What's the poop, skipper, 'sides me?' Before I could answer, Gable spurted out, 'That son of a bitch Mayer! I always wanted to see Siberia, but damn it, I never thought it would smell like this!' and he belched again."

Capra offered to go over the story line of *It Happened One Night*. "Or would you like me to read it to you?" he asked.

"Buddy," Gable slurred, "I don't give a fuck what you do with it."

Capra was fed up too. He had worked long and hard on this script. It was turned down by too many stars, shuffled from studio to studio, and now he had to deal with a drunken leading man who was being deliberately punished.

Mayer laughed alone. He had gotten rid of a rotten script and saved his precious Montgomery, and would make an idiot of Thalberg, who actually liked the bloody comedy. Best of all, Gable was suffering.

The story of a runaway heiress and a newspaperman traveling together from Miami to New York was mundane and boring, but the brilliant Capra forged ahead. His tools were weak—one bourbon-slugging leading man and a prissy leading lady who did not want to show her leg in the hitchhiking scene or remove any of her clothes for the "walls of Jericho." Colbert also insisted on a four-week deadline, because she had friends waiting in Sun Valley. There was plenty of ad libbing and last-minute changes—all of which came about spontaneously—and right.

Clark had to adjust to her left profile facing the camera at all times, but with his big-ear complex, he didn't protest. What the hell! "Let's do it," he said, "and get home in time for Christmas!"

Gable was approached by Capra's agent, Berg/Allenberg. They wanted to represent him, and Clark decided to sign with the biggest and the best. He spoke to Minna, who did not stand in his way. She was deeply hurt, of course, and claims she let Gable go because she adored him. Berg/Allenberg insists that they paid her $25,000. True to form, money or no money, Clark continued to see Minna, who, according to friends, was one of his "dear loves."

Gable's women had one common attribute—their bond of secrecy. Adela Rogers St. Johns's comment that any woman who had Clark Gable's baby would be proud to admit it is difficult to accept. He has proven to be the rare exception to all that is traditional. If he was unique on the screen, he was incomparable in his personal life. His protection by MGM defies that of the president of the United States, with the exception of John F. Kennedy, whose sexual prowess burst forth like the Fourth of July until the fireworks bored us. Perhaps it was the quantity and not the quality that lacked impact. They both had charisma—an indefinable magnetism that was everlasting after exposure. Unlike Kennedy, Gable was not the "rooster." He didn't hit and run. He was faithful to *all* of his women at the same time and willing to come back for more, but Gable was also a warm lover who made all his affairs important. The lady writer who said he was not a good bed partner until she looked up and realized it was Clark Gable on top of her undoubtedly summed it all up very simply.

Minna Wallis understood Clark's need for a prestigious agency to handle his career. Most assuredly it would be an insult to compare her to Josephine, but both made personal sacrifices for Gable and did not share his curtain calls.

Gable returned to MGM assuming his "probation" was over. It wasn't. Mayer cast him in the role of a dedicated intern in *Men in White* with Myrna Loy. "No," she said, "we weren't lovers. He wasn't my type, even though I found him extremely attractive." Clark didn't mind. There were other lovely little girls in the film who were more than willing.

The year 1934 began as badly as the previous year, maybe worse. He had little or no communication with Mayer. Jean Harlow got married. Joan Crawford was dating Franchot Tone. Irving Thalberg returned to MGM without the power he once wielded.

Clark was sent on tour to promote *Men in White*. This was an experience never to be forgotten. Yes, he made twenty-two movies. Yes, he co-starred with Constance Bennett, Jean Harlow, Joan Crawford, Norma Shearer, Barbara Stanwyck, Greta Garbo, Marion Davies, Carole Lombard, Helen Hayes, and Myrna Loy. Yes, he was the guy who put Norma Shearer in her place and socked Barbara

Stanwyck in the kisser. And yes, he was the one who kissed Jean
Harlow so passionately that the screen flickered. But Clark Gable
had never met his public face-to-face. He had been hungry, broke,
married, divorced, remarried; he made love to the most beautiful
women in Hollywood and taken most of them to bed; and he had a
head like a sugar bowl, a wife who was seventeen years older than
he, and two stepchildren. But moviegoers had never seen Clark
Gable for themselves in the flesh. For the record, every major star
was introduced to the American public this way, in New York City in
particular. Elaborate arrangements were made by the studio and the
publicity was grossly exaggerated, but unless one has been mobbed
and touched and kissed and grabbed and poked and stripped of buttons and cuff links and sleeves and shoes and hair, one cannot possibly imagine the terror and the realization of what one has become
during the long months locked up in a studio with only movie folk.
Suddenly the doors of the outside world open and a billion eyes stare
and two million hands reach out and ten million fingers touch like
ants and mosquitoes. It's hard to believe this is love and not war.

Gable was completely bewildered and confused. There was no
adjusting to the public's adoration of him after his exile by Mayer.
The contrast was too startling—the true meaning of it all beyond
comprehension. Ria accompanied Clark to New York but was kept
out of sight as much as possible and rarely mentioned in press releases. Never alone, Gable had little time to think—to put who and
what he was in proper perspective. On a merry-go-round of premieres, press parties, dinner dances, cocktail parties, Ria's friends,
and MGM's gala affairs, Clark had no peace. He was mobbed walking down Fifth Avenue, browsing in department stores, and dining in
restaurants. He was anxious to attend the theater, but his presence
was better than the stage show. People stared at him everywhere,
asked for his autograph, fainted, cheered, and begged for a glance.
He smiled until his dimples ached and laughed until his teeth wob-
bled like his knees.

Women, women, women everywhere, and they were all his, by
God!

Ria was able to accept what was happening and hoped this proof
of his popularity might lift his ego, put him in a livable mood, and
reduce his drinking, but the imbalance of his worth increased his
hatred for Mayer and sent him on a binge of women and bourbon.
Ria tolerated his disappearances because he always came back, in

need of her understanding sound advice. She was the mother figure who listened and never let him down when he was wounded and discouraged. She did not allow his attentions to other women to get under her skin. More than once she had walked into their hotel room and caught Gable kissing and fondling a girl; Ria pretended to be nearsighted. Her worst fear was a serious romance à la Crawford. Ria was over fifty and had no illusions about his comparing her to the lovely young women who would settle for just one hour with her husband. It would take only one very special lady to lure him away. She knew Clark better than anyone else and would recognize the symptoms. This was a very difficult time for her too. Gable was, after all, a thirty-three-year-old kid getting his feet wet in an ocean of publicity and loyal fans who slept in the stairwell of the Waldorf, jumped into his limousine, and screamed for him from the sidewalks far below his hotel window. His cigarette butts were worth more than gold.

It Happened One Night opened at Radio City Music Hall on February 23, 1934, with no fanfare. Gable was back in California, skimming through the mild reviews. After one week, the film was distributed around the country. Gable observed that ". . . The public is the only thing that makes stars. They want one thing one week and something else the next. It doesn't know what it wants or why it wants it, and neither does anyone else. You can't explain anything in this movie business . . ."

The silly movie about an heiress who lifts her skirt to hitch a ride, a newspaperman munching on a raw carrot, and corny goings-on in a cheap motel room with a hanging blanket separating the twin beds—his undressing without an undershirt (sales of undershirts dropped) and her undergarments flung over the "walls of Jericho"—clicked! It was what the American public wanted to see during the dark Depression. More than anything else, people needed to laugh, and they did during *It Happened One Night*. They lined up all over the country to see it. Critics took a second look. Mayer got a migraine to the tune of Columbia's success and Capra's creative ability, which substituted for Thalberg's intuition.

Gable kept a low profile, however, and accepted his role as the gangster Blackie in *Manhattan Melodrama* with Myrna Loy. Mickey Rooney made his movie debut. Carole Lombard's husband, William Powell, co-starred and would follow with Loy in *The Thin Man*, the beginning of the very popular team of Nick and Nora.

Joan Crawford was considering marriage to Franchot Tone when she and Gable co-starred in *Chained*. But their mutual attraction had not dimmed. "We lived with it," she said, "and grabbed every chance to be alone. Mayer was always waiting to pounce. Damn it, we were filming *Chained* and that's exactly what we were—chained by a studio that possessed us body and soul. We had no rights. Clark and I were scared shitless. No wonder our personal lives were all fucked up!"

Gable was truthful with Joan about his marital status. "It's over," he said. "Just a matter of time. Her daughter's getting married and will be leaving home. My father's found himself another bride. It's worth my buying him a house to get him out of my hair." Joan wanted to know if he was sure about divorcing Ria. "Yes," he replied, "but I'll never get married again. Never."

Joan didn't allow herself to believe that. She knew Clark liked to play, but he needed someone waiting at home. Was it worth waiting for him? Ria would not give up easily, and when she did, he would pay dearly. Then there was Mayer. Joan was sure he knew she and Clark were seeing each other and was testing their endurance by putting them together in another film. *Forsaking All Others*, a comedy, was rushed into production due to the success of the very funny *It Happened One Night*. If moviegoers wanted to laugh, MGM would comply—Mayer's indirect way of admitting that Gable was as good in light comedy as he was belting dames around.

As good?

Apparently so. He was nominated for best actor. "It was sheer luck," Gable said.

It Happened One Night was nominated in five categories—best actor, actress, director, writer, and picture—but the consensus was that it didn't have a chance of winning anything. MGM, however, was not taking any chances. They raised Clark's salary to $3,000 a week. He should have been thrilled. The fact that he wasn't happy disturbed him. "Every time I get more money," he told Joan, "something comes along to take the gravy." This time it was William's marriage and new house. And maybe more for Ria . . .

After Office Hours with Constance Bennett was Gable's last movie in 1934. While everyone in Hollywood buzzed about the Oscar awards, he decided not to go. He scowled. "Who wants to sit around and smile watching someone else win?"

Ria said it had been a long time between smiles, and then one night shortly before Christmas he came home with a grin from ear to ear. "After the holidays," he said, "I'm going to Mount Baker, Washington, to do *Call of the Wild*." She was happy if he was, and it turned out to be their best Christmas together. Ria wasn't trying to figure out his strange moods anymore. Odd things made him happy. A possible Oscar did not. More money did not. Why Jack London's *Call of the Wild*? Was he glad to get away from her? Or maybe the hunting was exceptionally good in Washington. Oh well, whatever it was that brought him out of his unpleasant moods wasn't important.

Or was it?

His co-star would be Loretta Young...

On February 27, 1935, the Academy Awards were presented at the Biltmore Hotel in Los Angeles. Voting polls closed at five on the day of the awards, and dinner was served at eight o'clock.

Nominated for best picture: *The Barretts of Wimpole Street, Cleopatra, Flirtation Walk, The Gay Divorcée, It Happened One Night, Here Comes the Navy, The House of Rothschild, Imitation of Life, One Night of Love, The Thin Man, Viva Villa!,* and *The White Parade.*

Nominees for best actress: Claudette Colbert in *It Happened One Night,* Grace Moore in *One Night of Love,* Norma Shearer in *The Barretts of Wimpole Street.* Nominees for best actor: Clark Gable in *It Happened One Night,* Frank Morgan in *Affairs of Cellini,* and William Powell in *The Thin Man.*

It wasn't the competition that bothered Clark. He felt that he had been humiliated enough and did not want his peers, especially Mayer, to watch him lose. Even Claudette Colbert was so sure she wouldn't win that she was taking the train to New York the night of the awards dinner. Somehow Ria convinced Clark to put on his white tie and tails. His stepdaughter, Jana, was sure he would win and begged him to go. He grumbled about having to sit around all evening in formal clothes, and he hated "putting on the dog" for those who would destroy him.

Clark was also aware that Hollywood took it for granted that his marriage was over. He and Ria had not been seen out together in a long time, nor had he attended her dinner parties, now much smaller and infrequent. There was no sign of a marriage at all, other than their sharing the same house. Gable knew all eyes would be on them. The only way he could get through the night was to fortify himself with bourbon.

When dessert and coffee were being served in the Biltmore dining room on the night of February 27, 1935, Columbia officials dashed on board the New York–bound train and delivered Claudette Colbert just in time to receive her Oscar. Embarrassed in a beige traveling suit, she wept and clutched the statue, excused herself, and was whisked back to the waiting train.

It Happened One Night was voted best picture, Frank Capra best director, and Robert Riskin best writer. By the time host Irwin S. Cobb read out the nominees for best actor, the crowd of a thousand was rooting for Gable to make it a complete sweep. In an awkward daze, he thanked the Academy and left the podium mumbling to himself, "... I'm still going to wear the same size hat... the same size hat..."

Gable had, in theory, beaten the system—one of the biggest in the world, Metro-Goldwyn-Mayer—and its almighty dictator, L. B. Mayer, who applauded as if he were responsible, and indeed he was. Thalberg cried. Crawford schemed. Ria clapped with gloved hands and knew her marriage was all over. Columbia's Harry Cohn shot Mayer a quick "Fuck you!", and Gable was in a sweat. He had defied all principles of acting—lived on bourbon, wore one outfit, worked only four weeks, and didn't make a pass at Claudette Colbert. All this won him the award for best actor. If he was drunk when he accepted the Oscar, he went all the way when the Biltmore dining room closed.

Ten years later he gave the statue to a little boy. "Having it doesn't mean anything," he said. "Earning it does."

CHAPTER SIX

Gable was very anxious to do *Call of the Wild* in Mount Baker, Washington. He was glad to get away from the studio as well as Ria's parties, but there was more to it than that. This episode in his life has been a mystery for fifty years. The circumstances are clouded, witnesses are coy, and the facts are foggy. It seems apparent, however, that Clark was involved with twenty-three-year-old actress Loretta Young. Maybe it is a tender love story. Maybe not. But the incredible Young played a memorable role in Gable's life.

Born Gretchen Young in Salt Lake City on January 6, 1913, she moved to Los Angeles with her mother and three sisters when her parents were divorced. The young girls were popular movie extras, and though Loretta chose to attend the Ramona Convent, she was home alone the day director Mervyn LeRoy called for her sister Polly Ann to appear in the silent *Naughty but Nice*. Loretta went in her place. At the age of fifteen she was Lon Chaney's leading lady in *Laugh, Clown, Laugh*. When she was nineteen, Loretta eloped with actor Grant Withers, who was ten years older than the bride. The marriage was annulled the same year in a highly publicized court trial. In six years Young appeared in more than forty films.

Her acting left a great deal to be desired. Bosley Crowther, *New York Times* critic, said about Young, "Whatever it is that this actress never had, she still hasn't got it." It was her high cheekbones, big gray innocent eyes, and virginal quality that lifted her to stardom. Her figure lacked curves but she wore clothes with flair. Loretta knew how to accentuate the positive and eliminate the negative with an irresistible innocence. Grant Withers referred to her as "The Steel Butterfly." She was also known as "Hollywood's Beautiful Hack."

Young cared little what anyone said about her. She studied the craft of performing before the camera and became a symbol of beauty, class, and refinement. She made the transition from silents to talkies with ease.

In 1933 Loretta Young co-starred with Spencer Tracy in *Man's Castle*. They fell in love instantly, their names linked in every gossip column. He had not reached her star status, but within weeks everyone in America would recognize Spencer Tracy, thirteen years older than she. The cast and crew working on *Man's Castle* thought they had seen it all, but watching Loretta and Spencer made them blush. They had eyes only for each other. Loretta would not marry out of her religion, and Spencer was also a devout Catholic. So what was the problem?

Spencer Tracy left his wife and moved into a hotel to be with Loretta. Mrs. Tracy announced the separation on the grounds of incompatibility. His only comment was "We'll try to work out our problems."

A casual guy with a bitter temper when he was drunk, which was most of the time, Tracy got into numerous fist fights with reporters and smashed a few cameras. His bad conduct was blamed on frustration and guilt, despite his wanting Loretta more than his career. The affair came to a heartbreaking end on October 24, 1934, when Loretta tearfully told the press she could not marry Spencer because of their Catholic religion.

A year later Young was in Mount Baker, Washington, five thousand feet above sea level, the highest movie location ever chosen. The expedition included one hundred players and technicians. Snowplows worked day and night over sixty-five miles of road to make way for the equipment. Owing to blizzards, production took three months instead of the anticipated six weeks. The unit was cut off from civilization and, when food ran short, had to forge on to the nearest town. The temperature, often ten degrees below zero, was so cold that it froze the oil in the cameras.

Director William Wellman said, "We had trouble on *Call of the Wild*, big trouble, on top of a mountain. Gable wasn't tending to business, not the business of making pictures. He was paying a lot of attention to monkey business, and I called him on it, lost my easy-to-lose temper, and did it in front of the company, a bad mistake.

"He was a big man. I am not, but there was a big something in my favor, his face. He made his living with it, mine behind the camera. He might have beaten my brains out. I don't know, but I do know that I could have made a character man out of him in the process." (William Wellman, A *Short Time for Insanity*, Hawthorn, 1974.)

Gable, who was always prompt, showed up late on the set and was not prepared with his lines. Reliable sources said Clark and Loretta Young were enjoying the long cold days and nights alone together. Without identifying the stars, Hollywood gossip columnists hinted at the hot combination in the state of Washington that should have melted the snow and ice by now.

Ria was prepared to admit that her gravest fear was reality. Clark returned to Hollywood in one of his darkest moods. A few months later Loretta announced that she was retiring from films for a year due to "health problems." The persistent rumor was that she was pregnant, and in 1935 this would have meant the ruination of Young's career. She simply disappeared and let reporters fight for reasons why she left town.

Hollywood writer Anita Loos wrote forty years later that Clark had had an affair with a co-star during the filming of *Call of the Wild* that resulted in the birth of a baby girl.

MGM offered him the role of Fletcher Christian in *Mutiny on the Bounty*. Gable declined. "The character is a pansy," he said. "And I'm not going to be seen wearing a pigtail and knickers!" Thalberg, however, talked him into it, and *Mutiny on the Bounty* was voted the best picture of the year. Gable was again nominated for an Oscar, but lost to Paul Muni in *The Story of Louis Pasteur*.

Gable was reunited with Jean Harlow in *China Seas*. A changed man, he took his work very seriously in this film, did his own stunts, and chatted quietly with Jean. Her third marriage, to Gable's favorite cameraman, Harold Rosson, sixteen years older than Jean, was on the rocks. They had all worked together in *Red Dust* and *Hold Your Man*. After less than two years of marriage, Harlow announced her divorce to the press. The gentle and likable Rosson would eventually film fourteen Gable pictures, but *China Seas* was not one of them. Jean and Clark, despite their heavy hearts, sat close together on the set and found solace in each other. He loved the Baby, and reminded her that he would always be there if she needed him.

When Gable left for a few weeks in South America, there was talk about his meeting Loretta, who, insiders insisted, was having his baby. She returned to Hollywood and resumed her career. Clark flew to New York and was seen having dinner with several lovely socialites. When he returned to Hollywood, he confirmed his separation from Ria, but refused to answer questions about anything or anyone else.

His new address was the Beverly Wilshire Hotel.

Loretta Young could not marry Gable, nor could she have an abortion, if the rumors of her pregnancy were true. Her religious beliefs were staunch. In an interview she said, "I'm a normal girl. I've fallen in love. If it were just a question of that, I'd have been married long before now. Falling in love isn't the whole of marriage. With me marriage is for life. I can't get a divorce because my religion forbids it. When I marry, I've got to stay married. I have no choice. You see, I wasn't married to Grant Withers in the Church. It was a civil marriage and, therefore, to the Church, no marriage at all. If I'd had to marry him within the Church, I might not have done it. I was only seventeen and I thought marriage would be a step into paradise. It didn't turn out that way. If I hadn't gone through it, I might have stepped blindly into another that would have been bitter."

In May 1937, Loretta adopted a twenty-three-month-old baby girl despite a California law forbidding single people to adopt children. "I fell in love with her in a San Diego orphanage," she said.

Director Wellman (*Call of the Wild*) commented, "Clark and Loretta were very 'friendly' during the picture. We were all locked in our rooms trying to keep warm for weeks. He wasn't himself. Something was bothering him and that's why we clashed. All I know is Loretta disappeared when the film was finished and showed up with a daughter who had big ears. She's grown up into a lovely woman who resembles her beautiful mother."

Loretta saw Spencer and Clark occasionally, but refused to be photographed with them. Finally, in 1940 she married advertising executive Thomas Lewis, who adopted little Judy. Watching the child grow up was a fairy tale for the romantics in Hollywood, because Judy Lewis might have been the daughter of two of the most famous stars in the world.

Loretta had fonts of holy water installed in her home and settled down to the marriage she had sacrificed so much to attain. She went on a campaign to abolish swearing, pornography, and immoral literature. On every movie set she had a "swear box." Monies collected went to a home for unwed mothers. Some actors handed her a ten-dollar bill and told her to lay off. Robert Mitchum, who didn't play

little games, asked her how much she charged. "Five cents for every
'damn,' ten cents for 'hell,' and twenty-five cents for 'goddamn,'" she
replied.

"How much for————?" he asked.

She smiled. "That's free."

Joan Crawford had a marvelous sense of humor about Loretta's
devotion to the Church. During one of her parties, a friend was
about to sit in a chair and Joan grabbed him just in time. "Can't sit
there," she said. "Loretta Young just got up and it has the mark of
the cross in the seat."

If Gable's marriage was hanging by a string when he left for Washington to film *Call of the Wild*, it was his relationship with Loretta
that cut it. Winning the Oscar gave him the confidence and power
he needed to break away. He had the best agents in Hollywood handling his career, and Mayer was eating crow. Ria's role as mother and
confidante was over, but no one could convince her of that. Rather
than return to Houston, she remained in Beverly Hills, waiting for
him to come back to her.

Joan Crawford decided *not* to wait any longer for Gable to make
up his mind. Despite her declaration when she divorced Fairbanks
—"I'll never marry again as long as I live. There is no such thing as
honesty or true love. If anyone ever catches me believing in anything, I hope they give me a good sock in the jaw"—Joan eloped with
Franchot Tone on October 11, 1935, while Gable was "thinking
things over" in South America.

"Thank God I'm in love again!" she exclaimed. "Now I can do it
for love and not for my complexion." The newlyweds moved into the
house she had shared with Fairbanks, because poor Franchot made
only $50,000 a year, compared to Joan's $250,000. Though she spoke
of her new interest in the arts, thanks to Franchot, on her wedding
night Joan was contacted by telephone once again regarding another
form of art she had been involved with as a starving chorus girl in
New York—porno movies entitled *Velvet Lips* and *The Casting
Couch*. She denied this to her death, but the flicks and stills existed.
MGM dealt with the blackmailers and obtained the films. MGM
officials claimed they viewed them and denied it was Crawford, of
course. The seriousness of the accusation was a threat not only to
Joan but to the studio. Exactly how much was paid and by whom was
hushed up. In later years reporters asked her if she had *really* posed

in the nude. Crawford replied graciously, "Bullshit!"

She would be plagued by her past, however. Her inability to have children she attributed to a "childhood allergy." Old friends claimed Joan had too many abortions. During her marriage to Franchot she had several miscarriages, and she waited for their divorce before adopting children.

But as she zigzagged from lovers to husbands and scandal to scandal, Joan and Clark protected each other's secrets and each other. They met 1936 with zest and confidence, and why not? Each had the largest dressing rooms on the MGM lot, a private table in the commissary, and better scripts. Their mates felt the aftermath... Franchot suffering from servitude and Ria struggling to explain her husband to the press. "I understand what happened," she said. "Clark was under tremendous pressure. It was a combination of too much work, too sudden success, and the fact that women fairly threw themselves at him all the time. Basically he has good Dutch principles, and no one could be sweeter at times, but he could also be stubborn and perverse. I tried to make him see that his happiness would have to come from within himself."

Gable enjoyed his first Christmas in fourteen years as a married bachelor. He took advantage of his freedom with young starlets, extras, and high-priced call girls. When he was asked why he paid for something he could get free, Clark replied, "Because I can pay them to go away. The others stay around, want a big romance, movie lovemaking. I'm not the world's greatest lover."

Sara G. was an extra in several Gable films. He knew her name on the second working day. She said he enjoyed sitting around listening to raunchy gossip—the harmless kind. "I think he got a vicarious thrill listening to the latest dirt about the supporting actors who got around... like George Raft, Gilbert Roland, Dennis O'Keefe, and George Brent. Clark said they had it made. Nobody cared what they did and they got away with more. He never talked about himself. This was part of his approach and his charm. Within fifteen minutes he knew I was from Cleveland, how old I was, where I lived in Hollywood, and how many roommates I had. He wanted to know what my ambitions were. In the middle of a conversation he said, 'I should go over my lines for the next take. Why don't we continue the discussion after work.' I said that would be fine."

"We'll go to your place if you don't mind," he whispered. "We

GABLE'S WOMEN

don't want to be disturbed by reporters and autograph hunters, do we?"

"Does that apply to my roommates?" Sara asked.

"Yeah, why don't you tell them to see a movie tonight. I won't stay late."

"Well, I . . ."

"When I leave the studio, it's nice to be alone. Makes me nervous having people stare at me. Besides, babe, I'm not divorced yet. You understand . . ."

Sara said that was how their affair started. He brought a bottle of liquor without asking what she preferred. Clark made his own drinks, poured one for her (Sara hated bourbon, but he never asked what she preferred), and sat down on the couch next to her as if he had been there many times before.

"Nice apartment," he said, looking around. "I must show you where I lived in the old days. What a dump!"

"Didn't you live with your first wife?" she asked.

"Yeah, that was a dump too. I had a few places. When I began making money in this town, I used to drive past those broken-down rooming houses. They've probably been condemned by now. So tell me, Sara, what're your plans? Acting? Singing? What?"

"I've taken lessons in everything," she said.

"No screen tests yet?" he asked, putting his arm around her.

"My agent's working on that."

"I see." He grinned, drawing her closer. "You're a cute little thing, but I guess you already know that."

He leaned over and kissed her. Sara described Gable as a powerful but gentle man. "He literally consumed me in his arms," she explained. "We didn't talk much after that. He fondled my breasts, but I still had my clothes on. I think he kissed me three or four times before looking at me with those piercing eyes and suggesting we take our clothes off. Clark had a superb physique, strong arms and legs, big feet, and a solid behind. He transmitted sex like sound waves. The act itself was important to him. That was all he wanted. There was no petting or foreplay. No romancing. No kissing during the act, which lasted less than a minute. When it was over, he asked if he could take a shower. We had a nightcap, and I believed him when he said, 'Maybe I can get you bigger parts at the studio. I can't promise anything, Sara. Will you see me again anyway?' I said I would. Clark didn't kiss me good night. The next day I'm sure he took another girl out—one of the extras who worked with me—but he was back in my bed later in the week.

"I liked Clark very, very much. I knew what he wanted, and he never pretended that he was looking for anything more. Naturally I preferred someone more romantic . . . the buildup, you know, but that wasn't for him. I know he tried to help me at the studio, because the casting director told me that Mr. Gable said I was on the ball, that I had spunk and he'd like me to work in his pictures. I got the old wink, which meant everyone knew we were sleeping together. I got more jobs than usual. To my knowledge, Clark never stuck his neck out and got a girl a screen test.

"Clark was separated at the time. He never spent the night with me, though, because that was too intimate for him. We never snuggled or smooched, and he never took me out in public. I don't recall his ever bringing food, either. Sometimes I cooked dinner, even though I couldn't afford anything fancy. He never offered me money or anything.

"Over a period of about four years we saw each other usually at my place, several times at his hotel suite at the Bel-Air. The first time he invited me there, I was thrilled to death. I fantasized about ordering room service and spending the night. It didn't happen that way. I spent a week's pay on a beautiful negligee—went all out. He told me to come in the back way because he had a private entrance. I remember he took my suitcase, but put it near the door, and I wondered why at the time. Wasn't it only natural if he took it into the bedroom? After a few drinks, we were intimate on the floor! Then he disappeared into the shower. I was about to hang up my new negligee when Clark came out of the bedroom wearing a shirt and tie. 'Glad you could come over,' he said. 'I have to rush off to a meeting, and I'm sure you're anxious to get home for dinner. Drive carefully, babe.' He gave me a pat on the ass, handed me my suitcase, and all but pushed me out the door. I felt like a damn fool. The next day he greeted me with a big smile. 'You look exceptionally lovely today, Sara. I'm a lucky guy.' That's all he had to say, and I forgave him. He could make a simple statement like that sound stupendous. He called me from the studio one evening and said his car broke down and he wasn't in the mood to fix it. Would I get a bottle of bourbon and two packs of cigarettes and pick him up? All the way back to my place he told me what a swell kid I was. There were so few around like me. Good friends were hard to find in Hollywood. He was in a very good mood that night, and we kidded around in bed, which was unusual for him. He was talkative, too, and told me not to give up hope of becoming an actress—if, that is, I wanted it more than anything else in the world, because that's what it was all about. He said there were thousands who would starve, steal, fuck, and kill to become a star, and unless I was willing to do all four, I'd have to get very lucky. I asked him if he did all those things, and Clark said, 'Not exactly. I didn't kill anybody. Sometimes I think that's better than hurting people, don't you?'

"I drove him within a few blocks of his hotel. After Clark got out of the car I realized he hadn't paid for the bourbon, the cigarettes, or the gas. I was practically broke. He forgot, that's all. I'd never ask him for the money.

"How did he get away with these things? Because he was so damn seductive. It was impossible to get mad at him. I don't think he ever meant to take advantage of anyone, but he did it all the time. As humble as he was, I got the impression he thought he was doing me a favor."

Sara was acquainted with other girls who went out with Gable. "We all felt the same way about him," she said. "He was one of the most exciting men in the world. He wasn't the most interesting or the most pleasing or generous, but he always came in the door with a big smile. Always optimistic and fun. He was the cleanest man I ever hoped to meet, and I told him so. Clark said he took five or six showers a day, sometimes more. He shaved his chest and underneath his arms. He liked clean women, and made a remark once that I forgot to shave the back of my legs.

One of the other girls wasn't a real blonde, and when he found out, he asked her why she didn't bleach her pubic hair. She did, but he never called her again. She asked me why the hell his first two wives were brunettes. I told her we didn't have to be psychiatrists to figure that one out. He married 'mothers' and it was okay if they had dark hair.

"I saw him after he married Carole Lombard. He still played around. If we were in a picture together, he always warned me ahead of time that she might be on the set and I was to be polite and refer to him as 'Mr. Gable.' I wasn't to stare at him, because Carole had eyes in the back of her head. She could spot one of his dames—like that, and he snapped his fingers. She was very jealous, he said. She looked us over, all right. She glared. That was a warning. She held his arm every minute to prove he belonged to her. Carole knitted a cock warmer for him and left it in his dressing room with a note. He showed it around. This was very funny, because the cock warmer was rather small . . ."

In early 1936 Gable was seen about town with the exquisite Merle Oberon. When they appeared at the Academy Awards banquet, tongues began to wag. Both were unattached and renowned for their passion. Maurice Chevalier, her co-star in Merle's first Hollywood film, said, "She was the most exotically beautiful woman I ever laid eyes on." Oberon claimed to be a Tasmanian aristocrat, educated in London and India. When Gable became acquainted with her, she was under contract to director-producer Alexander Korda, who would eventually become her first husband, but in 1936 she was enjoying intimate relationships with Leslie Howard and David Niven. Gable was unable to resist this mesmerizing lady, and Merle considered him "the sexiest creature on earth." An intimate evening with this sensuous twenty-five-year-old lady might not have been Clark's idea of raw satisfaction, but every minute was well spent. Merle Oberon was no ordinary woman. Her well-kept secret would not be revealed until after she died in 1979.

Her approach to sex was elegance—champagne and caviar, candlelight, soft music, silk sheets, silk robes with ostrich trim, French lingerie, incense—a banquet of love. Though Clark did not know Merle was a half-caste, she was only another woman to him. He knew about her affair with producer Joe Schenck, who was pot-bellied, balding, and unattractive. It was no secret that she was his mistress and the recipient of diamonds, furs, and expensive vacations on the Riviera. This meant one thing to Clark: She was no different from the others he'd slept with. The theme song was a change of pace, though. Theirs was a sexual attraction that lasted a few months off and on.

She and Clark would remain friends, however. Merle was a dear friend of Lady Sylvia Ashley's when Fairbanks was trying desperately to reconcile with Mary Pickford despite Sylvia's iron clutches. When Merle met Mary, they became very close, which proves the gracious-ness and warmth of Oberon, who was always welcome at Pickfair regardless of her friendship with Sylvia. Merle's aim in life was to rise to the crest of world society. After her divorce from Alexander Korda, she married wealthy Mexican industrialist Bruno Pagliai, who built her a palace, Ghalal, in Acapulco. She became an international hostess whose parties were unparalleled. She would have it all.

But Merle was a half-caste born in Bombay, the daughter of an Indian mother and a British father. She lied outright by introducing her dark-skinned mother as her maid. Merle's real name was Queenie O'Brien. She began her career as a dance hostess at the Café de Paris in London, where she caught Korda's attention in 1931. Her beauty so captivated him that he made sure Queenie O'Brien no longer existed. Korda chose Tasmania as her birthplace because it was remote and isolated. The curious would have a difficult task probing into the truth. He made her late father a major, not a British enlisted man. He was killed "on a hunt" rather than dying from pneumonia. Her "British" mother was left almost penniless, according to Korda's public relations staff, and thought it was best if Merle went to live with her godparents, Lord and Lady Monteith, in their Bombay mansion. This fairy tale was a far cry from the real poverty and filth of Merle's childhood, spent in the back streets and alleys of Bombay and Calcutta.

Clark never knew the truth. It might have made a difference knowing he had been with an Anglo-Indian woman. There is no denying that he was biased against Jews because he worked for them at MGM—L. B. Mayer in particular. To know them was all right, but to be ruled by them was degrading. His idea of the all-American girl was the White Anglo-Saxon Protestant.

Merle's half-breed status was not accepted in society during the Golden Era. A half-caste was an outcast. Clark had his principles even in the bedroom.

Gable also dated Ria occasionally. Out of respect for her, he was very discreet with Crawford and Young. Adela Rogers St. Johns remained ever faithful. When Clark heard that Mary Pickford was divorcing Douglas Fairbanks, he called her for a quiet evening together. She resented his obvious intentions. "He didn't want to go out," she said, "rather to stay home, if you know what I mean. He called often, and I made myself unavailable. I regretted it later. In fact, I must have been out of my mind."

Gable undoubtedly had his eye on Pickfair. Had he made it there as host and husband of America's Sweetheart, the thrill of it all would have lasted until her first ultra-formal dinner party and his having to stand in a receiving line. It was a whim—an egotistical challenge. Not one to give up easily, Clark decided not to pursue Joan Crawford's former mother-in-law.

An actress who prefers not to be identified described Gable after his separation from Ria. "He didn't stop when it came to women," she said. "I don't know how he did it. Dolls and booze to excess. He was like a kid in a candy store, as they say, but he had his own method of picking out sweet delicacies. At a party he could size up every woman in the room quickly. Within minutes he knew which one was leaving with him, and he hadn't met her yet. At other times he made his subtle approach with a look only he had. He'd say something flattering about her dress or maybe her hair, and never taking his eyes off her face, as if he were admiring the pores in her skin. He never said anything sexy because he reeked of it. He was like a giant magnet. I guess he did some chasing, and very few girls ran the other way. He didn't appreciate coyness, but understood shyness. He knew the difference. He was a very happy and contented man at this time. I don't think he was looking for a wife, because he had no intention of getting a divorce."

In a simple agreement, Clark gave Ria half of his earnings. If he was upset about this, he kept it to himself. In fact, he refused to discuss his separation. "Talk to the lady," he told reporters. Clark never said an unkind word about her, but he wasn't always as courteous. After making *Wife vs. Secretary* with Jean Harlow and Myrna Loy, MGM assigned him to *San Francisco*. It seems that Jeanette MacDonald insisted that he be her co-star. Gable wanted no part of it. "She sings and I listen. No thanks." Jeanette reacted to his refusal much as Marion Davies had. She wept dollars and said she'd go off salary until Clark was "available." He thought about it and still came up with the same answer, "No, I don't like sitting around and having to react to someone singing to me. Makes me feel like a lump."

When he found out Spencer Tracy was going to be in the film, Clark changed his mind. "I never forgot Tracy's performance in *The Last Mile*," he said. "And I'm still in awe of him."

Gable portrayed another gambler, MacDonald an innocent young opera singer who needs money so badly she lowers herself to a job in Gable's joint. Tracy was a priest who protects her virtue. The 1906 earthquake makes everything all right.

Gable liked Tracy. They had much in common. Both liked to drink too much. They had started out on the stage and shared fond memories of the theater. They were also very, very close to Joan

Crawford and Loretta Young. While they sipped and exchanged jokes, MacDonald sat alone with tears in her eyes. Gable said that nothing would have been different even without Tracy on the set. He did not take to Jeanette and that was it. She was one of Mayer's favorites, and therefore had one strike against her from the very beginning.

He began to wonder again if his luck was running out when Marion Davies wanted him for *Cain and Mabel*. Gable wasn't thrilled about the film, but he, Marion, and Hearst were good friends by now, and there was no friction.

Love on the Run with Joan Crawford was a picture both she and Clark quickly forgot. "The only thing we had going for us were the popularity polls," she said. "We were on top. But we were more frightened than we were in the beginning, when we had nothing to lose. We were typecast now. He was the tough guy with a heart of gold. I was the poor girl who makes good. This is what the movie-goers wanted. We talked a lot about what it would be like to lose everything. I'm sure no one else would believe our talks—Joan Crawford and Clark Gable terrified of having and being nothing. You must realize we were trained actors by now. True professionals. We had reputations to live up to. Nothing worse than being cast in B movies after straight A stuff. I remember John Gilbert had just died. He drank himself to death from a broken heart. He wasn't even forty yet. What a damn shame. Gilbert was the best. There was a hush in Hollywood when we found out he was dead. Clark hated Mayer even more—blamed him for destroying a great star. God, how we thrashed our lives out. What did the future have in store for us?"

During Gable's wild spree he attended Jock Whitney's gag party on February 7, 1936. Carole Lombard, whom he hadn't seen in a few years, arrived in a screaming ambulance, wearing a hospital gown, and entered on a stretcher carried by two attendants. Clark was dazzled by her daring prank, and though Carole's escort was Cesar Romero, Gable danced with her most of the evening, until he joked about her acting.

"You might make it someday, baby!"

Carole told him what he could do with his lousy opinion and stormed off the dance floor. She ignored him for the rest of the evening. They had been very cozy on the dance floor until she wiggled off in a huff. Clark had never been dumped so obviously and outrageously in his life. And he hadn't forgotten how Carole had turned him down flatly when she was divorcing William Powell. "I know how Gable operates," she said. "He waits until a girl is vulnerable and lonely before he moves in. When he got to the L's, this one didn't bite!"

Clark liked a challenge and called her for a date. Carole was surprised to hear from him after putting him in his place in front of the Hollywood crowd, but she couldn't deny her attraction to the "big lug." They began dating occasionally, and on Valentine's Day Carole sent him an old Model A with red hearts painted all over it. Not to be outdone, he picked her up that evening in a broken-down jalopy. Clark was in a tuxedo and she in a long gown, but they went in her "new car" to the formal dinner party.

When Gable was asked if he was in love with Lombard, he said, "No. I just like the way she wiggles her derrière in a tight satin dress."

Carole waited her turn with the press and made light of their "friendship." Bored with questions, she shocked reporters into complete silence with a casual quip: "Clark's not circumcised, but that's all right."

Their fights, however, were just as passionate. After one whopper, Clark woke up in his suite at the Beverly Wilshire early the next morning with a white dove staring him in the eye and six others fluttering overhead. Carole had arranged with the hotel staff to deliver these doves of peace to Gable as a symbol of "Let's forgive and make up." These were the first of many peace doves exchanged over the years. Gable had them caged and tended to "until the next time."

Carole, however, had no intention of becoming just another one of Gable's women. He was a married man with no intention of getting a divorce, and he insisted that in any case there would not be a third Mrs. Gable. Carole was game for almost anything, but not a one-night stand, for him or anyone else.

She was also dating the brilliant screenwriter Robert Riskin, who won an Oscar for *It Happened One Night*. (He was Frank Capra's partner and close friend.) Carole was not known for casual affairs. Her friends noticed a change in her after meeting Gable. She was in love, but in control. She was "in tune" with him, and what Clark didn't realize was that he was very much "in tune" with her, also. Carole did not rearrange her plans for him. She wasn't a last-minute date. When he flirted with other women in her company, she had no difficulty catching another man's eye and putting on a teasing performance herself. This was another first for Clark, who wasn't sure how to react. She dished it out as well as he did.

If Lombard wasn't with Riskin or Gable, she was dancing the Charleston at the Hotel Ambassador until dawn. This delightful, zany screwball had enormous energy that far surpassed Clark's. During Prohibition, she nipped on bootleg booze, played poker with the boys, but always wore a clinging dress to prove she was all woman.

She was born Jane Alice Peters on October 6, 1908, in Fort Wayne, Indiana. When she was six years old, her mother, Bessie, took Jane and her two older brothers to Los Angeles on vacation and never returned home. Bessie and her husband, Fred, did not have a good marriage, and he elected to stay in Indiana.

Jane was a spunky tomboy who tried to join her brothers' football team, was told to go home, but played anyway. There was no fence high enough to keep her out. She was either spinning cartwheels or wrestling with her brothers on their front lawn when movie director Allan Dwan, who was visiting a neighbor, thought she was the high-spirited girl he was looking for to play Monte Blue's daughter in *A Perfect Crime*. She was only thirteen years old. Jane wanted to be an actress, but continued on to high school. Three years later she was tested at Twentieth Century–Fox and signed a five-year contract for seventy-five dollars a week. The studio changed her name to Carole Lombard, and she was on her way with Edmund Lowe in *Marriage in Transit,* and Buck Jones in *Hearts and Spurs.*

When she was eighteen, Carole was in a serious automobile accident. A sharp piece of glass cut into the right side of her face from nose to ear. She endured four hours of pain without anesthesia while her face was being stitched. After the heeling process, she underwent plastic surgery. The procedure was a long one, and Twentieth Century–Fox dropped her contract.

When she recovered, Carole got a job with Mack Sennett, the famous comedy producer, whose Keystone Kops were the rage. For two years she appeared in two-reelers, engaged in pie-in-the-face routines and other silly antics. Joseph P. Kennedy, the late President's father, was head of Pathé and offered Carole a contract if she'd lose ten pounds. "For one hundred and fifty dollars a week I'd do almost anything," she said, "but not before telling Kennedy he wasn't so skinny himself!"

In 1930 a svelte blond Carole Lombard was signed by Paramount for seven years at three hundred and fifty dollars a week. After making two films with William Powell, *Man of the World* and *Ladies' Man*, she married him on June 26, 1931. Two years later they were divorced, but they remained dear friends.

Carole Lombard had no enemies. She was lively, frank, generous, funny, and humble. She enjoyed profanity even as a teenager, but she carried her four-letter words with dignity. One of her friends remembers the first time Carole rode a horse. "I don't know why the hell everybody thinks this is so great," she exclaimed in front of a crowd. "It's like a dry fuck."

Yes, Lombard was raunchy, tough, romantic, strong-willed, sexy, sophisticated, and hell on wheels. She never wanted to be a great actress or make a lot of money, and she rarely complained. Though she was one of the best comediennes in the thirties, Carole did not stand out in the public's eye. She was beautiful, but no one noticed. She had a curvaceous figure and slinky legs, but the critics never raved about these attributes.

At the beginning of her career she was suspected of being a lesbian, because she enjoyed the company of gays, male and female. After her divorce, Carole lived with her business manager, Madalyn Fields, nicknamed Fieldsie, who was over six feet tall and weighed well over two hundred pounds. Whenever the lesbian rumors reached her friends, they laughed. "Carole is capable of trying anything, but she's as straight as an arrow."

She was an excellent dancer and excelled at tennis. "Carole was good at everything," Bing Crosby said. "She had a delicious sense of humor and was one of the screen's greatest comediennes. She was also very beautiful. The electricians, carpenters, and prop men all adored her because she was so regular, so devoid of temperament and showboating. The fact that she could make us think of her as being a good guy rather than a sexy mama is one of those unbelievable manifestations impossible to explain."

Those who worked with Lombard were not offended by her profanity. How she said it took the edge off. Often it was her way of calming a tense situation, too.

Carole loved to start rumors about herself, and the one about keeping a dildo in her dressing room got back to her. She pretended to be furious, when actually she couldn't wait to show it to everyone to prove the rumors were true. She got the last laugh, though.

The dildo was black.

Lombard's parties were the talk of the town. "She was unique, to say the least," a friend said. "She'd tell us formal dress and serve dinner in bedpans. At more intimate gatherings, we'd all sit around having a drink. Each of us had our own little table. We'd be engaged in conversation without realizing dinner courses had been served one by one, very quietly. Carole invented TV tables, actually. She was way ahead of her time in so many ways."

She was the first to hire gay Billy Haines as her interior decorator. Billy was a big star in silent films, but banned when Mayer found out he was living with his homosexual boy friend. Haines was a talented decorator, but no one in Hollywood dared give him a chance—no one but Lombard, that is.

"After Carole's divorce from William Powell," Billy said, "she bought a simple medium-size house of her own and asked me to decorate it. Because Carole was different, I wanted to make her house match her screwball personality, but with the same good taste she possessed underneath all that spicy clowning."

Haines "blasted" bright shades of blue and purple against a background of white. This type of decor would become a fad in Hollywood, but Billy considered this lively contrast all Lombard. "She was one of the most beautiful girls on the screen. She photographed like a virginal princess, but she lived like a tiger and fluttered like a colorful butterfly. I accentuated the rooms with mirrors because Carole was a reflection of life. When the house was done and Carole gave me a check, I refused to take it. She had given me a chance and put her reputation on the line. I was in great demand after that. One of my favorite projects was the Mocambo nightclub.

"Carole's mother, Bessie, was a great gal too. She always had a numerologist and astrologer on retainer. They lived by the stars and adding up pertinent numbers, however it's done. They were always kidding me about not doing this or that on a certain day because Venus or Mars was in conjunction with another planet. They loved to play poker on Saturday nights, when odd-looking metaphysical folks would gather around the table and deal out the cards. Sometimes it looked like a Gypsy camp, but I found them fascinating.

"Carole was a believer, but she kept it to herself, for the most part. It wasn't like her to be serious about anything, regardless of what was going on underneath all that gaiety. I remember trying to

Clark Gable as a young boy in Ohio.

Courtesy Jane Ellen Wayne

A teenage Gable prior to his dental work.

Courtesy Jane Ellen Wayne

Courtesy Kobal Collection

Clark and Ria Langham, his second wife.

Courtesy Kobal Collection

Loretta Young and Gable in *Call of the Wild* (1935).

Courtesy Kobal Collection

The Crawford-Gable chemistry worked on and off the screen. Their affair lasted thirty years.

Jean Harlow, the Blond Bombshell, and Gable successfully teamed in several top-grossing films.

Courtesy Kobal Collection

Courtesy Kobal Collection

At the Encino ranch, Gable and Lombard tried to escape the Hollywood parties.

Lombard's jealous rages (usually justified) reduced Lana Turner to tears (*Honky Tonk*, 1941).

Courtesy Kobal Collection

Courtesy Kobal Collection

Dolly O'Brien was Gable's favorite New York City date after the death of Carole Lombard.

Courtesy Jane Ellen Wayne

Virginia Grey was one of Gable's companions in his search for another Carole Lombard.

Rhett and Scarlett. Gable and Vivien Leigh reportedly hated each other during the filming of *Gone With the Wind* (1939).

Courtesy Kobal Collection

Courtesy Kobal Collection

Anita Colby, dubbed "The Face" for her cover-girl beauty, was frequently seen with Gable.

Courtesy Kobal Collection

Gable married Lady Sylvia Ashley, but it was by no means a marriage made in heaven.

Courtesy Kobal Collection

The filming of *Mogambo* (1953) brought Gable and Grace Kelly together. Gable's charms more than the African sun melted the Ice Goddess' reserve.

Gable left Grace Kelly after the *Mogambo* filming to rendezvous with Suzanne Dadolle, the French "mystery woman" whose premature engagement announcement may not have been part of Gable's plans.

Courtesy Kobal Collection

Kay Spreckels, Gable's last wife and the mother of his only child, John Clark Gable.

Courtesy Kobal Collection

Marilyn Monroe with Gable on the set of *The Misfits* (1959). Monroe's depression over her failed marriage to Arthur Miller and her rejection by Yves Montand drove her into Gable's arms.

The King.

pin her down for a constructive discussion on the decor and she told me to go ahead with my own ideas."

According to Kenneth Anger's *Hollywood Babylon II*, Carole changed clothes in front of Billy and walked around the room in the nude. When she saw the surprised look on his face she said, "I wouldn't do this if I thought it would arouse you."

When her house was finished, Lombard's friends were anxious to see it. She arranged a party, but when the guests arrived, they were stunned to find that all the contents had been removed.

Yes, she was unique in many ways. Though she mingled with the Hollywood elite, Carole never failed to include plumbers, stagehands, painters, and gardeners in her lively gatherings. She liked everyone and couldn't have cared less how the snobs felt about it.

On the Paramount lot, she zoomed around on a motor skooter, another original idea that eventually became fashionable as well as convenient.

Carole's marriage to the very distinguished and proper William Powell was an odd one, considering how different they were. After they parted, she blossomed into a lovable lunatic. Now the question was, who would be nuts enough to marry Lombard?

Maybe singer Russ Columbo, who fell in love with her after his hot romance with Valentino's former girl friend, Pola Negri. Russ and Carole became inseparable. He carried his cigarettes in a $1,500 diamond-studded case, and he gave Carole similarly extravagant gifts. He lived with his parents in a mansion on Outpost Circle Drive, an exclusive Hollywood neighborhood. When Russ was twenty-six he signed a $10,000-a-week movie contract after starring in *Wake Up and Dream*. On August 30, 1933, he and Carole attended the premiere together. She was thrilled for him. "You wait, Russ. I predict you're going to be a star."

Two days later Columbo went to visit a friend who collected old guns. While the two men were admiring the Civil War relics, a pistol fired; the slug ricocheted off the table and struck Russ just above the eye. Two hours later he was dead. Carole was heartbroken. She attended the funeral with Russ's family and told friends, "His love for me was the kind that rarely comes to any woman."

The only member of the Columbo family who did not attend was his mother, who was blind and too ill to take the shock of her son's death. Carole helped with the charade that lasted eleven years—that

Russ was on a very successful European tour. Checks from his royal-
ties were sent to Mrs. Columbo every month, supposedly from Russ,
with a letter describing his exciting life abroad. Carole visited faithfully, and Mrs. Columbo died never knowing the truth about her
son.

Robert Riskin was the only other man who was linked with Lombard. Her friends insist that Carole frightened most men away—that
they couldn't keep up with her. She was funny, exciting, gaudy,
stunning, daring, and very, very bright—always a few steps ahead of
everyone else. The outlandish stories told about her were all true,
but Hollywood did not want her to change one little bit.

In 1936 Carole and ex-husband William Powell were both nominated for Oscars for *My Man Godfrey*. Neither won, but considering
their broken marriage, it was a memorable feat.

Though Lombard was featured in more than twenty-five movies
by 1934, she wasn't recognized, and the great John Barrymore was
aghast to find out that this "dizzy blonde" was to be his co-star in
Twentieth Century.

"I told Howard Hawks, the director, he was out of his mind,"
Barrymore said. "This kid can't act! I felt sorry for her and at the
same time had no intention of lowering myself to appearing with
what looked like a cute little flapper. Hawks took me aside and told
me to keep my mouth shut until we finished for the day, regardless of
what happened. I had no idea he had spoken to her about doing
whatever she felt like doing—that she should forget about acting
completely. Carole caught me off-guard. She was supposed to fly off
the handle in the scene . . . rave and rant at me. When she started,
she threw her arms in the air, kicked, screamed, and carried on like
a madwoman! I recall covering my balls instinctively. We went
through almost twelve pages of dialogue, too, without a mistake. We
did that scene only once. She was fabulous. Besides having great
respect for her as an actress, I fell in love with her."

Like the other actresses during the thirties, Carole never wore a
bra and preferred not wearing panties. In many ways she was like
Jean Harlow, who dressed for comfort, not sex appeal. A reporter
was eloquently descriptive of Lombard in 1936. "She looks New
Yorkish, talks Bostonish, and acts very Londonish," he wrote. "In
manners, she is brisk and slangy—an attitude which belies her
fragile type of beauty."

To create her stage name, this five-foot-one, 112-pound firecracker had concocted "Carole" from numerology and taken "Lombard" from a neighbor. Her family had money. One biographical account mentions that her grandfather founded the Horton Company in Fort Wayne, Indiana, after importing the first washing machine to the United States from Germany. On her mother's side, a great-grandfather established one of the first electric companies in California and helped finance the laying of the Atlantic cable. Supposedly, he was a director on the first board of New York's National City Bank.

Carole never discussed her wealth, but director Howard Hawks said she had "plenty of money" before she became the highest-paid actress in Hollywood.

William Powell was seventeen years older than Carole and Ria was seventeen years older than Clark, but Lombard was seven years younger than Gable. Those who knew them best think Carole was more the mother than either of his first two wives—that she had far more understanding of and compassion for Clark. It would take a long time, however, before either would show weakness in the contest of wits and spirit. For a while it was who could hold out the longest, or maybe who could hold *on* the longest. Whether Carole knew the extent of Gable's womanizing isn't known, but all bets were on her complete knowledge, because if anyone got around Hollywood, it was Carole. She didn't gossip, but she adored the latest dirt.

She and Clark dated, but not steadily. Carole still enjoyed the company of Robert Riskin, but as 1936 came to an end, she and Gable were very close.

Her friends did not think he was good enough for Carole. One of them said, "Gable did not have much respect for women. He wasn't very warm and considerate. I thought he was too rough and lacked sentimental values. Carole deserved more affection and attention. She came from a very close family, despite her parents' divorce. She liked to touch and hold. He didn't—except in bed. She remembered birthdays and anniversaries, and though she gave funny presents, they were thoughtful ones that had been carefully thought out, wrapped, and delivered on time. The only thing Clark remembered was his own birthday. Carole, of course, put on a great performance with him—like she didn't give a damn either. The Model A with the red hearts took a lot of time on her part . . . going to a junkyard getting the thing working and cleaned up. What surprised us was his turning around and giving her a jalopy, too. I mean, he had to part with a few bucks! And this wasn't like Gable. He was generous with food and booze, but gifts and affection? Nothing. Carole wouldn't have put up with this from any other man. She'd have booted him in the ass and explained the facts of life. Carole recognized the sensitivity underneath all that gruff exterior, but everyone knew he took women for granted, and Carole gave the impression she cared less. Clark didn't seem to give a hoot about anything other than what he liked to do . . . hunting and fishing, for example. Carole liked frilly clothes, nightclubbing, dandy parties, luncheons at the Brown Derby, and putting on one of her fashionable hats for cocktails with reporters. All of these things were not for Gable, with the exception of a party or two. She pretended to like his hobbies. Otherwise she'd never get to see him. So she bought britches and sport shirts and boots, learned to shoot a rifle almost like a pro, and he thought that was really swell. Carole wasn't obvious, though. He thought she went along for the fun, and she wasn't about to let him think any different."

Gable's friends weren't fond of Carole in the beginning, because he insisted on taking her on camping trips. This had always been "for men only," but now Clark usually wanted her to tag along. She was able to keep up with the jargon and taught the boys some new raw lingo. Her jokes were the raunchiest, too. Gable thought she was cute, but his buddies got bored and "turned off" listening to her swear like a sailor. One of Gable's friends said, "I never heard anyone talk like Carole—man or woman. She kept it up until I couldn't take any more. Every sentence was laced with 'shit' and 'fuck.' Clark was rooting for her. He encouraged Carole. She made him laugh all the time. He never got tired of her antics and four-letter words. We figured she'd get fed up with the bad weather, bugs, wet blanket, and roughing it in general, but she didn't. Instead, she went out and bought her own guns, reeled in the biggest fishes, and never got tired. I had nothing against her personally, but her language bored me, and I didn't think she belonged with a bunch of men in the wild."

When Carole was asked what she did to occupy her time lurking in the bushes if the ducks did not cooperate, she shrugged. "Sometimes we fucked. We did it twice in the rain."

The good times were few and far between during the first year of dating, because of hectic film commitments. They were usually alone together. If their friends did not appreciate the relationship, it worked the other way around, too. Clark wasn't comfortable with her intellectual and/or sophisticated chums. Carole had little in common with his heavy-drinking, sports-minded, women-chasing pals. The lovers were more contented and compatible alone.

He continued to tell the press, "I have no intention of getting married again, so why get a divorce?"

Carole, meanwhile, had to contend with the women who crowded around him at parties. One of her favorite wisecracks was "Here's one dame who isn't chasing you!"

She had no time for Robert Riskin now. It was difficult to see him as a friend, because he was in love with her. Clark managed his one-nighters, but very discreetly. Not only was he a married man, but there was Lombard to consider. He hadn't changed by any means where "dames" were concerned. Ria was his excuse for kissing and not telling, according to the girls who joined him in bed. These young ladies never betrayed him, because their careers were at stake too.

Joan Crawford, undaunted by Gable's fling with Carole, was having a delightful time with Spencer Tracy filming *Mannequin*. Her marriage to the quiet and gentle Franchot Tone was coming to an end. He found solace in the bottle while Joan got energized by Spencer, who drank heavily too, but Joan said it fit his personality.

"I was thrilled to work with him," she said, "but he turned out to be a real son of a bitch. When we began to film the movie, he helped me to conquer many fears. For example, I was terrified of horses, but he took me to the stables, and gradually I wasn't as frightened. Would you believe he taught me to play polo? Then he urged me to do radio, and I was scared stiff of microphones. As a movie actress, I didn't come face-to-face with them. They were overhead. Staring at one put me in a sweat. When Spence asked me to do a script on radio I said, 'No way!'"

He laughed. "Nothing to it!"

"Okay, I'll do it, but only if you're with me."

"Nothing to it," he repeated, with a big silly grin.

They got to the studio, and Joan asked him to give her time—not to rush her through the script. They rehearsed and rehearsed and rehearsed, because she continually blew her lines. Tracy was getting angry and very impatient.

"For Christ's sake, Joan, can't you read lines? I thought you were a pro!"

Everyone in the studio froze. Joan froze, but Spencer was disgusted. "C'mon, let's get this thing finished!"

Crawford burst into tears, ran out the door, and drove home. End of affair.

Crawford was hurt again when she walked into Franchot's dressing room and found him making love to a cute young extra.

"How could you possibly do such a thing?" Joan asked.

Tone replied, "I have to prove to myself that I'm still a man before I go home to you."

End of marriage.

After the judge granted Joan a divorce, he asked her, "You say that your husband caused you much nervousness and mental anguish. How does it happen, then, that you were publicized having a friendly dance with him in New York after these divorce proceedings got started?"

Joan glared at the judge and sat up straight. "Well! I certainly hope I'm intelligent enough to be friendly with my husband!"

Poor Franchot admitted years later that he had to get down on his knees to apologize when he was married to Joan. "It didn't bother me," he said, smiling.

To her death, Crawford maintained that Gable "had balls." This was edited out of David Frost's TV interview with her—the one and only time this expression was eliminated from her endless rambling about the love of her life. Sometimes she used it in reference to the bedroom, but more often to describe his attitude toward life. He did not take any nonsense from women, but Lombard was the exception.

Carole forged ahead without consulting him, pretending that she didn't care what he thought. Though he went his way and she went her way, they were seldom seen in public socially with anyone but each other, and the press followed them everywhere. Clark had privacy at his hotel, but Lombard was besieged by reporters at her home, where they lingered at all hours. Gable found it impossible to come and go without being questioned or photographed. Spending the night with her was virtually impossible. Carole did not want to spend too much time at the Beverly Wilshire. It was beneath her, and if there was one thing Lombard refused to do, it was pave the way for an eternal affair. She was in love with Gable and wanted to marry him, but Carole had the impatience of a mustang and the pride of a thoroughbred.

To avoid the glare and embarrassment of publicity, she moved into an English Tudor house in secluded Bel-Air. When Clark got tired of driving back and forth from Beverly Hills, he rented a house close to Carole's. It was Gable who confessed to friends, "Since our work conflicts, this is the only way I can get to see Carole once in a while." This was quite an admission for a womanizer like Clark, who never went out of his way for any girl—an indication that the unattainable King was vulnerable after all.

In September 1936 Irving Thalberg died of pneumonia at the age of thirty-seven. Clark was a visibly shaken usher at the funeral. That night L. B. Mayer was seen dancing joyfully at the Trocadero Club.

Thalberg had recognized that indescribable "it" in Gable that was shielded by his big ears and the hands of a sailor. Hadn't Warner laughed for days? Mayer would have ignored the screen test entirely, but Thalberg cast Clark opposite his wife in A *Free Soul*, which was the turning point not only in Gable's career, but in movie lovemaking in general. When Thalberg died, his discovery was the most valuable property in Hollywood. Mayer had the power to make Clark suffer, but would have a fight on his hands if he tried to destroy him.

Sid Graumann, who owned a chain of theaters, paid a visit to Mary Pickford and accidentally stepped into wet cement at the entrance to her dressing room. This mishap gave him an idea, and when Cecil B. De Mille's *Kings of Kings* opened at his new Chinese Theater on Hollywood Boulevard, Pickford was the first to "record" her footprints. Aside from the Oscar, this was the most prestigious compliment to a movie performer.

Ten years after Pickford charmed the country on newsreels as she placed her tiny shoe in cement, Clark Gable imprinted his big feet and huge hands with the inscription, "To Sid who is a great guy." He drew the largest crowd in history at this event. Carole took it in stride. "Wouldn't it be more appropriate if they took your cockprint instead?" she asked with a serious look on her face.

Gable grinned from ear to ear.

• • •

In April 1937, Clark was in Los Angeles Federal Court as a witness for the prosecution in the United States Government's case against Violet Norton, an English woman who claimed he had fathered her fifteen-year-old daughter, Gwendoline. Violet recognized her lover, "Frank Billings," when she saw *It Happened One Night.* She wrote letters to Clark, Mae West, Walter Winchell, Jimmy Fidler, and MGM. The district attorney of Los Angeles contacted Gable, who said, "I've never been in England."

"In that case," the district attorney said, "you'll have to prove beyond a doubt where you were in 1922."

"All over the Northwest. I was a drifter."

"You'll have to be more specific than that, and get witnesses to back you up."

Gable knew he was innocent, and laughed about it to Carole, who didn't think it was very amusing. "You'd better be telling the truth, you bastard!"

MGM attempted to contact everyone and anyone who might have known Clark in 1922. The Silverton Lumber Company sent copies of checks made out to him, but the most important witness was Franz Dorfler, who was living in Los Angeles.

On April 22, 1937, before an all-male jury, the trial began. It was established that Clark Gable had never been issued an American passport. He took the stand and related his early years from Ohio to Kansas to Montana to Oregon. Violet Norton insisted on taking a closer look at the man on the stand to verify who it was. The judge said, "Everyone in this court can see the witness is Clark Gable! Your request is denied!"

The key witness was Franz Dorfler. She was able to remember specific dates. Under oath she said that Clark was staying with her parents on the farm in September 1922, the month Violet Norton said she conceived.

Gable gallantly assisted Franz down from the witness stand.

Violet Norton was deported to Canada.

All smiles, Clark said, "As affairs go, the one she described was a long-distance project. It would have set a world's record."

With a straight face Carole said, "That's right. You have all you can do to make it at close range."

• • •

Gable had a great deal to be excited about. He was offered the role of an Irish statesman in *Parnell*—a part he thought would prove his ability as a dramatic actor. Joan Crawford was chosen as the married woman who destroys Parnell.

"I read the script." She yawned.

"Great, isn't it?" He beamed. "Baby, this will change my image."

"It stinks."

"Are you kidding?"

"Get Loretta."

"She has other commitments."

Joan smirked. "I'm sure she does, and you and Spence know every one of them, don't you? I would think you'd have better things to do than visit her on the set all the time. You and Spence never visit me!"

"That's after hours, baby . . . after hours . . ."

"Take *Parnell* and shove it!"

Clark was livid and didn't see Joan for a long time after that. Myrna Loy replaced her in *Parnell*. It was a terrible movie—one he tried to forget. Carole had stickers of *Parnell* made, and stuck them everywhere as a reminder that he wasn't God.

Clark, however, put the blame on Crawford, who turned down *Saratoga* because their relationship was so strained. Jean Harlow was second choice. She reported to work with her fiancé, William Powell.

Jean and Clark, happy at last—she with Carole's ex-husband and he with Powell's ex-wife. They all got along famously. Harlow was still the Baby, and she referred to Powell as "Daddy." He had given Jean a 150-carat star sapphire engagement ring, which, she swore, "I even wear in the shower!"

Saratoga was supposed to be fun. Harlow was delighted to be playing a rich girl instead of a whore for a change, but she had been ill with the flu and had yet to gain back her strength. She was edgy and tired. Gable assumed Jean was nervous from the strain of a thirty-day film schedule that had the entire cast and crew jittery. Her recent fight with Mayer was a threat to her future films at MGM, too. As *Saratoga* neared completion, Jean and Clark were doing a scene together. It called for him to sweep her off her feet and drop her on a chaise. But he noticed that Jean had broken out in a cold sweat and was going limp in his arms. Instead of throwing her down, Clark placed her gently on the chaise and waved his arms to stop the camera. Harlow started to get up and insist they continue. Then she collapsed. After she was revived with smelling salts, the director sent her home for a rest. Her mother, Mrs. Bello, took charge as a loyal Christian Scientist. The following Monday Jean did not show up for work. Mama Bello called the studio to say her baby was doing well and would report the following day. When Jean failed to appear and a studio messenger was sent away by Mama, Gable took it upon himself to visit Harlow.

"I'd like to see Jean," he said.

Mama Bello smiled. "She's sleeping."

"What did the doctors have to say?"

"Someday I must introduce you to Christian Science, Mr. Gable."

Clark rushed back to the studio and returned to the house with actor Frank Morgan and Jean's agent. It took several days for them to convince Mama to allow a doctor in the house. Harlow was rushed to a hospital, where she died. The cause of death is a mystery. Was it gall bladder? Was it her kidneys, as a result of Bern's beating? Both, undoubtedly. The fact that her bruised kidneys weren't functioning allowed the poisons from an infected gall bladder to enter the bloodstream, according to doctors.

Carole and Clark attended the very tragic funeral. Jeanette MacDonald sang "Indian Love Song," followed by Nelson Eddy's "Ah, Sweet Mystery of Life." The flowers that filled the chapel were estimated at close to $20,000, almost as much as the platinum blonde left behind. In her hand was a white gardenia with an unsigned note that read, "Good night, my dearest darling."

The *Los Angeles Examiner* wrote:

And when those of prominence had come and gone and the sorrowful relatives had driven away, the fans rushed through the unlocked gates and trudged half-a-mile up the hill to the vault where the body of their favorite film star lay in a beautiful casket.

There they scrambled madly for bits of flowers, ferns, that lay scattered on the lawn where a few moments before a lavish blanket of color had hidden the green grassway. Young girls and boys, women carrying babies, elderly women who found the climb a test of strength came to gather at the doorway of the church where the great had gathered an hour previously to pay their last respects to their friend and fellow worker.

The doors of the little church then were swung open and with hushed

lips and careful tread, Jean Harlow's fans filed down the aisle to stand for
a fleeting moment at the spot which a few minutes before had been the
garlanded bier of the film star.

Gable was too overcome with grief to comment. The terrible
death of Jean Harlow brought him closer to Carole. Much closer
than he had ever thought possible. Hollywood wasn't what it was
cracked up to be, was it? Life was shorter here than anywhere else in
the world. Poor Irving, poor Jean . . . poor everybody else . . .

Saratoga was finished using a double for Harlow, seen only from
the back. Several of the young blond hopefuls who tried out for the
part might as well have been auditioning for Gable's harem. He saw
to it that Virginia Grey was in many of his films, and Mary Dees,
who won the part, was another favorite of Clark's over the years.

Saratoga was released a month after the Baby's death, while the
public was still in shock. Gable grieved for a long time. He was
frightened and angry—appalled that the studio was taking advantage
of Jean's death by exploiting her last film appearance. He wondered
if anyone realized how admirably she had risen to the occasion when
she was so ill. For weeks he could see her vividly trying to get up
from the chaise to continue the scene. Poor Jean had been driven like
a lamb to slaughter. She was a baby with a woman's body, treated like
a common whore for the sake of the almighty dollar.

For a long time the lot was empty without Harlow slinking
around like a vamp. She had had the smile of an innocent and sincere child who needed love and care. Did she ever say to him that
she wanted anything else?

The fact that Mayer ignored pleas to have Jean hospitalized immediately—and only he could have enforced it—intensified Gable's
hatred of his boss. Clark knew that Jean had refused Mayer's offer of
a mink coat for a few hours in bed. She scorned him, hated him,
wished him dead, and said so. Mayer called her a cheap tramp. She
took great delight in having this chance to turn him down.

Yes, Gable had many reasons for despising Mayer—for his own
abuse, Thalberg's abuse, Gilbert's abuse, and Harlow's abuse.

Screenwriter Frances Marion wrote that Mayer could detect a
phony emotion more quickly than the directors and that he could
outact any actor. She cites his office performance for Lionel Barrymore—a scene from a script where a mother pleads for the life of
her son. "We were spellbound by Mr. Mayer," Marion said,

"... pitching his voice higher to achieve a feminine tone, sobbed out his pitiful pleas, then with tears streaming down his eyes, he fell to his knees on the floor, grabbed Lionel's hand and kissed it. 'Good God!' said Lionel."

She said that Mayer insisted that in the screenplays, all mothers must be saintly and all men true to their wives, which was rather paradoxical, considering his own roving eye. That must be blamed on those pretty little girls who served themselves on silver platters to the men who held the keys that opened the studio gates.

Marion went on to say, "I must betray a secret which some of us writers kept well hidden for years; we called these silver-platter girls 'Moos' when they became the bosses' sacred cows. Often we would tip each other off. 'Might be smart to write in a juicy part for So-and-So. She's L.B.'s latest Moo.' Once, a male scenario writer with a few drinks under his belt walked up to a luscious redhead sporting a diamond bracelet and a year's contract. 'Whose Moo is oo?' he asked. She snapped back, 'Don't get fresh with me or I'll tell Sam Katz on you!' And that was how we kept in touch with the transient love affairs on the Metro lot."

Mayer professed to be the father to his stable of stars, and in some instances he proved himself admirably. Strickling and Gable were observing (and trying to help) a newcomer to MGM, Robert Taylor, who was reeling through the studio treatment, but in Bob's case, Mayer was helpful and devoted. The story of Taylor, who was the lowest-paid Hollywood star in history, is so typical of Mayer, who refused to raise Taylor's thirty-five-dollar-a-week salary.

"Bob," Mayer said, "God never saw fit to give me the great blessing of a son. He gave me daughters—two beautiful daughters, who have been a great joy to me. They're now married to fine, successful fellows—top producers—Dave Selznick and Billy Goetz. But for some reason, in His infinite wisdom, He never saw fit to give me a son.

"But if He had given me a son, Bob—if He had blessed me with such a great and wonderful joy—I can't think of anybody I would rather have wanted that son to be than exactly like you. And if that son came to me and said, 'Dad, I'm working for a wonderful company, Metro-Goldwyn-Mayer, and for a good man, the head of the company, who has my best interests at heart. But he's paying me thirty-five dollars a week, Dad. Do you think I should ask him for a raise?' Do you know what I'd say to my son, Bob? I'd say, 'Son, it's a fine company. It's going to do great things for you—greater things than it has already done. It's going to make a great star of you. You'll be famous. That's more important than a little money. Don't ask for a raise, son.'"

When Taylor was leaving Mayer's office his agent asked, "Did you get the raise, Bob?"

"No, but I got a father," Taylor replied.

Mayer might have been stingy with the young kid from Nebraska, but he taught him how to budget what money he had—took the time to sit down with Taylor and work out a way for him to exist without going into debt. When the actor went into a slump, Mayer promised a plum role, and he always came through.

Taylor and Gable became very close friends. Both were Pennsylvania Dutch and down-to-earth. Neither ever "went Hollywood." They shared a close friendship with Howard Strickling, a love of hunting and fishing . . . and occasionally a girl friend.

III
SUPERSTAR,
SUPERSTUD

CHAPTER SEVEN

In the fall of 1938, columnist Ed Sullivan ran a "King and Queen of the Movies" contest in his syndicated newspaper column. Twenty million voters participated. Clark Gable and Myrna Loy were the winners. (Robert Taylor and Loretta Young came in second.)

Gable and Loy were crowned at a formal ceremony at MGM. Gable's title stuck for the rest of his life. Carole behaved herself at the coronation but told friends the next day, "If Clark had an inch less, he'd be Queen of Hollywood!"

The American public did not need verification that Gable deserved a crown. He had been King to them for a few years. What most people did not know (or care about) was that Carole Lombard was the highest-paid Hollywood star in 1937, at $465,000 per year. Her new Paramount contract was worth $2 million and included three films a year, beginning at $150,000 per film. And she was permitted to free-lance. *Film Weekly* commented, "... there is one very significant indication on a star's ranking—Hollywood's own opinion. Every producer and director mentions Carole's name with that mysterious professional enthusiasm whose authenticity cannot be mistaken. And they all declare that she is as fine an emotional actress as she is a comedienne."

If Carole was making more money than Clark, he offset that with the popularity polls, but their careers never conflicted. Only their work schedules. She was the extrovert who voluntarily gave sparkling interviews. He never did. She bounced around town. He didn't. She wooed the public. He claimed it was fickle. Carole loved life and she loved him. He wasn't very enthusiastic about life, but was falling in love with Carole despite himself.

Ria didn't think so. She had seen her husband through many flaming affairs, and this one, in her opinion, was no different. She and Clark discussed divorce, but neither did anything about it. She wanted him back and was sure he would eventually return to her. "He never did anything to embarrass me," Ria said, but she was very disappointed that Clark did not offer to see her children. When he left Ria's bed, he left her family, too.

While the talk around Hollywood was David Selznick's film adaptation of Margaret Mitchell's *Gone With the Wind*, Clark teamed with Spence and Myrna Loy. Tracy referred to *Test Pilot* as "another Gable movie"—half in jest, but he good-naturedly tried to steal scenes as only he could. In his death sequence, Tracy lay in Gable's arms long enough for one farewell, but continued to open his eyes for one more gasp. After a day and a half of filming, Clark shook Tracy and said, "Die, goddamn it, Spence! I wish to Christ you would!"

Gable was very much in awe of Tracy and couldn't stay mad at him for very long. "In one scene," he said, "Myrna and I were talking in the front seat of a convertible. Spence was sitting in the middle of the back seat. Myrna and I were having a 'hot' conversation. Spence only had one or two short lines, but the bastard was chewing gum. That did it! Nobody paid any attention to what Myrna and I were saying, because all eyes were on Spence chewin' on that gum. He didn't get the girl. He just stole the whole picture with no effort. There's no one like him in the business."

Gable was teamed again with Loy in *Too Hot to Handle*, an adventure melo about rival newscameramen. Clark became a national hero when the plane-crash fire went out of control and firemen prepared to rush in for Myrna, who was trapped.

"Keep the camera rolling, damn it!" Clark yelled. "I'll get her myself!"

When he appeared out of the smoke with Loy in his arms, Carole cracked, "You big ham!"

To get even with her for that remark, Gable held on to Myrna, whose arms were wrapped around his neck.

"You can let her down now," Lombard exclaimed.

Observers on the set of *Too Hot to Handle* were surprised that Carole was spending so much time with Clark during working hours. He had strongly objected to this in the past, but understood Carole's frustration and loneliness. She wanted to get married and he couldn't afford a divorce. Ria had stated her terms and was not about to change her mind. Carole was trying to avoid committing herself to a film contract in the event a miracle happened. She was anxiously waiting to find out if Clark would be offered the part of Harry, the hoofer in Robert Sherwood's *Idiot's Delight*. When the assignment was definite, she volunteered to help him with his dance routines.

Joan Crawford demanded the part of the phony "duchess" Irene in the film. When Mayer refused to discuss it, she cornered Gable on the MGM back lot.

"Must you wash your teeth in the drinking fountain?" she scolded. "Suppose someone sees you?"

"It's no secret," he said, putting them back in his mouth.

"What's doing with the Sherwood flick?"

"You don't know?"

"I know I want the part of Irene more than anything I've ever wanted, besides you."

"Norma's doing it."

Joan got off her bicycle and threw it on the ground. "Did I hear you correctly? Did you say that witch is going to play Irene?"

"It's a long story."

"What the hell's going on around here? Irving's dead but that bitch still gets the parts!"

"Are you crying?"

"What if I am?" she sniffled, burying her face against his chest.

"Don't do that," he grumbled, easing her away. "I think Carole's around here somewhere . . ."

"Fuck Carole. My career's more important!"

"Norma made a deal with Mayer, Joanie. Seems that mail's been pouring in about her playing Scarlett."

"What?"

"Do you want to hear the rest of the story?"

"Let's go to your dressing room. I need a drink."

"And I keep tellin' ya, Carole's on the lot. Will you sit down over here and listen?"

"Why do I have to sit down?" she asked, gritting her teeth.

"Because you'll be lyin' down otherwise. That's a good girl. Seems Norma doesn't think she's right for Scarlett and officially declined."

"*What?!*"

"That way, she'll pacify her fans and Mayer won't get lynched. Her reward is *Idiot's Delight*."

"What?!"

"Hang on to your falsies, baby, she also got the lead in *The Women.*"

"What?!"

"Joanie, you gotta remember, Irving left Norma controlling interest in MGM when he died."

"She rode into this studio on his balls, didn't she?"

"I hate to bring this up," he said glumly, "but you've been holding a grudge against Norma too long, and all because you made your movie debut doubling the back of her head. That was a long time ago."

"I'm sick and tired of playing second fiddle to her. If Selznick thinks I'll play Scarlett after that bitch turned it down, he's an ass."

"Try to get over this grudge, babe."

"You sap! The widow Shearer has you wrapped around her little finger too! She makes you look good, is that it?"

"I don't cast 'em, honey, I just play 'em."

"I'll get even."

"Now, Joanie," he said sweetly, looking around to make sure Carole wasn't within striking distance, "don't do anything you'll be sorry for . . ."

"Maybe the fucking widow won't be so haughty if I play Crystal in *The Women*. It's a small part, but I take away her husband."

"Christ, Joan, all the Scarlett rejects will be in that one. Are you nuts?"

"I've never been saner, and by the way, when do you want me to help you with Harry's dance routines? Great excuse to get together."

"Well . . . ah, you see, Carole's going to do that."

"I know them down pat. Why didn't you ask me first?"

"Because I'd like to be around to see my fortieth birthday."

Gable had several dance numbers—the most complicated with a chorus line of six blondes, to the tune of "Puttin' on the Ritz." At the end of the number, the girls carry him off-stage. Carole worked with him at home and at the studio. She arrived late one morning and found a chorus girl flirting with Gable. Without hesitating, Lombard screamed, "Get that whore out of here!"

The dancer was fired.

Carole kept her eye on Norma, who was getting over being rejected by Tyrone Power. This was, of course, an indication that the famous widow was looking for her next husband. After a love scene between Clark and Shearer, Lombard whispered loud enough for everyone to hear, "I hope you put extra glue on your false teeth, Pa."

The cast and crew on *Idiot's Delight* weren't tense, however, because Carole was as thoughtful and witty as she was jealous. Clark found an oversize pair of ballet slippers on his chair. He loved her gags, but the best was handing him a big bouquet of flowers when he finished the final dance number. She referred to him as "the prima donna," and Clark ate it up like a piece of his favorite chocolate cake.

Idiot's Delight was very successful and one of Gable's best. Though Gable was a hilarious Harry Van, he appeared tired and drawn on the screen. Undoubtedly, he was drowning his sorrows over Ria in the bottle. The big chatter around Hollywood was Selznick's *Gone With the Wind* and rumors that author Margaret Mitchell patterned her hero, Rhett Butler, after Clark Gable. During the filming of the light and frothy *Idiot's Delight,* negotiations were going on, and though Clark had not been approached, he felt the mounting pressure. "I can't win," he said. "If I get a raise, Ria gets more money. If I get the part of Captain Butler and share in the profits of *Gone With the Wind,* she'll ask for more than her share."

He had, of course, gotten rid of Josephine for nothing. His friends reminded him of this when he complained about Ria, but nothing could pull him out of his depression except Carole, who was always good for a laugh. What made him feel worse was the superb act she was putting on to cheer him up.

In late 1938, however, *Photoplay* magazine published an article that shocked not only the readers but Hollywood as well. It was entitled "Hollywood's Unmarried Husbands and Wives," revolving around such famous couples as Barbara Stanwyck and Robert Taylor, Paulette Goddard and Charlie Chaplin, Virginia Rice and George Raft, Constance Bennett and Gilbert Roland, and Carole Lombard and Clark Gable.

> ...just friends to the world at large—yet nowhere has domesticity taken on so unique a character as in this unconventional fold. For Clark Gable, Carole Lombard stopped almost overnight being a Hollywood playgirl. People are expected to change when they get married. The necessary adaptation to a new life and another personality shows up in every bride and groom. All Clark and Carole did was strike up a Hollywood twosome. Nobody said, "I do." Like any good spouse might do, Carole has ways and means of chastening Clark. When she's mad at him she wears a hat he particularly despises. Carole calls it her "hate hat." Yes, Carole Lombard

is a changed woman since she tied up with Clark Gable, but her name is still Carole Lombard. The altar record, in fact, among Hollywood popular twosomes is surprisingly slim. Clark is still officially a married man. Every now and then negotiations for a divorce are started, but until something happens in court, Ria Gable is still the only wife the law of the land allows Clark Gable.

The article pointed out the sad case of Jean Harlow and William Powell as a lesson to the Hollywood couples who were flaunting their affairs.

"For nobody, not even Hollywood's miracle men, has ever improved on the good old-fashioned, satisfying institution of holy matrimony. And, until something better comes along, the best way to hunt happiness when you're in love in Hollywood or anywhere else—is with a preacher, a marriage license and a bagful of rice."

This article was a number one scandal. Since the studios usually controlled what the fan magazines printed, it rocked the likes of Louis B. Mayer and his son-in-law David Selznick, who, by popular demand, wanted Clark to portray Rhett Butler. This would be out of the question now.

Ria consented to an interview and chose her words very carefully. "I've always told Clark he could have a divorce any day he asked for it. And he can. Today or tomorrow. But he's a businessman as well as a movie star. He knows one must be businesslike about these things. It's only fair. I gave him many years of my life and taught him a great deal."

Mayer cringed. The article was bad enough, but Ria made it clear that she was not standing in Clark's way if indeed he *really* wanted to marry Carole Lombard.

In defense of Gable, he did not want to give Ria half of the money that MGM put in trust for him. MGM didn't want to agree to this either, since it was their security should Clark try to walk out on his contract.

Gable and Lombard, meanwhile, tried to maintain their sanity. He enjoyed telling her about his escapades in bed and elsewhere. "I even did it in the swimming pool." He grinned. "You know, it's hard to do under water."

She smiled. "Yes, isn't it?"

His mouth dropped open. "What kind of a girl are you?" he exclaimed. "Doing a thing like that and having the nerve to tell me about it!"

Mayer insisted that negotiations with Ria become a serious matter. Gable's reputation was on the line. As popular as he was, moviegoers in 1938 would not pay to see anyone involved in scandal. Years before they had blackballed Fatty Arbuckle, despite the fact a jury found him innocent of murdering actress Virginia Rappe. And what about the It Girl, Clara Bow, whose maid exposed Clara's busy boudoir? She was single, but ruined for misbehaving.

Gable's past was catching up with him, but letters continued to flood MGM insisting that no one else could play Rhett Butler. Selznick was on the spot, too. He had been preparing for *Gone With the Wind* a long time and was anxious to begin production. He wanted Gable, but there was too much money involved should his Rhett get into a headline-making divorce. Clark had not accepted the role because he wanted Carole to play Scarlett and indicated those were his terms. Little did he know that he would have nothing to say about it.

Shortly after the *Photoplay* article was published, Gable made a simple announcement that he was going to divorce Ria, and lawyers on both sides began negotiations.

Carole and Clark began looking for a house in Bel-Air and Beverly Hills. They weren't desperate, because her home was adequate for the time being. Gable was anxious to "spread out" eventually, since he and Carole enjoyed horseback riding, dogs, and, above all, seclusion. When the one-eyed director Raoul Walsh heard that Clark was house-hunting he told the King that his twenty-acre ranch in the San Fernando Valley was up for sale. Gable had admired the place on his frequent visits to the Walsh hideaway, eight miles from Hollywood. In 1938 the Encino property was in the wilderness, filled with fruit trees and surrounded by mountains. The few ranches there were scattered and accessible only by one canyon road.

The two-story white brick Connecticut "farmhouse" was thirteen years old. The stables were big enough for ten horses, which fed on home-grown alfalfa and red oats. Orchards of oranges, lemons, peaches, figs, and apricots were beautiful. Huge pepper and eucalyptus trees provided shade from the sun's rays in the hot valley.

Since this was Walsh's second house, making the ranch livable year-round meant there was a great deal of work to be done—installation of furnaces, a larger kitchen, servants' quarters, and a care-taker's cottage. This was only the beginning, however. Additions and changes added up to one thing—money—and Clark's was tied up pending his divorce. "I've always wanted a place like this," he sighed. "It will be the first home I've had since I was a kid. Ma and I could be very happy here . . ."

It was Carole who laid out the $50,000 for his dream. She was investing in "her man," just as his two wives had done. This was a well-guarded secret, of course. Who would believe that Clark Gable was unable to raise the money? Josephine and Ria, undoubtedly. Ironically, whether he was poor or rich, unknown or famous, it was a future wife who came to Clark's rescue when he needed help the most.

Carole didn't care that she had to stake him. They were so happy and excited making plans, walking through the orchards, discussing color schemes and looking at tractors—until Ria announced that Clark had no right to "presume" anything regarding a divorce. She had been insulted and therefore was going to contest. Within days Gable gave a statement to the press:

> I regret bitterly that a short time ago a story was printed to the effect that I would seek a divorce from Mrs. Gable. Mrs. Gable and I had a fine life together until the time came that we both realized we could no longer make a go of it. After years of separation it is only natural that Mrs. Gable should institute proceedings that will assure her freedom

Ria simmered down and agreed to begin negotiations, but Clark's lawyers told him he would pay dearly for this divorce. MGM agreed to cooperate, and though Mayer was usually for the poor unfortunate wife in such matters, he had powerful motives behind his generosity and understanding. There is no evidence that he ever approached Clark about Lombard, who apparently had more friends at MGM than L.B. did! If he wasn't convinced she was the best thing that ever happened to Gable, he was the only one.

As for Carole, she was almost broke after extending herself for the Encino ranch. But she didn't allow this setback to diminish her poking fun at the King.

"God knows, I adore Clark," she told friends, "even though he's a lousy lay."

Gable was amused. "In that case, I guess I'll have to do a lotta practicing!"

Obtaining his freedom to marry Carole was all he wanted, or so he thought when it appeared that Ria would not cooperate. "But I never got a damn thing in life I didn't pay for," he said. Not only would the divorce hurt him financially, it would also put him firmly in Mayer's clutches. Gable went into a rage when he found out MGM was seriously considering loaning him to David Selznick for *Gone With the Wind.*

"I'll be tied up for a year!" Gable grumbled.

"Six months at the most," Mayer said.

"I want to know who's playing Scarlett!"

"Ask my son-in-law."

"I don't like Selznick, frankly."

"Neither do I. We agree on something."

"Don't I have a say in this matter?" Gable growled.

"No."

"I'm being bounced around like a tennis ball and I don't like it. I know for a fact that Selznick wants Gary Cooper."

"That's because my son-in-law's an ass."

"I'm second choice. Is that it?"

"Third. He couldn't get Errol Flynn, either."

"I happen to know for a fact that Warner Brothers was turned down when they offered Bette Davis and Flynn."

"You think you're the only actor in Hollywood!" Mayer bellowed.

"No, but you do. Now let's talk about Scarlett. You said something about a list of girls making a screen test." Gable looked at the names and shook his head. "Tallulah Bankhead? Is Selznick out of his fuckin' mind? Jean Arthur, Lucille Ball, and Susan Hayward? Who are they? Never heard of 'em. Norma Shearer and Loretta Young? Not wicked enough . . . on the screen, anyway. Forget Miriam Hopkins. Lana Turner. Is she the young blond kid? Yeah! Too cute. Joan Crawford, maybe."

"You know Joan better than anyone," Mayer said sarcastically. "She'll do anything to play Scarlett. Anything. Know what I mean?"

"Yeah . . . and Paulette Goddard."

Mayer laughed. "She's the favorite."

"What's so funny? She'd be great. Not as good as Carole, but this list is terrible! Are you preparin' me for Paulette?"

Mayer was still laughing. "She can't prove her marriage to Chaplin. They're living together, but Paulette insists they were married by the mayor of Catalina."

"So?'

"Catalina doesn't have a mayor. You should be so clever."

"Does that mean she's out of the running?" Gable asked.

"Unless she comes up with a marriage certificate, and that's not likely. If she were under contract to MGM, we would have protected her. That's our warm family policy."

"Yeah." Gable scowled, crumpling up the list of actresses begging for the part of Scarlett.

The screen tests began. As Joan Crawford put it, "All of a sudden every girl in Hollywood had a southern accent." She campaigned for the role and told Clark, "I know it's just a matter of time before you're Rhett Butler. I was in the mail room the other day and saw literally hundreds of thousands of letters insisting on it."

"What were you doing in the mail room?" Clark asked.

"I answer every one of my fan letters personally. Don't change the subject, darling."

"I'm sick and tired of this Rhett business."

"Not if I play Scarlett. We'll be great together. Dynamite."

"Yeah."

"You agree?"

"Yeah."

"You'll insist?"

"I can't do that!"

"Because of Carole? That's it!"

"Well . . ."

"Screw Carole. I love her dearly, but she's no Scarlett, for Christ's sake. There's magic between you and me, just as there is between Rhett and Scarlett."

"I made it clear there was no deal without Carole," he said.

"Don't be a fool!"

"I don't know what I am since this goddamn civil war broke out right here in Hollywood!" he said.

"Play it cool, darling, and we can have it all," Joan cooed.

"You'd better have your brakes relined."

While Clark was dodging Joan at MGM, Carole was fencing with Gary Cooper at Paramount.

"Tell them you'll play Rhett and then cancel out," she told him.

"Why would I do a thing like that?"

"So I can play Scarlett."

"But I may not play Rhett," he said.

"Christ, you've got a thick head! Paramount hasn't got anyone else to play Scarlett. I'm a shoo-in. When you back out, Selznick will have no choice but to sign Clark."

"I'm in the middle," Cooper said, scratching his head.

"All you have to say is 'Yup' and 'Nope.' Can't you do that for me?"

"Nope."

"You've got half of it right."

"Yup."

"Don't you take chances out of bed?"

"Nope."

"You owe me."

"For what?"

"Your fuckin' career."

"I don't get it."

"Who the hell carried you through *I Take This Woman*? Christ, that Clara Bow scandal almost killed you, Studs. You looked as if you were the one who took on the UCLA football team instead of Clara. Kissing you was like picking on a bone. But I got you through it, didn't I?"

"Yes. I was sick . . . very, very sick. I did need you, Carole. Remember our first date? You were just a kid . . ."

"And you were cheating on Evelyn Brent . . ."

"She didn't want me . . . turned me down . . ."

"Poor lamb . . ."

"I liked you from the very start, Carole. I could never understand what you saw in Bill Powell. He's a nice guy and all, but not for you. Guess we both made mistakes."

"The way I see it, you fucked your way into Clara's movies, but that was no mistake. After all, they don't call you 'Studs' for nothing."

"Clark didn't do so bad with Jane Cowl and Pauline Frederick."

"They took his pants off!" Carole exclaimed.

"Not the way I heard it."

"You've been jealous of Clark for a long time, and I think you're playing hard to get . . . trying to make Selznick squirm and Clark wait it out."

"Are you tryin' to rile me up?"

"How could I do that?" She laughed. "You're not even breathing."

"Do you really want the part of Scarlett that bad?"

"I do, because I can do it better than anyone else. And I don't trust Clark with Paulette or Joan for six fuckin' months. C'mon, Studs, tell Selznick you'll play Rhett. He doesn't want to share *Gone With the Wind* with Mayer. He'd love to release the film right here at Paramount. Clark isn't anxious to play Rhett, but he's in demand."

"MGM publicity."

"Jesus!"

Cooper frowned. "One and the same."

"There you go again!" Carole attacked. "You hate Clark. If it isn't bigger cars, it's a better gun collection. What is it with you two guys, anyway?"

"Ask him."

"I'll do that, because if I talk to you much longer, Studs, I'm gonna need oxygen."

"You've gotten me all mixed up," Cooper said. "What do you want me to do?"

Carole sat on his lap, put her arms around his neck, and looked him squarely in the eyes, noses almost touching. "I'm giving you a chance to give Clark some competition. Think of the free publicity you'll get. Cooper agrees to play Rhett. Cooper turns down Rhett. Selznick stuck with Gable. You'll be a hero."

"And you'll be Scarlett. She's a brunette."

"Who says she can't be a blonde?"

"Margaret Mitchell."

"Since when does a movie follow the book?"

"I gotta go home now," he said, easing Carole off his lap.

"I gotta go home now," she mimicked.

"Carole, I'd like to help you," he said, putting his arm around her. "But I have my reputation to think about."

"Since when?" she asked.

"I might do *Gone With the Wind*," he said, "even though I think it's going to be the biggest flop in Hollywood history."

"If you play Rhett, it will be," Carole said, kicking him in the seat of the pants.

Gable had no idea how his divorce was related to his role in *Gone With the Wind*. Once Mayer made up his mind to deal with Ria, he began negotiations with Selznick, and behind closed doors, Clark became Rhett. While he fumed, Ria would collect $300,000, and his contract and trust would be dealt with accordingly. Clark could live with this (did he have a choice?), but he could not accept George Cukor as the director of *Gone With the Wind.* "Why Cukor?" he wanted to know. "Everyone knows he's a woman's director!" Selznick replied, "He's the best."

Gable had barely gotten through Margaret Mitchell's best-selling novel about the Civil War and wasn't sure how to play Butler, but he had read enough to know that whoever played Scarlett O'Hara would be a threat to him.

If Carole was determined to become Mrs. Gable, and Ria was determined to be compensated for her years as Mrs. Gable, they both had a rival when it came to determination. A green-eyed twenty-six-year-old beauty was three thousand miles away in England, pining away for her married lover, who was making a movie in the United States. She had just finished reading *Gone With the Wind* and could identify with Scarlett. They thought and looked very much alike. She made up her mind in a split second, called her boy friend, and said she was sailing on the next boat for New York, adding, "Your agent is Myron Selznick, isn't it?"

"Yes, darling," was the reply. "Why do you ask?"

"Is he David's brother?"

"Yes."

"I should very much like to meet him."

"I'll arrange it, darling."

Laurence Olivier hung up the telephone and thought nothing more about it, other than that the woman he loved would be in his arms within the week.

In New York she boarded a plane for the first time in her life. During the fifteen-hour flight, with three stopovers to refuel before reaching Los Angeles, Vivien Leigh skimmed through Margaret Mitchell's book again and again, visualizing how she should portray Scarlett and how she should dress and fix her hair for the first encounter with Myron Selznick—who gasped, "My God, you are Scarlett!"

David Selznick said he would never recover from his first look. "I knew she was right—at least right as far as my conception of how Scarlett O'Hara looked . . ."

Vivien Leigh got one of her wishes when she signed a contract with Selznick for *Gone With the Wind,* but the other, to be with Olivier, was not easy. They were both married and trying to obtain divorces in England. Selznick explained that the code in the United

States was different. Americans did not take kindly to blatant adultery. He said Lombard and Gable were facing the same situation, but were not living together. They had been warned, also, to be very careful until MGM came to terms with Ria. Olivier was very gracious about the situation, but Vivien was extremely disappointed that she would have to be sneaky and not share a hotel suite with her beloved. When she was reminded that Paulette Goddard did not get the part of Scarlett because of her open affair with Chaplin, Vivien agreed to be discreet.

She became very attached to George Cukor, who coached her for the screen tests. She leaned on him completely.

Filming of *Gone With the Wind* began in January 1939. Gable accepted this assignment in worse shape than when he faced *It Happened One Night*. While the other players in the cast had to learn to speak with southern accents, Clark flatly refused. No one dared defy the angry leading man, whose attitude was stubborn and nasty. He had not yet met the irresistible Vivien Leigh, who was, by far, the most beautiful woman he had worked with to date. Everyone knew Gable's reputation with women, and regardless of Carole and regardless of Olivier, he would charm Miss Leigh, who would be his helpless victim.

Her first mistake was arriving late on the first day. Gable ranted and complained. As she walked onto the set, she could hear him cursing her tardiness, but Vivien approached fearlessly (she was breathtaking, of course), looked up at him, and said ever so sweetly, "I quite agree, Mr. Gable. If I were a man, I'd tell that Vivien Leigh to go right back to merry old England."

He turned around and gazed into her green eyes and between her breasts, taped together for cleavage. Neither said a word. What a glorious moment. He actually smiled, took her arm, and strolled around the set. It was magic, everyone said. Unfortunately, it was more like lightning that struck before the storm.

Clark might have tried his luck with Vivien had it not been for George Cukor, who worked with her conscientiously evenings and weekends while Gable complained about him to Selznick and Mayer daily. Finally, on February 12, less than a month into production, Cukor was fired. When Vivien heard the news, she burst into tears and ran from the set. She begged Selznick to change his mind. A few days later, Clark's good friend director Victor Fleming reported for work. Selznick insisted it was his idea—that Cukor went ahead with his own ideas, which were different from those originally discussed. The tension mounted, of course, because Fleming was a man's man, did not have sympathy for little girls wearing a dozen petticoats, and was more interested in guts than tears.

Cukor was shocked, to say the least. He said, "Perhaps Clark mistakenly thought that because I was supposed to be a woman's director, I would throw the story to Vivien—but if that's so, it was very naïve of him and not the reaction of a very good or professional actor. It is nonsense to say I was giving too much attention to Vivien. It is the text that dictates where the emphasis should go, and the director does not do it. Clark Gable does not have a great deal of confidence in himself as an actor, although he is a screen personality, and maybe he thought that I did not understand that."

Gable left the studio every night at six, just like Garbo. He made sure the "no overtime" clause was in all of his contracts. Vivien referred to this as "common." Factory workers punch time clocks— not dedicated actors, she said. The other players were amazed at his ability to get anything he wanted—no southern accent for Captain Butler, a change of directors, and then a complete new wardrobe and tailor.

He wasn't seeing the leading lady after hours, but Clark was widely believed to be sneaking off with one of the supporting actresses. Carole was suspicious, and wasn't very quiet about it at home. Gable was amused.

Carole was powerless to make a scene on the set, but she would be suspicious of Clark long after *Gone With the Wind* was finished. A male member of the huge cast said, "Carole was jealous of all the girls because Gable was on the verge of divorce and she wasn't absolutely sure he would go through with their marriage. She had come this close and was concerned that she'd catch him with another girl. Carole had her pride too. I understand she caught up to him, shall we say, when *Gone With the Wind* was in the can, but between Selznick and Mayer, Gable was thoroughly protected. MGM controlled the wives, sweethearts, and husbands of their family, believe me. Carole knew Clark played harmless games with girls and that he loved her, but they fought about this. Boy, did they fight. He was usually guilty. I'd rather not identify the girl he liked in *Gone With the Wind*. She was his type—blond, petite, and cute... probably his last sexual encounter before marrying Carole. I thought nothing of it. Others were shocked, because they didn't think he'd cheat on

Lombard. People don't change—especially a guy like Clark, who needed many women in his life. He had electricity and was always plugged in. Of all the actors in Hollywood, he was the one the studio worried about most."

Joan Crawford remembers Clark complaining bitterly. "He hated making *Gone With the Wind*," she said. "He absolutely detested Cukor, who was a discreet gay. He was my favorite director, God bless him, but George and Billy Haines were good friends. There was an underground rumor that Clark and Billy had a thing when Clark was desperate for a job. Clark was sure Cukor knew something, and that was the real reason he wanted to get rid of George, who called Clark 'dear' on the set. Mayer destroyed Billy's acting career, but the rest of us never forgot his kindness when we were nobodies. Clark was an extra in Billy's movie, *The Pacemakers*, in 1925. They were friendly. Billy was gay, and in 1925 jobs were hard to get. I tried to discuss the situation with Clark, but he was very upset. He also resented an English girl taking the part of Scarlett. And she went by the book—Margaret Mitchell's. Shit! That's not how movies are made. I begged Clark to remain calm and try to cooperate. He was stubborn and ready to pounce on anything."

Vivien Leigh did not think Gable was too bright. She said he was not a responsive actor. Victor Fleming did not agree. "Clark was unique at responding," he said. "That was his secret. He was an intent and genuine listener on and off the screen. I preferred giving the good lines to someone else because he was a genius at reacting— sometimes with a dumb look on his face or a smirk. It's not clear to me what Vivien meant, unless she wanted Clark to respond to her when he wasn't supposed to. She attended the Royal Academy of Dramatic Arts, was a polished stage actress and an artist, but Clark knew his limitations. He didn't try or pretend to be anything he wasn't. They were very well matched on the screen, but were worlds apart when the camera wasn't rolling."

What Vivien resented most was Clark's bad breath, caused, apparently, by his false teeth. The onion sandwiches he ate every day didn't help.

Ria Gable left for Las Vegas in January 1939, to begin divorce proceedings. Six weeks later Clark was a free man.

"How does it feel to be single, you big lug?"

"Swell, just swell."

"Oh, yeah?"

"Yeah."

Silence.

Clark waited for her to go for the kill. "Aren't you going to say anything?" he asked.

Silence.

"I was thinkin' maybe we'd get married on my first day off. That suit you?" he asked.

"Don't go out of your way!"

He laughed. "Look, Ma, that's the best I can do."

Silence.

"Suppose I leave it up to you." He smiled. "Would you rather attend the premiere of *Alexander Graham Bell* in San Francisco or run away with me?"

"Attend the premiere," Carole said.

"If you change your mind, we would head in the opposite direction . . . say, Kingman, Arizona, and get married. Howard can arrange it so we can drive down there and back in twenty-four hours without anyone knowin' about it."

"No honeymoon?" she teased.

"This is for the rest of our lives, get it?"

"When?"

"Howard figures March 29. Thanks to *Alexander Graham Bell*, we won't be filming. Nobody wants to miss the big premiere."

"I promised Louella an exclusive."

"You were that sure, huh?"

He got a pillow in his face, but before he could throw it back at her, she was in his arms.

At four-thirty on the morning of March 29, Carole and Clark left on the 357-mile drive to Kingman, Arizona. They were married in the home of a Protestant minister and were back in Carole's house within twenty-four hours. The following day the newlyweds had a press conference—he in a navy suit and white tie and she in a simple gray flannel suit. The third Mrs. Gable was all smiles, but did not have a juicy remark for eager reporters, who were used to a zany and outspoken Lombard. Clark was beaming but had little to say, which was no surprise. The press had one of the biggest stories of the year, regardless of the coy couple. They emphasized Carole's "new personality"—a quiet softness, a frustrated giggle, a gentleness about her that oozed happiness and an obvious determination to remain in the background.

Louella Parsons was furious that Carole did not call her in San Francisco.

"I tried to get through, Lolly, so I sent a telegram. I'll make it up to you, though, I promise you that. When I become pregnant, I'll call you from the doctor's office."

Louella hung up in a huff. Carole spent the next few months trying to make up. Louella and Hedda had the power to destroy any big star in Hollywood. Carole was a giver, and she gave plenty to soothe her dear friend, who was very attracted to Clark and resented his attentions to Adela Rogers St. Johns. Deliberately, Louella snubbed him in her columns and excluded his name from her list of favorite performers in 1939.

Clark affected Louella as he did most women. He flatly refused to talk to Sheilah Graham after her first column about him, in 1933. "Clark Gable threw his handsome head back and exposed a neckline on which a thin ridge of fat is beginning to collect," she wrote. Nor was he fond of Hedda Hopper. But Louella? She was different. A clever woman who was not easily fooled, she gave in to his charms. "It was a form of hypnosis," she said. "He could cast a spell on anyone. I found only one other man who could do that. Aly Khan. Aly was a prince and Clark was a star, but that had nothing to do with it. Clark wasn't chivalrous, cultured, or polished like Aly, but whatever the good Lord gave him—potency, might, and vigor—was enough. As close as we were, I was never immune."

Carole would not admit that Louella held a grudge for so long, because Clark had not seen to it personally that she got the scoop before anyone else . . .

After a hectic two days, Gable was Captain Butler again, with three months of filming still ahead. Marriage had apparently mellowed his attitude toward *Gone With the Wind*. When he objected to crying over Scarlett's miscarriage, Selznick asked Clark if he'd do the scene both ways. He did and admitted he was wrong. Rhett shed his tears.

The cast and crew were loosening up and decided to play a joke on Clark. It was Vivien's idea that he carry her up the long staircase at least ten times. She made sure something always went wrong. Gable was exhausted. Before he blew his stack, Victor Fleming said,

"The first take was perfect, Clark. Just perfect. The others were for laughs."

Such fun did not last long, however. Vivien mentioned Cukor's name too often in reference to how a scene should be done, and Fleming couldn't take her any longer.

"Miss Leigh," he shouted, "you can stick this script up your royal British ass!" He walked out and was replaced by Sam Wood. This put so much pressure on David Selznick, he came close to a nervous breakdown.

On June 27, *Gone With the Wind* was finished. Vivien Leigh sailed off to England with Laurence Olivier, and Clark was anxious to work with Carole on their new ranch so they could move in during the summer. Their plans for decorating and expanding were costly. There was little money left, so Carole signed with RKO to make four films for $600,000.

It was obvious at the casual press conference following their elopement that Carole had simmered down. It was, apparently, not only for Clark's benefit. Though she was pursuing a career, it wasn't her prime interest any longer. Nor was she a reporter's delight these days. *Modern Screen* was quite blunt about it:

> There are persons in Hollywood who are sore at Lombard. She doesn't care, however, because she probably doesn't know of her misfortune. If she did, she would doubtless do something about it because Carole is too good a business woman to willfully make anyone sore at her and too warm-hearted to deliberately give offense to anyone. It never pays to make enemies. Lombard knows all about this. Yet she is making folks mad. What's the matter with Lombard. That's what Hollywood is asking.
>
> Carole had long been a particular pet of the boys and girls who write stories about the stars because she was always cooperative, because she always gave honest, swell copy, told the truth and didn't blue-pencil every word she spoke that was more pithy than a nursery. Lately all is changed. There is, these days, an un-Lombardian evasiveness, a disregard of matters she once attended to richly and generously.
>
> Perhaps, you may say, Lombard has been shy of people, of the Press because she has not wanted to discuss her recent marriage with Gable. But that is no good, for Carole has gone out socially, and has given interviews since the beginning of her romance with Gable.
>
> They say that she is being counseled to be difficult, aloof, hard-to-get; advice which neither fits nor becomes a good fellow who is Lombard. But if she hearkens to this counsel, one might say, isn't she of the same stripes

herself? The truth of the matter is she doesn't hear it. Not properly. Not so she makes sense of it.

The article goes on to say that Carole was too busy arguing with Gable over which one killed the duck, too busy shopping for dinner, running around in an old car looking for dishes and linens, and fussing over Clark.

Adela Rogers St. Johns wrote, "Clark told his wife if anyone was going to do the swearing, he'd do it. He didn't want to hear any of it again from her and he didn't." Friends say that statement was for public consumption, because Clark liked Carole the way she was. He didn't want to read about their sex lives in Louella Parsons's column, but Carole knew better than anyone else what to say and when to say it. She was never caught off-guard, nor did she ever "blurt out" a tidbit. It was an act that the press heartily ate up.

Carole's attitude toward her new life as Mrs. Gable was not the least bit complex or bewildering. Nor had she changed. "Adjusted" is a better description, and wisely so. She had married a man who chased every gal in town but needed a mother. Lombard wasn't the type to wait in line or sit at home wondering if he was coming home for dinner. Gable knew it, too. If he loved her enough to make her his wife, she was willing to take care of him like a friend, sister, mother, and lover. "Mrs." was only something on a marriage license that meant very little. "There's a hell of a lot more to it than that," she said.

Carole was very organized in all aspects of her being and always had been. She fit into Gable's life and enjoyed it. No longer a single screwball working off her abundant energy dancing all night and lunching with Louella or Hedda, she concentrated on Clark because this made *her* happy. Their friends, the new house, his career, and their future revolved around Clark. She sent a red rose to his dressing room every day when he was working. Carole was continually giving him mementos of their love. Some gifts were fun. Others were mechanical tools or rifle attachments or the latest thing in camping equipment, since Clark was regularly making arrangements for their next outing. One of their favorite trips was sixty-five miles south of the Mexican border to La Grulla Gun Club. Gable frequently had the urge to go deeper into the mountains or farther south for duck and geese. Often they would have to take a private plane into these desolate places. More than once the hunting party experienced near misses in take-offs and landings. Or their station wagon broke down on lonely roads. Carole took these "inconveniences" with ease. She felt, as Clark did, that if anything fatal happened, they would be together. She was not one to express fear, since her philosophy was "One has the ability to work out personal problems, but if it has to do with cosmic influences, ignore them and go about your business." Ironically, if a near accident occurred in an airplane, Carole cheerfully, but seriously, told Clark they must never fly in separate planes.

She was most contented having him all to herself snuggling up in sleeping bags around the campfire and dining on canned baked beans. Or in an isolated cabin by the Rogue River. Or on a cabin cruiser in the middle of a small lake full of trout.

No one will ever know if Carole would have been such a good sport on these outings had she not loved Clark so deeply. She endured rattlesnakes (stepped on one), walked into a hornet's nest and was stung, waded in mud up to her waist, and learned how to cook over an open fire because she thought it would please the man she loved.

Maybe Clark made sacrifices for Carole. If so, they were too insignificant to mention. He admits wanting to share his outdoor hobbies with her and delaying trips if she was working on a film. It is possible he wasn't enthusiastic over Carole's annual parties and the few in between, but she tried to make them as informal as possible, with the exception of the obligatory dinner party for Hollywood big shots. This one was formal. Despite her love for pranks, Carole enjoyed putting on a slinky formal dress and playing hostess. She was a natural at public relations, manipulation, conning, and conniving. One famous example was her convincing Alfred Hitchcock to let her direct him in *Mr. and Mrs. Smith*. Hitchcock always made one appearance in each of his films, and on this occasion he merely tipped his hat to Robert Montgomery. Carole took charge. His walk wasn't correct. He didn't tip his hat right. He wasn't on cue. She made a major project out of it, but the annoyed Hitchcock did as he was told despite his not being known for his sense of humor.

Lombard could be as charming and sweet as she was witty and outlandish. It's doubtful that Clark suffered during the formal gatherings at the ranch.

The Gables also threw an annual outdoor party for friends. The Brown Derby catered the festivities in a large tent erected on the lawn. The best food in town was eaten on checked tablecloths. Can-

dles in wine bottles and flowers were on each table; a hot-dog stand
was nearby, and a dance floor set up for those who were willing to
put up with a band consisting of friends trying out their musical
talents from high-school days.

Always a topic of conversation were the famous doves, which had
multiplied and were penned for sentimental reasons . . .

There was a serious side to Carole, though she seldom revealed it
even to close friends. "Clark hasn't had a very happy life," she said.
"He needs someone to look after him, but don't tell him that."

Gable seldom talked about the hardships of his youth. His father
was willing to take his money now, but did not consider Clark a
successful man in a respectable trade. William never pretended
otherwise. He attended his son's premieres, but never in formal at-
tire, and he went in the back way to a regular seat. There would
never be a genuine closeness between father and son. If the early
years were strained, Clark had to live with the fact that William
knew about Josephine and Ria. These "useful" marriages made him
not only a sissy, but a gigolo as well. Though Clark referred to himself as "Mr. Lucky," he had little to show for his success aside from
the ranch. Ria and taxes took the bulk of his wages.

Carole hadn't done much better. In 1937 she paid 85 percent of
her wages in taxes. Typically, she said, "I don't mind. I'm proud to
be an American."

The Encino ranch was modest by Hollywood standards, but not
for the lack of or concern for money. The Gables preferred comfort to
luxury. Clark often looked at the orchards and fields of oats in awe.
After being owned and operated by MGM, he finally had something
that belonged to him. Yet he was terrified that his appeal would fade
and so would his beloved property. He needed Carole's strength because she feared nothing. She attributed this to her belief in astrol-
ogy, numerology, and the occult. (Her Libra and his Aquarius were
very compatible.)

Though Gable said he would never have lasted in films if it hadn't
been for *Gone With the Wind*, as 1939 came to an end he wanted to
forget that Rhett Butler existed. Mayer rushed him into *Strange
Cargo* with Joan Crawford.

"*Idiot's Delight* was terrible," she said. "Old beady eyes gave the
worst performance of her life!"

Clark scowled. "I wouldn't be so concerned about that. You really outdid yourself in *The Women*."

"You saw the rushes?"

"I'm talking about what happened on the set."

"I haven't the slightest idea what you're referring to, love."

Crawford had fought for and gotten the role of Crystal in Claire Boothe Luce's *The Women*, with Norma Shearer, Rosalind Russell, Paulette Goddard, Joan Fontaine, and Virginia Grey. Joan's part was small, but as the tough perfume salesgirl, she steals Norma Shearer's husband.

"I heard all about the knitting-needle episode," Gable teased.

"The afghan isn't for you, darling."

"You know what I'm talking about." Clark grinned. "Trying to distract Norma when you were feeding lines to her."

"I was doing no such thing. Can I help it if she's slow? I was knitting, that's all."

"Yeah, with needles the size of an elephant's tusks."

Crawford smirked. "Thank God that's over..."

"What did you put in the telegram to Norma?"

"Not an apology, that's for sure. I told her off. I told her how I felt about all the times I got screwed... that she'd be a shit extra around here if it hadn't been for dear Irving... that she had only two expressions on the screen—with her eyes open or with her eyes shut."

"I don't believe you did that."

"And more. I made up my mind to show her who was queen around here. She knows the score now."

"Sure!" Clark laughed. "I saw what happened the day you were late for those photo sessions. Everyone was amused."

"I wasn't going to be the first one there."

"Joanie, your dressing room was across the street from the photographer's."

"So?"

"Why did you need a limousine?"

"It's in my contract."

"For a U-turn?"

"You got it."

Clark's sides were splitting. "Round and round you went with Norma's car in front of yours."

"Behind mine."

"Yeah." He laughed. "Strickling turned out to be a traffic cop, but, Joanie, I saw it and couldn't believe it!"

"I blame you."

"Me?"

"You got Cukor fired and they gave him *The Women*. He wanted me to apologize because he was so goddamn upset about being kicked off *Gone With the Wind*."

"Your Georgie was where he belonged—with a bunch of cackling women and their knitting needles."

"We did it, you and me," she exclaimed. "I don't ever have to speak to the queen witch again, and you actually managed to get one of the biggest directors in Hollywood fired."

Crawford said nothing had changed between them. "*Strange Cargo* was good," she said. "Very good. Clark and I still had that magical aura on the screen. He was very relaxed in this one—didn't try so hard. Playing an ex-convict was his thing, though."

Carole was his life. There was never any doubt about that—but there were other women. *Always* other women—women who meant nothing. Maybe he didn't touch Vivien Leigh, but there were other lovely girls in *Gone With the Wind* who were too good to pass up. One of the best Gable stories, which his friends swear is true, took place in a hotel room when a dowdy maid walked in and found him still in bed. He grinned sheepishly. "Why don't you join me?"

"How much?" she asked.

"I would think, my dear, just being with me is payment enough!"

She didn't think so, and left the room.

Carole could do little or nothing about his harmless affairs. When she felt he deserved it, she let him have it. Their relationship was so unique, she never doubted their strong mutual love. This involved a deep understanding on her part. They wanted children very much. She gave up horseback riding because the doctor thought that might be the cause of her not conceiving. "We've tried every position there is," she said. "We'd fuck in a pile of manure if we thought it would work."

The spectacular premiere of *Gone With the Wind* was held in Atlanta, Georgia, on December 15, 1939. Carole, wearing black with sables, was presented with a bouquet of yellow roses when they arrived. "I'm going to let Mr. Gable do all the talking," she said graciously. "I love you all."

Later, at the Grand Theatre premiere, she was glamorous in a long slinky champagne gown with silver fox. Her rubies glistened in the spotlights as she clung to her husband when he stepped up to the microphones and said, "This is Margaret Mitchell's night and your night. Just let me be a spectator going in to see *Gone With the Wind.*"

Instead of watching the movie, however, he chose to have a long talk with the author, who refused to tell anyone else if she had Gable in mind when she created Rhett Butler. After all the guests were seated, she and Gable ducked into the ladies' room for complete privacy. Clark never revealed the entire conversation, but he told Carole and her mother that Scarlett represented Mitchell during her restless and fiery youth. She patterned Rhett Butler after her first husband, who, when she repeatedly rejected him, took her by force. Gable did not discuss it further, but indicated that it was a relief to know the author did not have him in mind for the role at the time she wrote *Gone With the Wind.* "It was tough enough knowing that the readers saw me as Rhett," Gable said.

At the Hollywood premiere, mobs of fans prevented him from viewing the film again. He remained in the manager's office until everyone had left the theater. Carole said, "We're the only ones who haven't seen *Gone With the Wind.*" Clark would not sit through it for another five years. Initially, he had refused to go to Atlanta. It was Carole who convinced him, and Carole who helped him get through the ordeal. When they returned to the ranch, he raved about his wife. "Everyone worshipped her," he said. She was oblivious to adulation. "Pa was the only one who was important," Carole said.

They did not attend the New York premiere.

Their first Christmas in the new house was a festive one. Carole was thrilled with a ruby heart from Clark, who threw in clothes and perfume. ("He's not the most generous guy in the world, you know" was a famous saying of hers.)

Gable was happy with his monogrammed pajamas and robes, but without sleeping bags and hunting and fishing equipment, it just wouldn't be Christmas!

The household staff knew his two quirks. Carole didn't have to remind them that he did not like the color pink, "and for God's sake never have his hats cleaned!" He was very meticulous about his extensive and expensive wardrobe. Carole howled with laughter every time she saw the soiled hats lined up like museum pieces. "Pa's funny," she said. "He wants his shoes shined before he feeds the chickens, and then puts on a dirty hat!"

When they were not filming, Carole and Clark worked around the ranch, but always dressed in the evening. She put a great deal of pride and love into decorating the house, especially the dining room, where dinner was a nightly ritual with or without guests. The weathered long refectory table, highly polished, was never covered with place mats or tablecloths. There was an off-white beamed ceiling, natural pine walls, an oversize white brick fireplace, and antique captains' chairs around the table. Clark's was the largest.

In a sunny living room, the carpet and sofa were bright yellow, while the furniture added splashes of red and green. Clark was very proud of his gun room, where he spent his alone time. There was a secretarial suite and servants' quarters on the ground floor. Upstairs were the two master bedrooms. His was brown and beige, with a tufted brown leather headboard on a double bed. Carole's suite was a masterpiece in white chintz, organdy, marble, with fur rugs, crystal chandeliers, floor-to-ceiling mirrors, and a four-poster bed.

There were eight rooms in the house, none for guests.

Gable could be seen on his tractor early in the morning. Carole romped with the dogs, cut fresh flowers for the house, and planned her husband's meat-and-potatoes dinners. Spareribs, baked beans, and apple pie were his favorite.

There were many hunting and fishing trips: sleeping bags, cheap motels, canned food, poison ivy, and rattlesnakes. Carole braved them all. Clark never went without her. They could, by now, arrange their filming for time off together, but if she was working, he waited patiently for her to finish.

The year 1939 had been very good—a year that brought them their dream house, their idyllic marriage, and *Gone With the Wind*. Carole made two successful films—*Made for Each Other* with Jimmy Stewart, and *In Name Only* with Cary Grant. On New Year's Eve they drank to many children and . . . another Oscar for Clark.

Gone With the Wind received ten Academy Awards, but best actor was not one of them. "Clark was crushed," Crawford said. "He felt he had put everything into it. Robert Donat won for *Good-bye, Mr. Chips*. What could I say? He would gladly have traded in the one for

It Happened One Night. He didn't think he deserved that. The best of us have been through it. Liz Taylor got an Oscar for the dreadful *Butterfield Eight,* but really won it for *Cat on a Hot Tin Roof* the year before, when she was blackballed after the Eddie Fisher–Debbie Reynolds thing."

Gable was happy for Vic Fleming, who won an Oscar, but fumed when Vivien Leigh accepted her award. What embarrassed him most was that best actor was one of two categories that did not win for *Gone With the Wind.* He felt that Selznick had not campaigned on his behalf. For the rest of his life, Gable would be reminded so often that he did not win the Oscar for portraying Rhett Butler because we, his fans, thought he had walked away with it easily.

Carole went back to work in *They Knew What They Wanted* with Charles Laughton. Her appeal at the box office was slipping, because her marriage came first. Not being a mother left her with a feeling of uselessness. "They were forever checking sperm," a friend said. "She eventually took the blame for being infertile, to cover up for Clark. Carole didn't want his masculine image damaged even in their circle of friends. They wanted children so badly. Clark was proud of her as an actress, but wanted Carole to retire with their kids, make a film occasionally. Regardless of that tough exterior, he was a very insecure man. She knew it and might have put him down as King of Hollywood for fun, but she made sure he was King at home. Maybe that's why he wanted to keep her there."

Clark filmed *Boom Town* with Spencer Tracy and Hedy Lamarr. Tracy was bored again because this was another "Gable movie." He knew that Clark had signed a new contract for $7,500 a week; it called for only two films a year and gave him top billing. As for Hedy and Clark, there was no chemistry. They would star again in *Comrade X* as a sensational team, but he found her dull off-camera. By now Carole knew the type of woman who appealed to Clark, and Hedy wasn't it.

The year 1940 did not bring an addition to the Gable household, nor healthy fruit trees nor plentiful eggs. They raised and slaughtered steers, but didn't have the heart to touch the meat because the animals had been pets. Fans in buses, in cars, and on foot invaded their privacy. Clark was forced to fence in the ranch and install an electric gate. Intruders still managed to get onto the grounds, but the servants were not allowed to touch them, for fear of being sued. Only the police were permitted to deal with trespassers, while Clark and

Carole hid behind locked doors. Day and night, admirers waited at the gate for a glimpse of Clark Gable and Carole Lombard.

"We'll have to move," he said.

"I know, Pa."

"No fun anymore. Might as well be living on Hollywood and Vine."

"We'll look at property further out."

"Is there any place they won't find us?"

"I don't think so, Pa, but we'll try."

Gable put the ranch on the market, but was appalled by the offers and decided to remain where they were. He built a house on the property for his father. There would be talk again and again about selling, but Clark never did.

Having their home on the tourist map caused a great deal of tension in the Gable home, but Clark's romping with other women caused most of their marital conflicts. Carole was always on guard. She never caught him in the act, supposedly, but had keen intuition and ways of knowing her suspicions were not groundless. Besides the chorus girl in *Idiot's Delight,* there were others who were fired because of their indiscretions with Clark. Whether Carole had anything to do with this or MGM officials handled the matter *before* she found out isn't known. His heavy drinking blurred his discretion at times. Mayer let it be understood that there would be no more scandal where Gable was concerned, and much of this responsibility was left to Howard Strickling and his staff, who remain loyal and mum. "Gable was a promiscuous man," they will admit. His buddies called him a royal "cocksman." Carole said Clark had been "sex starved" most of his life. No one has figured out that statement to this day, unless it was Carole's wild sense of humor.

Hollywood insiders gave the marriage a solid chance of lasting if Mrs. Gable learned to live with her husband's infidelities.

Clark's co-star in *They Met in Bombay* was Rosalind Russell, one of "Hollywood's Three Nuns." Who could be any safer? Carole wasn't sure, since the other two "nuns" were Irene Dunne and Loretta Young! But Russell was everyone's jovial friend, who arrived on the set with a smile and a few jokes, enjoyed her work, and went home without getting involved in love affairs and petty gossip. She had an "I don't give a damn" attitude toward Hollywood. "I played a career woman in twenty-three films," she said. "I've been every kind of executive and I've owned everything—factories and advertising agencies and pharmaceutical houses. Except for different leading men and a switch in titles and pompadour, they were stamped out of the same Alice in Careerland. The scripts always called for a leading lady somewhere in her thirties, tall, brittle, and not too sexy. My wardrobe was a set pattern: a tan suit, a gray suit, a beige suit, and then a negligee for the seventh reel near the end, when I would admit to my best friend on the telephone that what I really wanted was to become a dear little housewife."

Her one and only marriage was a happy one, which was unusual in Hollywood, but not for this well-balanced delightful clown, who was aware at the onset how Mrs. Gable felt about Mr. Gable's leading ladies. Rosalind told Carole that Clark was a puppet during their love scenes. "He's easy to follow." She laughed. "One for the money, two for the show, three to get ready, and four to go! He does the same thing with Norma Shearer and Myrna Loy."

Carole smiled. "Yes, but he's quite original with most of the others."

The Gables celebrated their second wedding anniversary on the set of *They Met in Bombay*. The party, arranged by Carole, was catered by the Brown Derby. Hedda Hopper reported that the Gables were happier than on the day they were married. Carole had no movie commitments, in anticipation of becoming pregnant. She tempered her tongue, but would catch friends (and Clark) off-guard if the mood struck her. During a chichi dinner gathering at the ranch, Carole said to a guest, "Pass the fucking salt, please." All eyes were on Clark, who looked up from his plate and said casually, "Pass Ma the fucking salt." Then it was the gravy and the sugar. When dinner was over, Gable laughed himself silly.

Carole could behave for days or weeks, without a blue peep or outrageous gag. No one was expecting anything out of the ordinary at the Fred MacMurrays' party, because his wife did not approve of swearing and Carole respected that. The evening was hot and humid, and the guests were seated around the pool when the Gables arrived. Carole was wearing a new expensive flouncy white evening gown, but that didn't stop her from jumping into the pool. Clark burst into gales of laughter. "Isn't she beautiful?" He beamed. "She's fantastic! She's my girl!" Carole changed into a pair of Fred's pajamas, which she wore for the rest of the evening. The gown was ruined. "I'll order another," she exclaimed.

"But you did it deliberately," a friend said. "Do you think Clark will pay for it?"

"Of course not, but it was worth it! He loves women who make him laugh, so I have to be the champ."

After their second anniversary, Carole signed for *To Be or Not to Be* with Jack Benny, and another called *They All Kissed the Bride*. "Maybe if I keep busy I'll get pregnant," she said. "Pa and I don't want anyone knocking on our door unless they're invited, because we're busy making babies. You might as well know that Sundays are reserved for that. This kind of fucking is very scientific, you know!"

Clark was not happy with *They Met in Bombay* and was anxious to do another picture right away. He chose the part of a ruthless frontier gambler in *Honky Tonk* and asked his friend Jack Conway to direct the film. MGM offered to find something better, but Clark said he had more faith in a good director than a good script. Conway, a hearty drinker and womanizer, worked with Gable on five films, including *Saratoga* and *Boom Town*.

"I know I'm sticking my neck out on this one," he told Carole, "but I'm going to fight for it." Clark remained adamant about *Honky Tonk* and wanted to begin filming immediately. Mayer relented, but did not offer him an established leading lady. He cast a newcomer instead—a decision that would have a drastic effect on Clark's life.

Lana Turner was a beautiful, wistful twenty-year-old blond divorcée who had done fairly well for herself in second-rate pictures. After *Ziegfeld Girl,* MGM decided to let her soar into the heavens with their other stars, and what better vehicle than Clark Gable?

Labeled the "Sweater Girl," Lana was discovered by the publisher of the *Hollywood Reporter* while she was sipping a Coke at the Top Hat Cafe near Hollywood High School.

"Would you like to be in the movies?" he asked her.

"I'll have to ask my mother," she replied.

Lana made her movie debut when she was sixteen and signed a contract with MGM a year later for a hundred dollars a week. She had auburn hair until the studio chose her for one of the blond dancers in *Idiot's Delight* with Clark Gable. Reluctantly, she changed the color of her hair. Instead of doing the movie, however, Lana went into a hospital for minor surgery. The operation described by Turner, however, was by no means an emergency, and MGM gave her a bonus. This led to speculation that she was the chorus girl who was fired by Carole for "trying to make out with my husband!" The consensus is that she was not the one. The few who claim she was base their opinion on the fact that *Idiot's Delight* was her big chance. Why would she elect to have voluntary surgery instead? And why would MGM give her a bonus for doing so?

Most significant is Turner's decision to remain a blonde. This new image gave her an outgoing personality that upset Mayer, who told her to "stop running around until all hours with men." She obliged by falling in love with handsome attorney Greg Bautzer. Mayer didn't have a chance to intercede, because Joan Crawford made up her mind that no teenager was going to move in on her territory. She summoned Lana to her home. "I told her that Greg was in love with me," Crawford said, "that he liked to date and have a good time, but occasionally got overly dramatic about it, and usually with girls who were young and gullible. Lana was stunned, poor dear, but it was best that she found out before getting hurt."

Lana bowed out of Bautzer's life and married Artie Shaw, whom she divorced a year later.

Clark Gable was her first famous leading man. After only a few days of filming *Honky Tonk*, rumors of a romance were so rampant that Carole threatened to confront the "lovers" on the set and "kick them both in the ass!" Her fights with Clark were bitter and explosive. "I'll have her fired!" she threatened.

"You can't do that," he argued.

"Then I'll have you fired!"

MGM stars were protected from all dangers, including their spouses, and a quiet alert was called on the set of *Honky Tonk* whenever Carole drove through the studio gates. Her visits ended when Lana, rehearsing a love scene with Clark, spotted Carole and ran to her dressing room in tears. Consequently, the set was off-limits to outsiders, including Mrs. Gable.

Lana described how she looked over her shoulder and saw the "beloved Carole Lombard" glaring at her. "I felt faint and went to my dressing room. Jack Conway asked me to come back, but I told him I couldn't do that. I had to get hold of myself. My knees were shaking. Finally someone knocked on my door and told me it was time to resume work. Carole Lombard was gone."

Lana apologized to Clark, who whispered, "I understand . . ."

Over the years she has denied there was anything between her and Gable. "Ours was a closeness without intimacy," she said.

"There was a dear loving for him but not an affair."

While on tour to promote her recent autobiography, Lana said in a television interview that she had a reputation for being a sexpot, but she never was, and that she never had much feeling about sex.

A well-known Hollywood producer said, "I wish movie queens would tell the truth in their books. To hear them tell it, they're all virgins except Shelley Winters. As for Lana Turner, she was a delectable woman who liked men. Gable, Taylor and Power were mad for her and I'm sure she wasn't immune to them. I got the feeling Lana was a candidate for the convent, but that wasn't the way it was when she was one of the most desirable women in Hollywood. I felt the same way about June Allyson's book. She made it sound as if her relationship with Alan Ladd was sharing an occasional ice cream soda."

Choreographer Jack Cole said, "I've worked with them all—Rita Hayworth, Betty Grable, Lana Turner . . . the whole bloody bit, and what's very curious, well, Lana Turner's a little different because she really liked men, she liked to fuck a lot. But most of the others, it's the idea of it." (John Kobal, *People Will Talk*, Knopf, 1986.)

MGM finished *Honky Tonk* in record time to separate Turner and Gable, who were so hot on the screen, the studio was forced to consider pairing them again right away. Lana was rushed into *Johnny Eager* with Robert Taylor, who said, "She wasn't very career-minded, and preferred men and jewelry over anything else. Lana wasn't as 'busty' as her pinup pictures, but her face was delicate and beautiful. I have never seen lips like hers, and though I was never known to run after blondes, Lana was the exception. I couldn't take my eyes off her, and there were times during *Johnny Eager* that I thought I'd explode. Her voice was like a breathless child. I don't think she knew how to talk without being sexy. When she said, 'Good morning,' I melted. She was the type of woman a guy would risk five years in jail for rape."

Acting daily with Lana frustrated Taylor. He took it as long as he could, and when he discovered she was making no effort to ignore his attentions and was physically drawn to him, he knew he had to be alone with her. "She became an obsession," he said. "I *had* to have her . . . if only for one night."

Lana admits a very strong attraction to Taylor, but denies any involvement despite his asking his wife, Barbara Stanwyck, for a divorce so he could marry Turner. The Taylors separated for a few days. (Barbara was rushed to the hospital with a serious cut on her arm, which she said happened when she tried to open a window and the pane shattered.) To this day, Barbara Stanwyck refuses to speak to Lana Turner.

An actress friend who has a list of Gable movies to her credit but prefers to remain anonymous speaks casually about the King. "When Clark said he had them all, he did. He wasn't bragging. He was remembering the good times. Lana Turner was a very special lady and he was nuts about her, but I don't think she was a threat to his marriage."

Carole didn't agree. She was angry and then deeply hurt, an emotion that she rarely, if ever, displayed. MGM officials kept their eyes on her rather than Lana and Clark, because word was spreading around town that Carole was "going in for the kill." She rose above the occasion and accompanied Clark to the premiere of *Honky Tonk*. They held hands during the entire movie. Reporters noted that it was quite unusual for Gable to attend premieres and display such affection toward his wife in public. A few weeks later, Carole went into another rage when she found out that Clark and Lana were going to co-star in *Somewhere I'll Find You*.

The bickering and battling began all over again. Gable took these outbursts in stride. If having affairs with other women meant nothing to him, then why should it mean anything to Carole? Knowing his logic added fire to her fury, but she would have to live with it because MGM's demands came first, above and beyond hers. The fact that *Honky Tonk* had made Lana Turner a top star and the public clamored for more of her in the arms of Clark Gable was strictly business. Accepting this with grace and poise wasn't Carole Lombard Powell Gable, who blew her stack if Clark looked at another woman. She wasn't herself these days. Friends thought she was too quiet, sometimes sad and pensive, not so bouncy and optimistic. Not one to complain or explain, Carole spoke only about wanting a baby more now than ever before . . .

December 7, 1941. Bombs, not beds, shocked the world, and Hollywood was suddenly just another town of Americans anxious to volunteer for the war effort. The Gables sent a telegram to their friend President Roosevelt, asking how they could be of service. The reply was: "Entertainment. Stay where you are."

They got involved with the Hollywood Victory Committee. Clark was appointed chairman of the Screen Actors Division. Aside from exchanging personal Christmas presents, the Gables sent cards to friends noting a donation to the Red Cross or enclosing a war bond. Clark gave Carole a pair of diamond-and-ruby clips that matched her ring and ruby heart. She gave him an engraved gold cigarette case.

Clark spoke to Carole about enlisting. "I've got to get into this war," he said. "I can't sit on my ass."

"You'll do what you want to do anyway," she said.

"I know, but I wanted to talk it over with you first."

Carole was approached about a war-bond tour in her home state of Indiana. She accepted and wanted Clark to go along, but he was scheduled to begin *Somewhere I'll Find You*. Carole's mother, Bessie, and Clark's personal public-relations man, Otto Winkler, agreed to accompany her.

It was the first time the Gables would be separated for any extensive period. They had quarreled bitterly over his attentions to Lana Turner, and Carole did not want to leave town. She managed one joke before her departure—a blond dummy in Gable's bed with a note: "So you won't be lonely." She gave her secretary five notes for Gable—one for each day she would be gone—and she sent flowers to his dressing room.

On January 12, 1942, Carole boarded the train without fanfare. Friends assumed she was depressed over leaving Clark, but this time she didn't try to pretend otherwise. She called from Salt Lake City, Ogden, Utah, and Chicago. On the fifteenth she arrived in Indianapolis for the rally and sold more than $2 million in war bonds.

"I'm anxious to get home to Clark," she said. "Let's fly back."

Winkler didn't like the idea and tried to talk her out of it. Carole suggested flipping a coin, and she won. Bessie hated planes and tried to convince her daughter to rest up on the train. "I don't like choo-choos," Carole said, and made reservations on TWA. Bessie, who was a proficient numerologist, jotted down the flight data and came up with a fatal number. She showed it to Carole, who was a believer but laughed it off. At four the next morning, January 16, they boarded the plane. She sent Clark a telegram about her change in plans, asking him to meet her at the airport at eight that evening.

What was Clark doing while his wife was away for five days? Supposedly he was in Washington, D.C., trying to get into the Air Force by pulling a few strings. He returned to Hollywood the day after Carole's departure. The press and his friends do not give the same account of what he did or where he was, other than filming *Somewhere I'll Find You* with Lana Turner.

Clark planned a welcome-back dinner for Carole at the ranch, with a few close friends. The house was filled with fresh flowers and the dining-room table set elegantly. To get even with her little prank, Clark put a male dummy with an erect penis in Carole's bed.

It was Howard Strickling who got a call that Carole's plane was down near Las Vegas. He chartered a plane and called Clark. It was a silent flight to Las Vegas. What was there to say? Gable was not one for small talk or the "everything will be all right" routine.

Search parties were being organized to climb the snow-covered rocky mountain. A Western Airlines pilot had seen Carole's plane hit Table Rock Mountain and burst into flames. Clark insisted on going with the rescue party, but halfway to the crash site, an MGM official said to him, "Carole wouldn't want you to see her in that plane wreckage, Clark." Gable thought for a moment and turned back. It was a blessing that he did. He was spared the agony of seeing Carole's charred, decapitated body, a script nearby, a remnant of her ruby clip (Clark's gift to her), and strands of long blond hair.

On the way down the mountain with the bodies, the rescue party stopped at a way station and sent a telegram to Clark: NO SURVIVORS. ALL KILLED INSTANTLY. The next day he was driven a few hundred feet from the crash site by a pilot who explained to Clark what had happened and said, "There's no chance that Carole suffered for even a second. All twenty-two passengers didn't know what happened."

Clark accompanied the bodies of his wife, her mother, and close friend Otto Winkler back to California. He wore Carole's burned ruby clip around his neck in a gold locket. Unable to go back to the ranch alone, he stayed with friends until after the funeral. Carole had requested to be clothed in white and placed in a modestly priced crypt in Forest Lawn Memorial Park, Glendale, California.

Clark received thousands of telegrams, but the one he treasured most read: "Mrs. Roosevelt and I are deeply distressed. Carole was our friend, our guest in happier days. She brought great joy to all who knew her and to millions who knew her only as a great artist. She gave unselfishly of her time and talent to serve her government in peace and in war. She loved her country. She is and always will be a star, one we shall never forget nor cease to be grateful to. Deepest sympathy."

The Defense Department offered a military funeral, but Clark

declined. He followed Carole's wishes, and on January 22, 1942,
services were held at the Church of the Recessional in Forest Lawn.
There were no prayers or hymns, only the Twenty-third Psalm and a
favorite poem of Carole's. When it was over, close friends took Clark
back to the ranch. Later that evening his secretary gave him the fifth
and last note Carole had left behind. His sobs echoed through the
house and into the valley. . .

CHAPTER EIGHT

Joan Crawford said Gable came to her the night Carole was killed.
"They were so right for each other," she said. "Terrible, terrible,
what happened. He was so drunk and he cried. There was nothing I
could say. Nothing meant anything to him anymore. He wanted to
die. A stranger walked through my door that night and never returned—in the physical, maybe, but he was never, never the same.
Clark was a walking corpse. He had every right to drink that night.
How else could he have survived that horrible ordeal? But he kept
right on hitting the bottle. He was in another world and never came
back to us."

Gable took long drives by himself, walked around the ranch with
Carole's dog, drove to Oregon by himself for some fishing, and
avoided mutual friends whose presence reminded him of the good old
days. Yes, finally Gable could reflect on the good old days, but the
hurt was indescribable. He never complained. He didn't have to. His
loss and grief and loneliness were etched on his face and set in his
eyes forever. When liquor failed to drown his sorrow, Clark bought a
motorcycle to "blow his mind." He almost succeeded in killing himself before MGM demanded he stop the recklessness. He was forbid-
den to ride a motorcycle again. (It's been said this was in his
contract.)

Carole left her estate to Clark. Her brothers, deliberately eliminated from the will, never spoke to Clark again. He had invited them
to Carole's homecoming dinner, but after the funeral the friendship
ended. It's possible they resented the serious quarrel over Lana
Turner—the obvious reason Carole rushed back home to her death.
Then there was a rumor that Clark was with another woman the
night his wife was killed. After all, he had sent someone else to the
airport when the plane was delayed en route.

Regardless of the facts, Carole died for love, pure and simple.

She couldn't wait the extra day to see Clark. It's conceivable he had a last-minute quickie before his wife came home. If true, only he had to live with it for the rest of his life.

Adela Rogers St. Johns came to see Clark at the ranch. He wanted to give her something of Carole's, and they went to the frilly white glamorous bedroom that was so very typically Lombard. Nothing had been touched. There were still traces of spilled face powder on her vanity. It was not a shrine, he said. Her will had to be probated. Still, there was warmth in knowing everything was as she had left it. St. Johns accepted two of Carole's books: *The Clouds of Unknowing* and *Cosmic Consciousness.*

Other friends were not so understanding about Carole's room. Probating her will was one thing; spending so much time there was another. It was his subconscious shrine, all he had, really, except for a few strands of blond hair clipped in death. Her room, however, was alive with the aroma of her favorite perfume, Chanel No. 5, and the powder puff that had touched her face when she was breathing and vital and beautiful.

It wasn't only her bedroom. It was the house and the gardens and the stables and the fruit trees and the knickknacks. Everything represented Carole Gable. Clark searched for another house in Beverly Hills, but didn't have the heart to leave Encino. He finally gave Carole's possessions to friends and changed nothing in the house, including her room.

This was their home.

On February 23, 1942, he reported for work on *Somewhere I'll Find You.* Mayer told everyone on the set to pretend nothing had happened. Above all, no pity or tiptoeing around. He had a private talk with Lana and asked her to go along with Clark's emotions. "If he wants to work, work. If he wants to leave, let him. If he wants to talk, talk. Go with the flow. I understand he doesn't like to eat alone, so if he asks you out, go."

Clark invited her to the ranch for dinner, but he never mentioned Carole. Lana tried to be cheerful and talkative. He responded.

Crawford formally invited him to her home for dinner. "He came almost every night until he finished filming," she said. "Clark could drink a quart of booze before dinner. He told me it was all wrong and then he cried. There were times he stayed until dawn, but talking was good therapy for him."

Joan volunteered to take Carole's assigned role in *They All Kissed the Bride,* and donated her salary of $125,000 to the Red Cross. She was facing the realization that marriage to Clark might be a dim prospect. They made love occasionally, but their passion was turning into a deep and lasting friendship. Often she tried to lure him from the bedroom because there was so little satisfaction in it for her.

Clark finished *Somewhere I'll Find You* and devoted his time to fishing the Rogue River. He told his buddies, "I'm going to enlist in the Air Corps, but not until I get my head together and sort things out." MGM announced his next film would be *Shadow of the Wind,* but Clark had no intention of doing anything other than fight in the war. "I don't expect to come back," he said. "And I don't want to come back."

On August 12, 1942, he was sworn into the Air Corps as a $66-a-month forty-one-year-old buck private. He could have had a commission, but chose to earn it at Officers Candidate School in Miami Beach, Florida. He was one of the oldest enlistees, but wrote friends that he enjoyed the young men and didn't mind sleeping in a three-bunk room or getting up at five in the morning. He allowed a military photographer to take a picture of him shaving off his famous mustache, but made it clear that he did not want any more publicity.

It wasn't easy for Clark Gable, movie star, to go through the rigors of calisthenics, marching, and inspection. The other men were aware of his age and rich life in Hollywood. They expected him to get preferential treatment. He knew he was being watched and tested, which made it even more difficult.

The women in Miami Beach hung around the barracks to get a glimpse of their sex idol. Very few recognized the tall thin movie star in his baggy khakis and crew cut. His eyes were tired and his face was drawn. Some in the group did not think he'd make it. One recruit said, "Gable was a mess. I thought he'd collapse, but he kept going."

His letters indicated fear of failure. Long after lights-out at night, he sat in the bathroom studying the complex manuals. "I have to try harder than anyone else," he said, "because of who I am. Can you imagine the publicity if I flunk?"

He graduated on October 9, volunteered for aerial gunnery duty, and was sent to Tyndall Field in Panama City, Florida. As a first lieutenant he grew another mustache, had his uniforms custom-made, and sent home for his English shoes.

On December 18 he returned to the ranch for a few days. At a party in his honor, Clark was delighted to see Virginia Grey again. It had been a few years since she auditioned for Jean Harlow's double in *Saratoga*. She didn't get the part, but the sixteen-year-old Virginia attracted Gable, who arranged bit parts for her.

The blond and willowy Virginia bore a striking resemblance to Lombard, whom she imitated in her quest to attract Clark. She appeared with him in *Test Pilot* and *Idiot's Delight*. He considered her his protégée, of sorts. Insiders had thought she had a better chance of marrying Gable than Lombard did, and they were quite surprised that Carole did not have Virginia fired from the chorus line in *Idiot's Delight*.

Grey was one of Clark's favorites for many years, but was not seen with him publicly until after the war. It was taken for granted that she reminded him of Lombard. Or was it the other way around? Did Clark find Virginia in Carole? Both women were peppy, witty, and blond. Virginia played similar roles—the smirky foul-mouthed dame, the other woman, or the tough broad with a cynical tongue. She was not as soft, lithe, or talented as Carole. Unfortunately, Virginia's luck in movies matched her luck in love. She always got supporting roles, never the lead.

Grey never married. In between Clark's marriages, it was Virginia who strolled proudly on his arm and was expected to be the next Mrs. Gable. Now in her early seventies, she's a bitter woman who never stopped loving Clark.

In December 1942, however, Hollywood thought Grey was the perfect substitute for Carole.

On January 7, 1943, Clark Gable received his gunnery officer's wings and was sent to Polebrook, England, eighty miles from London. On May 14 he made his first mission in a B-17 over Belgium. He doubled as gunner and photographer on four more over the Ruhr Valley, Gelsenkirchen, Nantes, and Villacoublay. On one flight a German shell missed his head by only inches, but he wasn't fazed. The Germans put a $5,000 price tag on Captain Gable—dead or alive. "I'll never bail out," he said. "Hitler can have me dead or not at all."

To say he was fearless is an understatement, but he wanted nothing to do with heroism or medals. He didn't give a damn, because if a five-foot-one blonde weighing 110 pounds could brave a seventeen-hour flight in bad weather to save her marriage, he'd make it up to her by facing death head on. He defied all odds and looked for trouble, volunteered for the most dangerous missions, saw his war buddies wounded and killed . . . and wondered why he was spared. The men close to Gable during the war knew he had a death wish. He wanted to be a good officer first and then get more than his share of liquor and women. One of his fellow officers said, "I was compelled to ask Clark why he chose the dogs when so many pretty girls were drooling all over him. He said the ugly ones were really appreciative and were no bother. He didn't have to try very hard to please them. Another time he was going out frequently with one of the homeliest girls I've ever seen. She turned me off at first glance, so I asked him again, 'Why her?', and Gable said, 'She's there.' I figured he must be pretty good. He had an insatiable appetite for food and plain women. There was something very lonely about him, though, and he had a faraway look. He'd be listening to me and not be there somehow. He was punishing himself, but never talked about Carole Lombard. He wore a locket around his neck and told someone that was all he had left of her. I know he didn't want to go home . . . back to Hollywood."

Director Frank Capra saw Gable in the lobby of the Grosvenor House in London and asked the commanding officer how Clark was doing. "How's he doing?" The General scowled. "He's scaring the hell out of us, that's how he's doing. The damn fool insists on being a rear gunner on every bombing mission. He's a hot potato! And I'm pulling every string to get him out of my command, I'll tell you that. Guy gives me the willies. Know what I think? Gable's trying to get himself killed. Yeah! So he can join up with his wife."

On November 1, 1943, Captain Gable was back in California, in a daze, happy and sad, proud and depressed, handsome and gray at the temples, nervous and composed, friendly and distant, smiling but forlorn, lonely—very lonely and busy. Shattered. Virginia was waiting with a new puppy to replace Carole's dog, Commissioner, which had died while Clark was away. She had recently moved into a home nearby.

Joan Crawford had taken husband number three. On July 21, 1942, she married actor Philip Terry. "At last I'm in love."

John Wayne said, "I knew what kind of marriage it was going to be when I saw her walk on the set. First came Joan, then her secretary, then her makeup man, then her wardrobe woman, then Phil Terry carrying her dog!"

In 1943 Crawford asked to be released from her MGM contract. She had been overlooked for the roles she wanted and there was every indication that Mayer's favorite was Greer Garson. When Joan asked to break her contract, he tried to change her mind. She was adamant, and he let her go.

Gable's ranch had flourished while he was gone. His father and the servants wanted him to come home to fresh fruit and vegetables and blooming flowers. Clark was very grateful and seemingly at peace with himself. "I'll be goin' to the Pacific soon," he said. "We're needed there badly." No one argued with him or asked, "Haven't you had enough?"

MGM tried to give him an incentive to stay alive and well by offering him a twelve-year contract calling for only two films a year and shorter working days. He was guaranteed $7,500 a week for forty weeks, to commence the day after his discharge. He didn't turn it down, but said he was going to fight in the Pacific if they wanted him. He hated L. B. Mayer and MGM more than ever, if that was possible.

The ranch became his haven. All he wanted was to have Carole back, but Clark no longer had a chip on his shoulder. Nor did he feel sorry for himself after seeing the dead and wounded in England. If there was a God—and he wasn't sure—the notion that he had been singled out to be the grieved widower of such a vibrant and loving girl no longer tortured him. He was only one of many.

On January 15, 1944, L. B. Mayer was asked to preside over the launching of the ship *Carole Lombard*. Irene Dunne stood next to him, and Clark Gable, his fists clenched at his sides, gave a brief speech. When Dunne formally christened the ship, Clark could no longer control himself. He sobbed openly, tears streaming down his face. It made a heart-wrenching front-page picture. Millions wept with him that day.

Gable was not recalled to active duty and was discharged on June 12 with the rank of major. His Report of Separation was signed by Captain Ronald Reagan. On a New York vacation he became reacquainted with society hostess Dolly O'Brien, and he attended a Christmas party at her West Palm Beach home, but he preferred spending the holiday with close friends at the ranch. He began assembling a circle of women friends that would be quite extensive.

Dolly, a blue-eyed blonde, was a former Powers and Conover model whose picture appeared on no fewer than seventy magazine covers. Her second husband, yeast millionaire Julius Fleischman, gave her a $5 million divorce settlement. (Fleischman died a short time later, leaving an estate of $66 million.) Dolly married actress Mae Murray's former husband and dancing partner, Jay O'Brien, who was a favorite of Elsa Maxwell's and a friend of Gable's. (Clark felt comfortable with the ex-wives and widows of old friends.)

Dolly was a bouncy society darling who liked the company of young men because they kept her youthful and vibrant. She was six years older than Clark, but Dolly never showed her age. He relished her socially prominent circle of friends, who were catered to at nightclubs, yacht clubs, and country clubs. While Dolly enjoyed the winter warmth in Florida, Clark waited for a movie assignment, drank very heavily, and never missed a good party.

One of his frequent dates was Kay Williams, who might have been just another blond divorcée under contract to MGM had she not put Gable in his place when they met.

"Why don't you get undressed?" he suggested.

"Why don't you shit in your hat?" Kay replied.

Another cool lady was Anita Colby, fashion consultant and coordinator for David Selznick Studios. She was thirty years old, blond, and a former Conover model who appeared on the covers of twelve magazines in one month. Known as "The Face," Anita was outgoing, bright, and very ambitious. No one knew the intimate details of her personal life. She was never married or seriously involved, but men were attracted to the beautiful and mysteriously aloof Anita, who thrived on her career. Like Kay Williams, Colby loved to have a good time and gave the impression that she danced from the party to the bedroom. She didn't, and this fascinated Clark.

Though he had been with countless women, Gable could not remember being single. Franz Dorfler overlapped into his marriage to Josephine, which overlapped into his affair and marriage to Ria, which overlapped into his affair and marriage to Carole Lombard. He had never experienced the freedom of bachelorhood. Women had changed during his two decades of wifely protection. Women had survived the Great Depression and were in charge of the country while their men were overseas fighting a war. They were wearing pants, working in factories, driving taxicabs, tending bar, proving themselves valuable in big business, and leading the popularity polls in Hollywood.

Betty Grable was the Pinup Girl. She was glamorous, but movie-goers could identify with her hash-slinging style. Grable danced, sang, and read her lines as if she didn't give a damn, and she didn't. She couldn't have cared less about awards. Who needed one when she had the Army, Navy, and Marine Corps on her side? It was Joan Crawford who was voted best actress for *Mildred Pierce* in 1945, because Mildred baked pies to get what she wanted. She fought hard to make a life for herself and did not take money for granted. She was betrayed, but she was a survivor.

Greer Garson as Mrs. Miniver portrayed another woman who survived. She didn't bake pies. She dodged bombs in England, but protected her family first and foremost.

Protect and survive. If you want something said, ask a man. If you want something done, ask a woman.

Americans wanted realism during wartime. They flocked to see John Wayne fighting on all fronts, and balanced their emotions with musicals and religion: with *Yankee Doodle Dandy, The Song of Berna-dette, Going My Way,* Abbott and Costello, Bob Hope and Bing Crosby on the road to somewhere, and the all-American Van Johnson in his red socks, Peter Lawford's lovesick eyes, and Cornel Wilde's dashing romantic passion. Marital plots in movies were no longer frivolous. Wives and husbands were separated by a war, and the other woman emerged. This was a fact of life.

Ray Milland got the Oscar for best actor in *The Lost Weekend,* the story of Gable's life these days. While Joan was snuggling up to her Oscar (literally), Clark was driving recklessly up Sunset Boulevard, heading the wrong way in his Duesenberg. When he realized his mistake, he tried to turn around, but swerved into a tree. Fortu-nately, the accident occurred on the property belonging to Harry Friedman, vice-president of the Music Corporation of America. Friedman called Howard Strickling, who was there in minutes. Gable was taken to Cedars of Lebanon Hospital with cuts on his leg and face. The story released to the newspapers described a helpless Clark doing his best to avoid a car coming in the wrong direction. MGM took Gable's clothes away and told him to remain in the hospi-tal for several days to evoke sympathy. Even though he had two hol-low legs and rarely showed the effects of too much liquor, this accident had been long overdue. His commanding officer had been relieved to see Clark leave England. Now he was MGM's bad boy, with Spencer Tracy a very close second.

After three days in the hospital, he told his secretary to get him some clothes and insisted that the doctor prepare his release papers.

MGM decided it was time to put him to work, and Adela Rogers St. Johns was assigned to find him a good property. Clark told her he wanted to depict a man down on his luck. "A guy who has courage and principle, hope and confidence regardless of the odds. He doesn't compromise. He doesn't give up."

Adela understood what Clark wanted, but couldn't find the right story. Mayer took charge and cast him opposite Greer Garson in *Adventure*. Gable hated the film and disliked Garson. As the philosophical sailor Harry Patterson, he falls in love with a prissy librarian (Garson) who "helps Harry find his soul." Victor Fleming, who directed *Adventure*, lost touch with the spiritual aspect, and there was little left but a corny plot.

Garson was terribly miscast following her Oscar-winning *Mrs. Miniver, Good-bye, Mr. Chips, Blossoms in the Dust, Random Harvest*, and *Madam Curie*. She had been discovered on the London stage by L. B. Mayer, who worshipped her. She was, he said, a great lady. The pedestal he built for her was so high and mighty, however, that Garson was resented by the other members of the MGM family. Gable put her in the same category as Vivien Leigh—English girls taking away good parts from American actresses. "A good time to Miss Garson," Clark said, "is tea time."

Adventure was a bad movie, but the studio's publicity was worse: GABLE'S BACK AND GARSON'S GOT HIM. Critics added, ". . . and they deserve each other." Clark was angry, embarrassed, and crushed. He would never get over the slogan. His homecoming film should have been a blockbuster, but he refused to pass a movie theater with *Adventure* on the marquee. His fans didn't let him down, however. It was a box-office success.

Gable rushed off to the Rogue River in Oregon and found another girl friend, Carol Gibson, who was good at reeling in big salmon. Though Clark preferred blondes, "because brunettes look dirty to me," he was smitten by the tall and slender girl, who loved the outdoors and was an excellent sportswoman. Clark purchased some property near Grant's Pass, Oregon, and gave friends the impression that he had fallen in love with Gibson, who lived too far away to compete

seriously with the sophisticated beauties available to Clark in Hollywood.

Because these ladies were frequent guests at the ranch, he had
an enormous swimming pool built, but was less than enthusiastic
about it. When it was completed, Anita Colby sent him a regulation-
size dinghy. He had moorings built on either side of the pool for
guests who enjoyed paddling the boat back and forth.

Since Gable was rarely seen in the pool, it was taken for granted
that he disliked swimming. Not true. What very few people knew
was that he had a suite with its own private entrance at the Bel-Air
Hotel. He swam a great deal there late at night, according to the
hotel staff, who provided him with absolute protection. This was his
hideaway. Out of respect for Carole, he did not rendezvous with his
women at the ranch and preferred the privacy of the Bel-Air rather
than risk being seen at the apartment buildings or houses where the
girls lived.

Aside from his new swimming pool, the house and grounds remained the same. He still took pride in showing Carole's room to
those who dined with him at the ranch. It was, four years later, just
as she left it. Hollywood respected Gable's lingering love for his late
wife and did not gossip about Carole's toiletries, atomizers, and
towels neatly displayed to her liking. The room was spotless, and one
felt as if she were about to return at any minute. He bought every
film she had made and viewed them when the mood struck him. She
was as much a part of him as she always had been. Any woman who
tried to be like her was often put down. One of his dates who never
swore came out with a four-letter word, and he didn't like it.

"How can you say that after being married to Lombard?" she
asked.

"That's different," he said. "She could make 'shit' sound like
'sugar.' "

Virginia Grey was able to get away with acting and talking like
Carole since she was so much like her. Virginia was working at it
these days, and conveniently lived just down the road from Clark.

There were no hard feelings among Gable's women—on the
surface, anyway. His social life was no secret. Several girls were
often invited to the same party. Others were good friends. Though
Gable was legally available to marry, his heart lay shattered on a
mountain near Las Vegas. This was no secret either. He didn't have
the ability to love.

Kay Williams and Dolly O'Brien would remarry and divorce before he was able to put the pieces of his life together. Joan Crawford left Philip Terry in 1946, and for the first time in her on-again-off-again affair with Clark, they were both single. On April 25, 1946, Joan testified at the divorce hearing that her husband kept her a virtual prisoner and criticized every script sent to her. She had lost twenty pounds from physical and mental anguish. "I'll never go through this again," she told reporters, who wanted to know if that meant she would never hear the Wedding March again.

She shrugged. "Maybe that's the trouble. I never had any music at my weddings."

Joan could see Gable in the open now, but they preferred to be alone because of his never-ending feud with Mayer. She was very interested in handsome attorney Greg Bautzer, who was a ladies' man in his own right. He remained a bachelor until he married the exquisite Dana Wynter, leaving behind many broken hearts. Joan might have become Mrs. Bautzer after a four-year courtship, but did not appreciate his attentions to another woman at a dinner party. Joan drove home that night. Several miles from Beverly Hills, she asked Greg to get out of the car to see if one of the tires was going flat. He did, and she left him stranded. This was the beginning of her peculiar behavior. Hollywood blamed it on the Oscar. Joan gave a better performance after the awards that she didn't attend because she "had a temperature." Actually, she was scared to go, but greeted fans and reporters at the front door and posed with Oscar in bed. This statue gave her power, and she used it. Nobody was going to push Joan Crawford around anymore—no man, no producer, no director, and no son or daughter. She was making the nightclub scene with gays and unhappily married men, to show Hollywood who the best actress was. And Gable was running around in circles trying to forget who the best actor had been.

"I hate heels, and this character is a heel!"

"Wakeman's novel about Madison Avenue is brilliant," Mayer said. "You became a star playing a bastard. What's wrong with it now?"

"The book is filthy rotten!"

"That's why you're perfect for it, Clark."

"Take your book, your script, your adulterous heroine, and shove it!"

"I had no idea you were so proper." Mayer smirked. "I can always get Errol Flynn. He's not a crybaby."

"That's right," Gable bellowed. "He fucks them!"

"I'm serious about Flynn. You've been bitching about *The Hucksters* too long. I want to start production."

"You forced me into *Adventure* with a limey virgin, but I went through with it, didn't I?"

"Not without a fight, but then you always face a new script with a chip on your shoulder. I don't know what the hell you worry about. Do you remember what Sam Goldwyn said about you in the thirties?"

"I'm not interested."

"I don't care if you are or you're not. I'm going to tell you anyway. Sam said, 'When Robert Montgomery walks on the screen, you know he's got balls. When Clark Gable comes on, you can hear them clacking together. That's the difference.' "

"As an actor," Gable said, "my mouth is open, not my fly."

Mayer laughed. "Don't give me that sanctimonious crap, Clark. I know about you and Louella."

"I don't give a damn if you do or you don't. It was cheaper than buying her off. She wasn't very happy about not getting the scoop on Carole and me . . ."

"I wasn't throwing dirt in your face. Just pointing out that you can't come in here with a halo over your head and expect me to see it. What is it you don't like about *The Hucksters?*"

"The female lead, for one thing. I won't tolerate acting an affair with a married woman."

"Only in real life, eh? What else?"

"The guy I play is oversexed. He's a satyr."

"So? You should be able to do the part without looking at a script."

Gable ground his dentures together. "Make her single and give my guy some character and you might have a deal."

"Might?"

"Your brains are horny. You've got a bastard in this story who doesn't know how to fight another bastard. That doesn't make sense. I want to retaliate at the conference table when the boss crucifies me. I don't care how it's done."

"As I see it, you want to be a kinda bastard who kinda likes to fuck and kinda wants to get even with his boss. Is that it?"

"Kinda."

"You're kinda castrating the novel," Mayer remarked. "That's what you're doing—castrating the whole damn project! Is that what you're trying to do?"

"Hell, no. If I wanted to castrate something," Gable said, walking out the door, "it would be you."

Mayer wanted him for *The Hucksters* without giving in too easily to Clark's demands. He did, however, ask writer Luther Davis to revise the script. Gable stalled until he got what he wanted, and, though not satisfied, he finally agreed to do it. He tested with Deborah Kerr, another English actress, who would play the female lead, and a fairly new MGM starlet, Ava Gardner, for the role of the sensuous singer who loses her man to the wholesome Deborah. But Ava didn't like *The Hucksters* either. She resented being typecast as the good-natured girl who's never good enough for the hero. She was willing to go on suspension if it came to that.

Clark called Ava.

"I hope you'll reconsider," he said.

"I'm fed up."

"Baby, when you've been around as long as I have, *then* you can say that."

"The only reason I have for doing that fuckin' movie is because you're in it."

"Best reason in the world!" he exclaimed. "We'll have a good time. You'll see. No booze on the set? Like hell, baby!"

"I gotta tell you this," she said. "When I first came to Hollywood I saw you driving down Sunset and I almost crashed into the car ahead of me."

"Then do the movie with me, Ava. You're only twenty-four years old. Plenty of time to find a good script. I'm not quite as fortunate, kid."

Deep sigh. "All right, you talked me into it."

Gable and Gardner were attracted to each other from the start. She was unhappily married to bandleader Artie Shaw, who wanted her to be a cultured lady. She was bored with books, classical music, and Emily Post, never one to put on airs or pretend she was anything she wasn't. No one in Hollywood was quite as direct and unpretentious as Ava Gardner.

She was born in Boon Hill, North Carolina. When she was eighteen her sister's husband took pictures of Ava and put them in the window of his photo studio in New York City. Someone from MGM went into the shop to find out who she was and gave her a screen test. She left for Hollywood.

While Ava was on a tour of the studio, Mickey Rooney took one look at the chestnut-haired green-eyed beauty, ogled her magnificent high, firm breasts and small waist, and knew he had to have her. Dressed up like Carmen Miranda, Rooney walked off the set of *Babes on Broadway* and asked for an introduction. He courted Ava with champagne, caviar, crêpes suzette, limousines, flowers, double dates with Hollywood stars, and hundreds of marriage proposals. Mickey was four inches shorter than Ava, but he came on like a tornado that engulfed her so suddenly, she said yes. A friend reminded her, "You said you were going to marry the biggest movie star in the world and here you are!"

"Yeah," Ava said, "but why couldn't he be tall, dark, and handsome like Clark Gable?"

She didn't marry Rooney to further her career, but she did marry him because he was a star. Ava cared less about fame. Though she loved dancing, parties, and laughter, she looked forward to being a good wife, taking off her shoes (she hated them), and stirring up a big pot of homemade spaghetti sauce. This was not for Mickey, who considered home a place to sleep and little else. Unfortunately, he enjoyed his cronies and rarely took Ava with him.

She divorced Rooney several months later and dated many men until Howard Hughes captured her. He bought Ava a house and left a plane at her disposal. The restless Ava managed to sneak away from her bodyguards when she got bored waiting around for Howard to make one of his infrequent appearances. When he found her with another man, he slapped her so hard he dislocated her jaw, but Ava picked up a heavy brass object and knocked him out cold. Hughes had an obsession for big breasts, and Ava's were classic. He proposed to her many times, but despite his millions, Ava preferred her freedom. "He didn't like women who drank," she said. "There was never a drop of liquor on his private planes." But theirs was a satisfying sexual relationship, and Howard was her type—tall, dark, and handsome.

By the time Ava met Clark, she was ready for him. They were both passionate and good drinkers, and did not take their affairs seriously.

She used profanity like Lombard, fought with Mayer, and wasn't sure she belonged in Hollywood. Gable sensed her nervousness and remained by her side on the set of *The Hucksters*. She, in turn, saw tragedy in his eyes and assumed his hands and head shook because he suffered from hangovers. He said it was the Dexedrine he was taking to lose the weight he had gained from too much drinking. The camera could not do many close-ups of Gable, and this endeared Gable to Ava. Both were unsure of themselves and fluffed their lines often. She blamed herself for being terrified of their love scenes. But it was Clark who apologized. "I'm sorry," he said. "I wasn't thinking straight because I was so damn concerned about you. I know you don't think you're an actress. Well, I'm not sure I'm an actor."

Gardner became one of his favorites. He had his harem and she had her stable. He taught her about acting and the art of discretion. She found the latter rather difficult to grasp, but Gable was a perfectionist.

Robert Taylor was attracted to Ava while they were filming *The Bribe*. On the verge of divorce, he saw her regularly. "I seem to follow in Gable's footsteps where women are concerned."

The Hucksters did not get rave reviews, but it was a good film, and Gable felt he had redeemed himself after the disastrous *Adventure*.

Kay Williams married millionaire sugar heir Adolph Spreckels, who was notorious for fighting with his wives. Clark wished her well and left for Phoenix, where he met the Jones sausage heiress, Betty Chisholm, a thin athletic blonde who was an excellent golfer. A classy widow with charm and wit, she became one of Gable's women. By now he had one in all corners of the country, with the exception of New York City, where he met Millicent Rogers, the Standard Oil heiress. This interesting brunette was as zany as she was rich. In her mid-forties, Millicent loved to shock society by wearing costumes instead of designer gowns to formal affairs. Would she arrive as a squaw or as an Egyptian princess? Gable got a kick out of her, but she had a serious side, too. Millicent fell in love with him. He asked her to visit him in California in the near future.

Dolly O'Brien married for the fourth time. Only Clark's most intimate friends knew that she had turned down his proposal and how deeply hurt he was. An anonymous actress said, "Maybe he did and maybe he didn't propose to Dolly. It was easy for him to say so because she married someone else. I got the impression he wanted us to think he was making an effort to settle down. Clark wasn't posses-

sive, and yet there were times he acted like a sheikh. God forbid if a
girl left him for another man. He drank so much and loneliness
caught up to him. If the setting was right, he might have proposed
marriage. Poor Clark was in the pits. He wasn't a good lover and he
knew it. When Dolly married someone else, he made a funny remark
that maybe he didn't satisfy her in bed."

After a four-month vacation to the Rogue River and then to Phoenix for some golf with Betty Chisholm, he came back to the ranch,
Virginia Grey, and Anita Colby.

He began *Homecoming* with Lana Turner, who had divorced her
second husband by now and was madly in love with Tyrone Power.
It's doubtful that Clark and Lana had anything more than a platonic
reunion, since she was counting the minutes until she would be
reunited with Ty in New York City. While she was in Gable's arms
in the touching film *Homecoming,* Power was in the arms of actress
Linda Christian, whom he would marry. "Tyrone Power was the
love of my life," Lana says today. "He was the one who broke my
heart."

To spite him she married millionaire Bob Topping.

In 1948 Clark made *Command Decision* with an all-male cast that
included Walter Pidgeon and Van Johnson. It was a good picture, but
Gable cursed, "I can't wait for the day I throw my dentures in
Mayer's face!"

His close friends saw very little of Clark from 1947 through 1949.
He was fair game for such beauties as Paulette Goddard, whom he
dated off and on. Whether she was ever legally married to Charlie
Chaplin isn't known, but she was headed for another divorce from
her third husband, Burgess Meredith. Goddard was one of Hollywood's most determined go-getters and Gable was at the top of her
list of conquests. Her friends insisted that if she didn't get the man,
she'd get the usual car or diamond ring. Clark's friends said, "No
way!" Paulette was unexpectedly dismissed when Clark drove her to
the airport. Reporters were on hand when she asked him to kiss her
good-bye. He refused. She laughed it off: "Well, that's that! So long,
sugar!" After Goddard boarded the plane, reporters asked Clark if he
was planning to marry her. "No," he replied. "We're longtime
friends. That's all." Unofficially he told a friend that Paulette came
on too strong and he had to go out of his way to avoid her.

One of the reasons Gable wasn't seen in his usual haunts was Errol Flynn, whose house was a haven for pretty girls, liquor, and dope. If Clark had any guilt about his association with women, he felt like a monk during his escapades with Robin Hood.

Ann Sheridan said the powder room at Flynn's house was bugged. "The girls didn't know this," she said. "Errol's parties were mostly singles, and no one knew who would end up with whom most of the time. We'd talk it over, but the worst was we really raked them over. When I think back ... oh, my, the things that were said demeaning their manhood! Errol made the men promise not to tell anyone about it. I found out years later quite by accident.

"In the late forties it was a coincidence that so many of us in Hollywood were going through divorces, changing studios, and watching the star system gradually fade away. We clung to each other. Errol was good company. He was the kind of guy who could make anyone forget their problems. Yet he had been through hell during his trial for statutory rape, and though found not guilty, he was ostracized for several years. Errol told me he put a gun in his mouth and didn't have the nerve to pull the trigger. He hated himself for being a coward.

"I often wondered what would have happened if Errol had married his fair maiden, Olivia de Havilland, who was so in love with him and he with her, but she was afraid of Errol. He played such nasty tricks on her. One day he put a big dead snake in her panties, laid out with her costumes in her dressing room. She was terribly shaken. This was Errol's way of getting her attention because he didn't know how to express love.

"Since I worked primarily at Warner Brothers with Errol, I didn't know Gable well. In the late forties we were all hopping from one studio to another. Errol and Clark drank and smoked excessively and shared the same women. David Niven said to me, 'Take a good look at those two handsome legends because they're about to fall apart. It's a bloody shame.'

"I could remember the first time I saw Errol Flynn. He was the most beautiful man I had ever seen. Perfect. Flawless. He was a rebel. But he did not have that startling effect that Gable did when he stood in a doorway. I have yet to figure it out. When I first saw him, my heart stopped beating. Errol made it beat faster. I didn't stare at Flynn, but my eyes were glued on Gable. This was one of the discussions the ladies often had in the ladies' room at Errol's home. What the hell was it about Clark that stopped the world?"

It was only a matter of time before Millicent Rogers showed up in Hollywood for an elaborate and extensive campaign to marry Clark. She bought a monkey and "wore" it on her shoulder wherever she went. She gave Clark expensive jewelry (he gave her nothing), wooed his friends, servants, and secretary, and, sadly, followed him on the nights he wasn't with her. Millicent didn't know Gable very well, and soon dropped out when she found him with another woman. She is significant for trying harder than the others and diving into the affair totally before becoming a recluse.

Dolly's marriage was over before it began, and she was back in Clark's life. But Dolly was wiser than Millicent. Before she would consider Gable for her fifth husband, she made it clear that he would have to live in the East—New York, Palm Beach, or Newport. From there they could hop on a ship to Paris, Monte Carlo, and the Riviera. That was very nice, he said, but not an easy drive to the MGM studio.

Before leaving on a European vacation, Clark went to Grant's Pass to see Carol Gibson, who had no desire to be part of his glamorous life in Hollywood. Their favorite pastime was getting a group together, taking a boat down the river, and camping overnight along the way. Carol's father, Rainbow Gibson, owned an inn on the Rogue where Clark stayed for many years on his fishing trips. He was at home with the Gibsons and considered building a cabin nearby. Maybe there was a future for him with Carol . . .

On July 12, 1948, Clark sailed for France, where Dolly O'Brien was waiting for him. He began a whirlwind of parties given by Elsa Maxwell, golfed with the Duke of Windsor, spent leisure hours at the casino playing baccarat, drove to Switzerland in an open car, and thoroughly enjoyed Dolly's company. "She's the funniest and wittiest woman I've ever known," he said. Candid pictures of the couple proved they were happy together—always laughing and too busy having fun to bother posing. Dolly wasn't one for intimate romantic dinners. No sir! She adored a distinguished crowd of pleasure-seeking thoroughbreds and was not a lady to fawn over any man. It was Gable who went to Dolly from the beginning.

It was a splendid vacation, perhaps the best. Unfortunately, William Gable died, and Clark left for home immediately. His father's third wife had passed away a few months previously (Clark did not attend her funeral), and the house built for them was sold at a loss because Clark hated bargaining. Money was something he kept in a safe deposit box or in his pocket. No one could convince him to invest, nor did he have a financial adviser. He was a very frugal man. Lombard laughed uproariously every time she saw *Idiot's Delight* and heard him say to Norma Shearer, "Hey, I paid three bits for that, baby. It's the most expensive thing I ever gave to a dame!"

He was generous with his servants and his secretary, but not with his women. Carole was the exception, after a good deal of cajoling. But then, Clark did not spend on himself, except for clothes, his custom-made English shoes, fine luggage, and sports cars. He was a good mechanic, and said he balanced his sanity by taking a car apart and putting it back together. If he couldn't fix an engine, it was time to buy a new automobile, but he never gave up until it was hopeless —his way of proving to himself he needed a new car.

His personal secretary, Jean Garceau, nagged Clark until he eventually allowed her to buy blue-chip stocks. She said he never carried his own checkbook. "He couldn't be bothered," she said. He thought a great deal of Jean and promised to buy her a Paris original when he was in Europe. Rushing home for William's funeral prevented him from keeping the promise, but he managed to find time for shopping in an exclusive show in Beverly Hills and chose a very costly Paris gown. Jean was overwhelmed. After ten years she knew him only too well.

Garceau had been working for David Selznick when Carole hired her as a personal secretary in 1938. Jean shared the triumphs and tragedies that Clark endured. She remained in charge of the ranch when he was in the Air Corps, and she was the one who gave him the last note from Carole after she was killed. No one, with the exception of Howard Strickling, was as sincerely devoted and loyal to Gable as Garceau. He, in turn, had respect for Jean and did not expose his casual affairs to her—only the regulars.

Anita Colby was one. She was his best pal, and though she loved Clark, she wasn't in love with him. Anita was a gracious hostess, and he chose her for the more influential parties. She did, of course, bear a remarkable resemblance to Carole Lombard. When Anita decided to further her career and settle in New York City, Clark felt a surge of panic. Anita was different from the others; like Dolly, her life did not revolve around him, nor did she share his bed, which seems inconceivable. That was Anita.

A short time before she left Los Angeles, Clark proposed to her. His speech was apparently thought out very carefully—a warm and genuine reaching out. Anita was shocked. She assumed, since theirs was a chaste relationship, that Clark understood how she felt. As he described their future together, Anita wasn't so concerned about the sincerity of his words so much as she was over his apparent desperate loneliness. She worried about leaving him in the clutches of so many women who were in love with the movie star and not the softhearted pathetic man. Anita said she wasn't ready for marriage and didn't think being anyone's wife was part of her future. She was a business-woman foremost, but she hoped he would visit her in New York and continue their friendship. Clark was depressed and remained silent after his proposal. Anita was blunt about his drinking too much. So far as she was concerned, this was a serious problem. He tugged at her heart with "That's because I'm so lonely." He was too vulnerable.

"Don't rush off and do something you'll regret," she warned. "I worry about that more than anything else where you're concerned."

Oddly, the two women he considered marrying preferred life on the East Coast to life with him.

Poor Virginia. She wanted to hear those glorious words of pro-posal with all her being. But she waited patiently, unaware that Clark had said them to anyone else. His harem was getting smaller, and Virginia believed that when the time was right, he would marry her. That was an unspoken understanding between them.

Then quite suddenly Crawford and Gable emerged from their closet. He arranged a birthday party for her at the ranch, and they were seen in public from time to time. This was the closest they came to marriage. Joan said, "We had both been around the block a few times. I was in my mid-forties and he was almost fifty. We un-derstood each other. That was the problem. We understood each other too well."

CHAPTER NINE

Television began taking its toll on the movie industry. L. B. Mayer was forced to face MGM's deficits, which amounted to $6.5 million. Their movie-contract stars, producers, and directors were not winning Oscars or making the prestigious "ten best" lists. The artistic Irving Thalberg was never replaced. Mayer, not one to take the blame for anything, had been more interested in his stable of race horses and courtship of a new young wife. When the decline of MGM became public knowledge, he began a search for another Thalberg, and hoped it would be Dore Schary, who had just resigned as production head of RKO. Mayer offered him the job of vice-president in charge of production for $6,000 a week. Schary signed a contract on July 1, 1948, but though he put MGM in the black again, he was not popular with many of the contract players, including Gable, who turned down the lead in the multimillion-dollar production of *Quo Vadis*. Schary was ready to put him on suspension. That was fine with Clark. "I'm not going to be seen in Roman garb with my bloody knees sticking out," he bellowed. "It's not my thing and I won't do it."

"You have a point," Schary said. "Bob Taylor would make a better appearance, but if you should change your mind..."

Clark sneered. "Don't count on that. Why the hell can't you find something decent for me to do?"

"I'm looking. In the meantime, how about *Any Number Can Play* with Alexis Smith?"

"Jesus Christ! Another reformed gambler?"

"Until I can find what you want, Clark. Deal?"

"Yeah..."

The only good thing about *Any Number Can Play* was that it couldn't be any worse than *Adventure*. While Clark waited for that Oscar-winning script, Schary asked him to film *Key to the City* with

Loretta Young. Gable wasn't thrilled about this one either, but he was very fond of Loretta and wanted to work with her again. She was married to Tom Lewis, who adopted her "adopted" daughter, Judy. During the production of Key to the City, Loretta was rushed to the hospital suffering from a miscarriage. She had given birth to a son by Lewis a few years before. Loretta recovered quickly and was back on the set, where a good time was had by all. Clark fell off the edge of a park bench when she edged too close to him, and the artificial fog was so thick he disappeared. They both took their time and didn't care how long it took to film the movie. She demanded the right to leave with Clark at five, even though her contract did not have the no-overtime clause. "I don't like working when he's not here," she said. "When someone else feeds me his lines, it's not the same. . . . I don't react the same."

When the movie was completed, Loretta and Tom had a party to celebrate. Clark came alone.

Spencer Tracy wasn't in on the fun anymore with Young. He was too busy making movies with Katharine Hepburn, the love of his life.

Actor Frank Morgan and director Victor Fleming died suddenly, and Clark Gable mourned his dear friends. He went into another deep depression, smoked and drank more heavily than before, and raced his Jaguar XK-120 sports roadster in the desert. He was growing increasingly discouraged, as an actor and as a lover. Fascinating scripts were as hard to come by as fascinating women. He was bored and tired and very lonely. The girl most likely to reach the altar with Clark was still Virginia Grey, who at thirty-two was so desperately in love with him. He had been a widower seven years. It was time for marriage. It was time to stop running. It was time to make peace with himself. It was time to marry Virginia, give in, accept the fact that she was the closest he would ever get to Carole's image. Virginia was willing to give up her career, which consisted of supporting roles and not many of those. Clark began to see her on a steady basis. There was no announcement or formal engagement. Just that blasted understanding. Virginia did not care how much he drank. She'd known him intimately for sixteen years. When he talked about Carole, she listened and added her memories of a dear friend. Yes, they had shared many years with Lombard. Virginia spent hours trying to look like her (she did), talk like her (she did), walk like her (she did), and dress like her (on a limited budget). Friends were sure that Clark would marry Virginia any day.

He managed golf outings with Betty Chisholm and fishing trips with Carol Gibson. Another Joan came into his life—Joan Harrison, a beautiful British writer-producer who was associated with Alfred Hitchcock for many years. Still, it was Virginia he chose to be with most of the time . . .

Shelley Winters, a Hollywood beginner in 1949, met Gable when Yvonne de Carlo invited her to an intimate dinner at Errol Fynn's (Shelley Winters, *Shelley*, Ballantine Books, 1980). When Shelley pulled up to the house, Gable opened the car door and Shelley fell out. He caught her just in time, got his wristwatch entangled in her wool shawl, and had to be disentangled by Flynn, who asked Shelley if she had done it on purpose.

"I knew Mr. Gable would catch me," she said.

Gable grinned. "I would catch her anywhere, anytime, under any circumstances."

Flynn took her arm. "After three double martinis," he said, "I'm surprised he was so alert."

Yvonne took Shelley aside and asked, "Which guy do you want?"

"Do I have a choice?"

"I think Errol likes you, so I'll make the big sacrifice and take Gable."

Each couple sat at the far end of a long couch to watch a film. When the movie was over, Clark left with Yvonne. Shelley spent a long and beautiful weekend with Flynn, who wanted to give a party in her honor for the Hollywood press. "I'll get Clark Gable to be your escort," he said. "Then I'll get jealous and have a make-believe fight with him, and the press will have a field day."

On the night of the big party, Clark picked up Shelley in a navy blue Rolls-Royce.

They went to Romanoff's where restless and very nervous, Shelley asked, "When are we going to Errol's house? What are we waiting for, Mr. Gable?"

"Am I boring you?"

"No, you paralyze me. I'm sure if we wait too long, the Rolls is going to turn into a pumpkin and my gold lamé dress will disappear."

He pinched her on the fanny and said, "Shelley, that feeling of unreality is an occupational hazard. Every time they say, 'Cut,' and it's the last take of a movie, I feel I'll never be hired for another one, and I'll be back tomorrow doing extra work again. All actors feel they're not entitled to happiness and all that money, that some evil God will take away from us when we do get it. And please call me Clark."

When they arrived at the party, Gable asked her to dance and held her very, very close. He kissed and whispered in her ear. Then Errol cut in. They danced for a while until Clark cut in again. Errol got angry and said so. Gable mumbled obscenities, and the two men got into a heated argument. Before they exchanged blows, police arrived, handcuffed Shelley, and drove off. She cried all the way to the Hollywood Canteen, where, the officers said, she would have to entertain for an hour.

It was all arranged. All a joke. She was furious, upset, and confused, but Shelley sang at the policemen's benefit for the USO. The officers were waiting to take her back to the party. They told her that Errol and Clark had played many jokes on them.

She found Flynn's house a shambles, but he was drunk and happy. Gable was in the same condition. "As long as they spell your name right," they cheered.

The next day she was a household word after her name appeared on the front page of all the newspapers. Scripts were delivered to her house before she had a chance to have a cup of coffee, and a star was born.

In the summer of 1949, Clark attended a proper dinner party given by Minna Wallis. One of the guests was Lady Sylvia Ashley, whom Clark had known casually as Mrs. Douglas Fairbanks, Sr. Sylvia was, if you can believe it, another Lombard look-alike, but without the softness. She was ten years younger than Clark, divorced twice and widowed once. Her jewels were outrageous. When asked how much they were worth, Sylvia thought "about half a million," maybe more. She wasn't a dishy dame, but if you could concoct Gable's type of woman, Sylvia was a combination of Lombard, Dolly, Anita, Millicent, and Ria. She had class, money, beauty, wit, intellect, charm, and guts.

Born Sylvia Hawkes in England, she was the daughter of a footman and pubkeeper. Sylvia made her debut on the London stage in the successful *Midnight Follies* with Dorothy Field. Billed as "Silly and Dotty," they sang ballads and played the ukelele. In 1925 Sylvia appeared in *Tell Me More* at the Winter Garden, and to make ends meet she modeled lingerie. Hawkes was a very ambitious and determined young lady. The theater was grand and applause somewhat appealing, but they could not compare with nobility. Every English girl knows that. Watching the King and Queen was a way of life—a goal for those who considered themselves worthy, and Sylvia did. She was blond, thin, and shapely, and she carried herself well. Maybe Sylvia was a footman's daughter, but no one would know when, at sixteen, she married Lord Anthony Ashley, heir to the ninth Duke of Shaftesbury.

Lady Sylvia Ashley!

This might have been good enough for most eager young ladies, but seven years later she fell in love with Douglas Fairbanks, Sr., who was still married to Mary Pickford. Quite an affair, insiders said. What a shock, outsiders gasped. Poor Mary. She understood her husband, who at fifty-one wanted a last fling at youth. Sylvia was a mere twenty-three, but she'd never been married to a world-renowned movie star—especially one married to America's Sweetheart. Weren't the Douglas Fairbankses considered Hollywood royalty? And wasn't Pickfair their equivalent to Buckingham Palace? Sylvia had her title; now she wanted fame. It wasn't an easy task pursuing a married man who was making a film with his famous wife six thousand miles away, but after *The Taming of the Shrew,* Douglas left for England "on business." When he called Mary to tell her he was not returning to Pickfair, she was consoled by Buddy Rogers, who had been in love with her for a long time.

To avoid a scandal, Mary spoke to Louella Parsons, an old friend. "My marriage to Douglas is over," she confessed. Parsons tried to play it down, but reporters, hungry for the sordid details, followed Mary everywhere. Trying to maintain her dignity, she told them, "Where there had been only heartbreak"—she wept—"and hope, a full-size scandal stares me in the face." She relied on Buddy Rogers for sympathy and fell in love with him. This was Doug's freedom, of course.

Lord Ashley accused Sylvia of adultery with Fairbanks, and three years of disgrace on both continents followed. Finally, in 1937, Sylvia married Doug and Buddy married Mary. Everyone settled down happily except poor Sylvia, who hated having to give up her title of "Lady." Sacrificing was not her style. In 1939, Fairbanks died of a heart attack. Five years later Sylvia married Edward John Lord Stanley of Alderly. Within months, however, he charged her with adultery and began divorce proceedings, which lasted four years. In 1948 "Lady Ashley" settled down in the $50,000 Malibu beach house left to her by Fairbanks.

Less than a year later she set her sights again. This time it was Clark Gable.

Following the dinner party given by Minna Wallis, he took Sylvia out occasionally, but not more often than the others. They weren't even mentioned in the gossip columns. Clark was just as attentive to Joan Harrison and Betty and Carol and, of course, Virginia, who was simply waiting for him to name the day.

On December 17, 1949, Gable's biggest alcoholic binge began at a party given by agent Charles Feldman. Sylvia's behavior was shocking. "She was practically on top of Clark," a guest said, "and he was responding. They were acting like horny teenagers, and Sylvia was the aggressor. We knew he was plastered, but we had never seen him like this before. It was different. Clark wasn't himself somehow. Not in control. It was something to see a woman taking advantage of him! I felt very uneasy about the whole thing."

The next day Gable called Howard Strickling. "I'm going to marry Lady Ashley," he slurred.

"Who?" Howard asked.

"Sylvia! Lady . . . Sylvia . . . Ashley! I want you to make all the arrangements, and tomorrow won't be too soon."

The reaction was the same from his close friends when Clark invited them to the wedding. "I'm marrying Syl," he said.

"Who?" was unanimous.

MGM's publicity staff hoped to talk Clark out of it. Everyone tried to convince him to wait a few days and think it over. Sylvia, however, was with Gable every second, and to the "Are you sure?" question she responded urgently, "Sure he is."

Three days after the Feldmans' party, Clark married Lady Ashley at the home of a friend. She wore a navy wool dress and he wore a navy suit. They sliced a four-tiered cake with a Spanish sword. The newlyweds spent their wedding night at the ranch and boarded the Lurline for Honolulu three days later. Mobs of fans were waiting everywhere to get a glimpse of the new Mrs. Gable. MGM was so concerned about the drunken groom that they sent Strickling to Hawaii as chaperon to make sure the honeymoon went smoothly.

Virginia Grey received a telephone call on December 20. "Gable just got married" was the message.

"This is a joke!"

"No."

"Who?"

"Lady Ashley."

"Who?"

"Sylvia Hawkes Ashley Fairbanks Stanley."

Virginia was devastated. Her telephone rang constantly, and when she chose to answer she said, "Yes, yes, I know! Clark married Lady Ashcan!"

The honeymoon proved that Clark and Sylvia had little in common. While he sat in the sun, she sat in the shade wearing a hat and gloves to protect her white skin. He played a little golf. She preferred not to. Clark lived on booze. When he wasn't sure what happened, Howard was there to remind him. As for Sylvia, she looked after Sylvia. That was the vast difference between the two blond Mrs. Gables. Carole devoted her life to Clark. Sylvia would fit him in to her liking. Two weeks later the newlyweds sailed home.

As soon as Clark had a minute alone, he called Virginia, who asked him, "Why?"

"I was drunk," he replied. "Can you forgive me?"

"Don't ever call me again," she said.

"I didn't know what I was doing."

Virginia repeated herself, "Don't ever call me again!" He did, of course, so often, in fact, that she was forced to change her phone number. He approached her on the street and in restaurants when "Syl" wasn't around, but Virginia refused to have anything more to do with him. Several days later she got a call from a friend who asked if it was all right to give Robert Taylor her telephone number, and she agreed. He called and said he would bring over some steaks, wine, and records. It was obvious to Virginia that Bob did not want to be seen in public until his divorce from Barbara Stanwyck was final. So they spent their evenings at her place.

"Bob was a big mystery to me," Virginia said. "After our first evening together I left the room for a minute, and when I returned he had disappeared. Taylor had simply decided it was time to go home. When he called a week later he never mentioned the incident, but he would disappear like that often. He reminded me of Clark. You could get to know them so far and then the wall!"

Taylor did most of his movies on location. When he returned, it was Virginia he called. "Bob and I missed each other because I had to keep changing my telephone number," she said. "Clark would not leave me alone. I explained this to Bob, who was just as sensitive as Clark. He actually thought I was trying to avoid him. Yes, they were very much alike. I don't think it was a routine, but Bob would say things like 'Gosh, I was lonely up there in Utah. Wish you had come along.' He didn't ask! Or 'I came back on Saturday and tried to call.

You weren't home.' I was. Things like that. They always made me
feel as if I were on their minds all the time—that I was the one
avoiding them. They were both very insecure and gave the impression of helplessness."

It was a difficult time for Virginia Grey. She believed that Gable
had been drunk, but the marriage had taken place, and so far as she
was concerned, the hurt and humiliation were almost too much to
bear. She had listened endlessly about Carole. She would not sit still
while he moaned over Sylvia. Virginia wasn't the only one who decided not to see Gable. Many of his close friends were not comfortable with him these days, and they were very annoyed at Sylvia, who
wanted them out of his life anyway. She also made up her mind to
bury Carole Lombard once and for all. She had no intention of being
identified with anyone, especially Clark's former wife. Sylvia considered his past life a blackboard full of white memories and began eras-
ing them fast! She made it fairly obvious to Clark's old chums that
they weren't her type and did not make an effort to get to know
them. After numerous introductions, she failed to remember their
names. There would be no more comparisons to her husband's old
way of life. There was too much talk about hunting and fishing. Too
many prospects for "roughing it." She wanted Clark to begin again—
new friends, new hobbies, new furnishings, and a new outlook.

Crawford had little to say except "If I were still married to
Douglas junior, Gable would be my father-in-law."

Maybe Joan thought Clark's marriage was a big joke, but his servants didn't when they watched Sylvia putting Carole's mementos
away in storage. Clark had given her complete charge of the house,
to the amazement of everyone. There was nothing left of Lombard
except the dining room, which was a bit too informal for Sylvia, God
knows, but she removed Carole's treasures and touched nothing else.
She naturally took over the white bedroom—and painted it pink!
Gable hated pink. Carole was allowed only her collection of pink
Staffordshire, which was stored away by Sylvia. Everything "Lombard" was replaced. The servants expected Clark to protest when she
suggested another dining room more to her liking, and so they built
an extension. In some ways, Sylvia took her time as gradually her
antiques and English furniture arrived by the truckload.

The biggest surprise of all, however, was "Syl's" taking over
Clark's gun room for her paintings. "I don't know how the hell that
happened," a friend said. "I wasn't the only one who almost passed

out. She made it look like a French drawing room, for Christ's sake. If she was going to leave anything for last, it should have been Clark's gun room. I don't think she did anything without his prior knowledge, though, even Carole's horrid pink bedroom. That was enough to make anyone vomit. I'll give her credit for the English rosebushes she planted all over the place. They were lovely, but not Gable. Nothing was, anymore. He looked great, though. I'll say that much for him. He came back from the honeymoon in a good mood and looking better than I had seen him in years. Then he kinda gave in. He didn't fight anymore. I don't know if he made up his mind this was it—with Sylvia, I mean—or he felt very guilty about marrying her in the first place. She had exquisite taste. Her furniture was the best you could buy, but when she had the bright living room redone with her antiques, it lost its charm. The whole house did, except for the old dining room, which was rarely used. She had her own that was done elegantly—more to her liking. She was very uneasy having anything of Carole's around. I can understand that. She married a guy who was obsessed with a butterfly that didn't fly high enough and collided with a mountain. I don't know how often we all talked about it and how Sylvia could never get rid of Carole. She could take Clark to Tibet and Lombard would be there. I, frankly, did not see the resemblance, but he did. Sylvia was hard-looking to me. She wasn't delicate or tender or pliable. Well, as I said, her putting Clark's guns in the shed, or wherever, was the epitome."

Sylvia had a guesthouse built despite Gable's distaste for anyone spending the night on his grounds other than the servants. She even tried to get rid of Jean Garceau by suggesting she work at home. The office was made into a sitting room. It took Gable a while to realize this was all wrong. He needed Jean close by. She agreed to work in the guesthouse.

Then there was the dinner menu. No more meat and potatoes, baked beans, or spareribs. Instead Sylvia served French gourmet or English dishes. The food was not the only thing continental. So were the invited guests—the Ronald Colmans, the David Nivens, the Charles Boyers, the Fred Astaires, the Tyrone Powerses, Clifton Webb, Joan Fontaine—all European or so inclined.

But the most offensive sight was Clark carrying Sylvia's little diamond-collared terrier while his wife spent lavishly on evening wear. It did not take long for him to remind her, "You're richer than I am, right, Syl?"

"Why bring that up, Bird?"

"I want you to feel free to spend your million," he said.

She gasped. "You'd ask me to sell my jewels? My securities? My beach house?"

"Something like that. Your choice, of course."

"I'm somewhat taken back."

"So am I when I see the bills, my dear."

"I'll see what I can do, Bird."

"I'll drink to that!"

Gable felt much better about his career when MGM put him in *To Please a Lady* with Barbara Stanwyck. He portrayed a racing driver and she a newspaperwoman. With these two pros, the film was already a success. As he had done in *Night Nurse* thirty years earlier, Gable let Stanwyck have it. "You'd better listen to what I'm saying or I'll knock that smile off your face," he growled.

She smirked. "Knock it off."

He did! With one swift swing of his right arm, she went spinning. Moviegoers loved it! Gable was back in his original form, all right, and making sure dames didn't get away with any smart talk! *Motion Picture Exhibitor* wrote, "Gable is his charming best. Miss Barbara Stanwyck in a flip characterization which counts. In their first scene, Gable slaps her face and she comes back for more."

As soon as the movie was finished and Sylvia was sure there was no romance between her husband and the recently divorced Stanwyck, she left for Europe to disentangle some of her assets. Clark spent the three weeks she was gone with friends and conferring with Mayer and Schary. "I liked doing *To Please a Lady*," he told them. "Haven't enjoyed myself so much in years."

Mayer smiled. "More than *The Hucksters* with Ava?"

"That's different!" Gable snapped. "I liked both of them, actually."

"Your British wife's teaching you some good manners, I see. Well, you can't have Ava. She's too busy screwing around with Frank. Besides, I think you're overdue for a rugged role . . . you know, on location someplace where you can fish and hunt in your spare time."

"Your thoughtfulness astounds me." Gable scowled. "It bothers me more, though. Let's have it."

"Always suspicious." Mayer smiled. "What I have in mind is a role you can get your teeth into—a rugged trapper hunting for pelts in Indian country. Here's the script. You'll like it, but you'll like

Colorado even more. That's where you'll be filming."

Gable glanced through the script and nodded. "Not bad. I'll look it over tonight. On the next one, try to get Ava."

Schary pretended not to hear any personal innuendoes. He was too square, but as Gable was leaving he said, "Hey, did you see *Quo Vadis* with Bob Taylor?"

"He was the guy for the job," Clark said. "Bob's your knight in shining armor."

"Aren't you a bit disappointed about turning down the part?"

"I'm not comfortable in iron jocks, Dore."

"Give my regards to your charming wife."

"Yeah . . ."

Sylvia returned in time to accompany Clark to Durango, Colorado, for *Across the Wide Missouri* in July. He was anxious to drive despite the rough terrain, but she felt ill at the very thought. "I'd prefer taking the train," she said.

"The train? With all that goddamn baggage? We're only staying two months."

"That's a long time." She smiled demurely. "Must you drive, Bird?"

"I was looking forward to it, yes."

"In that case, I can take along a few more things."

"I'm not hiring a private train for you, Syl. Just a private compartment."

She laughed because he could be so witty. "I know, I know," she chirped. "Do you mind taking Minnie with you in the car?"

"Take the dog on the train, for Christ's sake."

"But she's so attached to you, darling. How can you be so cruel?"

The car was so overloaded with trunks and suitcases, Gable could barely see through the back window. "Are you sure this is everything?" he asked, holding the little terrier.

"Well, I have some shopping to do, but I'll manage somehow on the train. Somehow, someway, I'll manage."

"Yeah," he groaned, trying to fit himself into the front seat. "You don't need much where we're goin', Syl. All you need, really, are some britches, sweaters, and boots."

Sylvia was more interested in kissing her little pooch, Minnie, bye-bye. And then Clark. "Safe trip, my darling!" She waved. When he was safely on his way, Sylvia went on a shopping spree in Beverly

Hills for a complete western wardrobe. With an exorbitant amount of excess luggage, she boarded the train, which would be the last of her luxuries for a while.

"Jesus, Syl, we're not moving up here," he said when she arrived. "I thought I brought everything in the car."

"Aren't you silly, Bird. How could I come to beautiful Colorado without my easel and oils?"

"Yeah," he said, waving to some husky men to help him unpack again. Meanwhile, Sylvia reached for the smelling salts when she saw the rustic cabin assigned to them.

Clark was very busy filming and not paying much attention to anything else. The frilly lace curtains came first. Then the landscaping. Sylvia had layers of grass put in and trees planted, and supervised the garden herself. It all came together one morning when Clark peeked through the opening in the drapes and saw trees that hadn't been there when he went to sleep. Beautiful green grass, too, nicer than he had at home. The flowers were blooming, but he couldn't remember anyone putting seeds in the ground.

Then came breakfast, served with Sylvia's best china, silverware, silk napkins and tablecloth, candelabra, and finger bowls. He had a drink, gulped down some black coffee, and left for the day. Maybe all of this would disappear by the time he got home.

It got worse. Sylvia served him cocktails in her best crystal!

"We're having dinner with the others," he said. "It's ranch style."

"Is that the name of the restaurant?" she asked.

"No, my dear. We all sit at a long table with the crew and eat what's served on big platters and in big bowls. Maybe you'll have to serve yourself."

"That might be fun once in a while," she chirped.

"Every night, my dear. Each and every night."

At least this gave her a chance to wear her new western outfits —a different one each and every night. Clark could almost accept this, but bringing the dog to the table was too embarrassing for him to take. Sylvia took a nibble and then little Minnie took a bite. The crew kidded him about this unmercifully. No one dared mention the frilly cabin, which stuck out like a sore thumb. Clark tried to escape with his fishing gear, but Sylvia tagged along. She hated the sport, so she sat under a tree wearing her hat and gloves. Sometimes she brought along her needlework.

It never occurred to her that Clark enjoyed the rugged outdoor life—his way of relaxing and getting paid for it. It didn't occur to her either that he resented living any differently from the others working on the film, not to mention the added expense of redecorating the cabin and landscaping the grounds. One of the technicians tried to make Clark feel at ease about Sylvia's fussing.

"I told him it was very nice that his wife tried to make a dreary place look more comfortable," he said. "She really went to a lotta trouble. Gable said, 'Yeah, there goes the profit!'"

He endured it for two months, and it's up for grabs who was happier to get back to the Encino ranch, he or Sylvia. She considered the eight weeks in Colorado a disaster. Clark considered it the end of his marriage. Sylvia, however, did not grasp what was happening. He drank beer when she and her friends sipped champagne. At one of her catered pool parties, Clark rode his horse into the sunset. One of the British guests said, "All we could see was the horse's ass. I do believe he was trying to tell us something."

Clark told his wife her "personal" servants had to go. They were an added expense and he had managed with his staff very nicely over the years. She gave in reluctantly. When Sylvia said she was inviting her family "again" for a visit, Clark said, "The guesthouse isn't a guesthouse anymore. It's Jean's office." From the day they returned from Hawaii, Clark had no privacy. Sylvia's family came to the ranch and lingered for an eternity. As they were going out the door, friends from jolly old England were coming in the door with their luggage.

Clark was giving his wife a message and a warning. She was miffed, but assumed he was in a bad mood after filming the not-so-hot *Across the Wide Missouri*. He had yet to pack his guns and rods for a long-overdue trip to the Rogue. It was all Sylvia could do to survive Colorado. She hated sleeping bags, fish scales, guns, canned food, bugs, tents, worms, golf, Clark's old hats, dirty fingernails, and muddy shoes.

If Hollywood snickered at Clark's carrying little Minnie, they got a bigger laugh when he fell asleep at the opera while Sylvia dug her elbows into his ribs. She pretended to be amused when the incident made the gossip columns—Clark Gable, in white tie and tails, snoring at the opera. Sylvia expected him to pretend, for goodness' sake, but Clark wasn't going to do that anymore. Maybe this was a sign that he was bored with Sylvia's way of life, but it became very apparent when a fishing buddy asked him, "Are you thinking of building on your Rogue River property?"

Yes, he was.

"Do you think your wife will like it in the country?"

"That won't matter at all," Gable replied.

When one of Sylvia's friends offered her and Clark a villa in Nassau for the Christmas holidays, he agreed, but they came home barely speaking. The servants heard loud bickering about what he should wear to such and such a dinner party. He told her he was perfectly capable of dressing himself properly for any occasion and "butt out!" She wanted him to change the cut of his clothes, but he refused. When Sylvia didn't take the hint, Clark told her never to approach the subject again.

She had yet to recognize the seriousness of Gable's protests, but felt she should try to get him out of such a glum and cranky mood. For his fiftieth birthday, Sylvia decided to give him a party with *his* friends instead of *hers*. She'd surprise him with his favorite dish, chicken and dumplings. Maybe the guests and menu weren't the crème de la crème, but the table setting was. She might have given in this once for a less formal setting, considering the common meal being served. Not Sylvia.

She had just hired a new cook, and Clark suggested it might not be a good idea to have a party under the circumstances. Naturally, Sylvia wasn't the least bit concerned. Who the devil worried about chicken and dumplings, for heaven's sake? The house was filled with fresh flowers, the fireplaces flickered during the cocktail hour, and Clark seemed more relaxed and content than he had been in a while.

Then Sylvia announced that dinner was served and the guests sat at their place settings in the dining room. The serving platter was put in the middle of the table. *Voilà!* Or was it *merde?* A foul odor filled everyone's nostrils. The ladies felt sick and put down their forks while the gents, including Clark, dove in. He hadn't had a decent meal in a year! No one could pretend politeness. There was gagging and coughing. The ladies covered their noses with hankies or napkins, and the men wiped their foreheads. One of the servants apologized, with the explanation that the new cook had prepared the meal a day ahead of time and did not refrigerate it overnight.

Clark pushed his chair back and left the room. He did not return until much later in the evening. He was not amused. He had warned Sylvia about new cooks, but what hurt him most was her carefree attitude toward his friends, as if they didn't count. As if chicken and dumplings didn't matter. He was well aware that this would not have happened at one of her own dinner parties.

He decided that night he needed to work—to get his mind off the formality of life that presented itself day after day with Sylvia. Two months after the disastrous chicken-and-dumplings party, he agreed to do *Lone Star* with Ava Gardner. He had no intention of having Sylvia around to distract him. In April 1951, he came home one night, told her he wanted a divorce, and locked himself in his room. Once he had made up his mind, there was no turning back, no discussion, no argument. That was that. Sylvia talked to his friends, who were blunt. It was all wrong to turn his life around so drastically, they said—to change the ranch he loved, to crate Carole's knickknacks, to keep him away from the woods and streams, to remove his guns, criticize his clothes, and allow her relatives and friends to invade the privacy he treasured.

Sylvia admitted she had been warned, but she felt uneasy being surrounded by memories of Lombard.

She was reminded that Carole had changed for Clark. She had never fished or hunted, worn britches or camped in the rain. Who knows if she liked spareribs or canned beans? She was smart enough to know that whatever made him happy would make her happy. Through it all, however, Carole never lost her identity.

Sylvia hoped it wasn't too late. She asked their mutual friends to intervene. "Please talk to him," she pleaded. "I love him very much."

Gable refused to discuss it. He wanted Sylvia out of the ranch as soon as possible. She left for Nassau hoping he would change his mind. When she returned, all the locks had been changed. Lady Ashley was locked out, and the servants had instructions not to allow her inside. On May 31, 1951, she filed for divorce in Santa Monica, and left for Hawaii the next day with the Vanderbilts on their yacht *Pioneer*.

Ava Gardner and Clark Gable resumed their close relationship in *Lone Star*. She was seeing the very married Frank Sinatra, who could not break away from his family ties. MGM was furious over the public affair that was causing such a sensation. Ava had a toughened attitude toward life. She resented Sinatra's stalling while she received threatening letters and phone calls from irate people who referred to her as a bitch, a homewrecker, and a whore.

Gable had aged considerably and was drinking heavily throughout the film. A rumor that he was in the first stages of Parkinson's disease persisted because his head shook uncontrollably. Ava's heart went out to him. She handled Clark gently and calmly. They lunched together and discussed their "fuckin'" problems, which seemed endless. Spencer Tracy dropped by and helped them laugh through their sorrows. Ava told him about a scene where she walked happily down the street after spending the night with Gable. "Schary cut it out," she complained.

Tracy said, "Yeah, since Dore took over, nobody gets laid at MGM."

Gable was in his favorite element. Both Spencer and Ava were good for the soul, he said.

On June 22, 1951, midway through *Lone Star*, L. B. Mayer resigned.

"Christ!" Gable moaned.

"You don't like Dore-e-e?" Spencer joked.

"From Mayer to Schary's like going from shit to manure."

Ava had been at the studio only ten years, but she was hardened and one of the boys. They could talk freely with her. In fact, she made Tracy's hair stand up straight more than once. He, of course, could take anything—even the dialogue in *Lone Star:*

GABLE: You're a lot of woman . . . you're a strange woman but a lot of woman.

GARDNER: You know, you're a strange man, but quite a lot of man.

After that scene, Tracy said he'd meet them for lunch—off the set.

Ava concentrated more on Clark than she did on her lines. He was bloated, overweight, and the wrinkles were more pronounced. The makeup people said, "Gable doesn't look like Gable anymore." Ava didn't think so. Gable would always be Gable, she said. But Gardner? How long would she survive the drinking, the late nights and heavy affairs? Was she worried? Not because of vanity, but the camera was cruel and the public was crueler. Hell, why did men grow old so gracefully? Gable was one, she thought—the gray at his temples, the sheepish grin, and the twinkle in his eyes. She turned on the charm and praised him, knowing someday a young actor would look at her and say, "Gardner doesn't look like Gardner anymore." Ava protected Clark, pretending that his head didn't shake during the love scenes. And she made him feel like the man she knew he was.

When *Lone Star* was finished, Ava found Sinatra and the press waiting. Gable had compassion for her, but business occupied his time. Knowing that Schary's taking over meant more problems, he signed with the most powerful agent in the country—MCA. Then he called Sylvia to pick up her things at the ranch, but she stalled. He knew what that meant. She was holding out for a reconciliation or a huge settlement, so he took the situation into his own hands. After drawing out all his money and throwing it into a suitcase, he left for Lake Tahoe, Nevada, and checked into the exclusive Glenbrook Lodge. He established residence and filed his own divorce suit in October. When the lodge closed for the winter, he moved to the Flying M.E. Ranch in Carson City. By law he could not leave the state of Nevada for more than twenty-four hours. Friends drove down for a visit with his guns and fishing equipment. He had his license plates changed and settled down for the required six weeks in Carson City, where he met Natalie Thompson, a pretty young brunet divorcée. Thinking he had outsmarted Sylvia, he was feeling pretty good until he received word that Jerry Geisler, Sylvia's attorney, obtained an injunction against his Nevada divorce action. Clark was advised to come home and wait for a trial date. Natalie followed him to Beverly Hills, and they became a steady couple.

Gable's harem had disbanded. Virginia refused to speak to him. Dolly and Anita were enjoying themselves in the East. Joan Crawford was still around and willing to see him, but the Lady Ashley drinking spree showed a very weak streak in Clark. She had her own professional problems. As for the one-nighters—well, that was Gable's style. Natalie did not last long. He might have pursued her one more time if she had stayed in Carson City. Clark was eager to get his divorce over with and to restore the ranch's decor back to the way it was before Hurricane Sylvia, and get that "goddamn good motion picture that will get me out of this slump."

It was a brighter day when he could look into his gun room and remember how proud he was of it. The antiques were crated and Carole's possessions brought back into the house and placed according to her wishes. This was home, and no one would try to change it again. The servants and Jean were more comfortable, too, when the ranch was back to normal. Clark was back on the plow, playing with the dogs and caring for the other animals. He was not able to get to the Rogue while negotiations with MGM were going on and, of

course, there were phone calls back and forth from attorneys on both
sides. He was anxious to do a film with Ava Gardner right away. Joan
Crawford wanted him for *Sudden Fear*, but RKO told her Gable was
too expensive these days. She went into a rage when Jack Palance got
the part, but he helped get her a third nomination for an Oscar. She
lost, and blamed that on not having Gable as her co-star.

Clark's fifty-first birthday was a quiet one. Jean and a friend
baked him a coconut cake. Laughingly they agreed it was better than
the chicken-and-dumplings party last year.

He didn't get Gardner for his next film. It was a big disappointment. She was about to marry Sinatra but there was hope of getting
her for *Mogambo*, the remake of *Red Dust* that was in the talking
stages.

During the MGM negotiations, Clark heard from Sylvia's attorneys. She had broken an ankle and was in Doctor's Hospital in New
York City, but willing to discuss the terms of the divorce. At first
Clark refused to see her, and then he changed his mind. When he
walked into Sylvia's hospital room, they were all over each other
again, his lawyer said. "Clark and Sylvia were like two kids," he
explained, ". . . laughing, joking, gabbing. I wanted to get the matter
of the settlement over with. It got to a point I thought they were
going to call the whole thing off! They were having a great time
telling jokes, calling each other by their silly affectionate nicknames.
They didn't care about talking business. After an hour of this kidding around, I reminded Clark we had a dinner appointment. He
told me to go on back to the hotel and he'd be there shortly. I had to
call him several times and he was still with Sylvia. Finally he showed
up all smiles. He said everything would be all right. . . that Syl
wouldn't make any trouble. She wanted to be fair."

On April 21, 1952, Clark met her in Santa Monica Court, where
she received an uncontested interlocutory divorce decree and a
$150,000 settlement, to be paid over a five-year period. In all fair-
ness to Lady Ashley, she could have gotten much more. Sylvia
wanted him back and hoped by proving she wanted "almost" nothing
from him, he might realize her unselfishness. The scene in the hospital room was more her doing than his, and he played the game to
the hilt. When it was all over, he refused to discuss Lady Ashley—
as if their marriage never existed. The amazing Sylvia married
Prince Dimitri Djordjadze when the divorce was final. She was more
satisfied with a title, and this time around Sylvia scored.

• • •

It was actor Stewart Granger who spoke to Dore Schary about the remake of *Red Dust*. Following the very successful *King Solomon's Mines*, Granger wanted to return to Africa with *Mogambo*. Schary went ahead with the script, but decided it was Gable whose career was in danger. He sweetly told Granger that several months away from his wife, Jean Simmons, might jeopardize their marriage, and "besides, Gable needs all the help he can get right now." It wasn't that simple, however. Schary told Clark he would get his wish—Ava, big-game hunting, and *Mogambo*. Gable was delighted, but Schary wasn't finished. "The Mau Maus are rebelling," he said, "so there will be a delay."

"Don't you think we should get started before they go on the warpath?" Gable asked.

"Yes, but we haven't found the right location as yet, nor have we cast the part of Linda."

"Then I'll go up to the Rogue."

"No, you'll go to London and make *Never Let Me Go*."

"That's a good title. Sounds like my life. Why me?"

"Do you want *Mogambo*?"

Gable smiled. "Sure, but I have to pay a price. Is that it?"

"Look at it this way, Clark. Gene Tierney will be your leading lady, and if you make the film, there's a big tax break in it for you. From England you'll have time for a vacation before reporting to Africa for *Mogambo*."

"Yeah."

Two weeks after his meeting with Sylvia in court ("She should have paid me alimony!"), Gable sailed for France on the *Liberté*. In Paris he met a tall and beautiful Schiaparelli model, Suzanne Dadolle, who offered to show him around. She was blond and twenty-seven and, yes, she resembled Carole Lombard. Clark felt that his life was turning around. He loved Paris in the springtime, was falling in love with Suzanne, and was very elated to find the *Mogambo* script waiting for him at the Hotel Lancaster. As he read over the dialogue, he thought about the nude Jean Harlow inside the crude rain barrel and how they laughed despite her life with Paul Bern and his suicide. The Baby needed someone to love her so desperately, and Clark tried. How silly and young they were through it all. Some things never changed. He was still drinking too much and loving too hard, but Clark was content for the first time in years. Beautiful

Gene Tierney was waiting for him in London, Ava was preparing to leave for Africa, and he was dancing in the streets with a young French girl on Bastille Day.

His friends had to sit down when he wrote home that he had given Suzanne a huge topaz ring. Gable raved about Dadolle. He was captivated, but how many French girls did he have in his long list of girl friends? "Clark was a little boy," a friend said. "He just never grew up. She fascinated him because she was European. I never asked him what she thought about his shaving the hair off his body because it looked dirty to him. Europeans like body hair. He told me the boys in the Air Corps were shocked because he shaved his chest so often and took numerous showers a day. Clark had a thing about looking dirty."

Though Gable had been stationed in Europe during the war, he had been in an alcoholic daze—the frightening missions, his dreadful choice of women, as if punishing himself for Carole's death, his raging temper when the wounded lay suffering, the dreaded fear of going home to an empty ranch and the wrath of L. B. Mayer. How many lifetimes ago was it? Walking in the Paris sunshine, it never happened. Europe had few scars left. They were there, of course, like the ones he had. But he felt carefree again—not interested in Dolly's society friends or Elsa's parties. They had their place in his life, but Sylvia had taught him a good lesson. It's nice to visit the grandiloquent, but not to live with them.

In mid-June Clark checked into the Dorchester in London to prepare for *Never Let Me Go* with Gene Tierney, who played his Russian ballerina wife. Gene, recently divorced from designer Oleg Cassini, was traveling with her mother, who was an observant lady. On the set she told her famous daughter, "You could have Gable if you set your mind to it." Gene wasn't interested at the time, having been introduced to the one man who was more charming than Clark Gable and could back it up in the bedroom with no rival—Prince Aly Khan.

"I knew Clark was vulnerable," Gene said. "We had dinner one evening and he told me how much he loved and missed Carole Lombard. I found him to be tough on the outside and gentle on the inside. He had a quality that was hard to resist, but my mother was too anxious. I don't think she realized Clark always romanced his leading ladies. He and I laughed about our beginnings in Hollywood. We both had physical drawbacks that might have kept us off the screen—my teeth and his ears. We had a good laugh about that. He was a thoughtful man. My feet were blistered from extensive ballet lessons, and he remembered to bring back some salve from Paris that helped a lot."

As was Gable's pattern, if he couldn't bed down his leading lady, a bit player would do very nicely. He hated the damp weather in London—one good reason to lounge in front of the fireplace in his Dorchester suite when he wasn't filming. Then there was Spencer Tracy, who needed a drinking companion while he waited for Katharine Hepburn to arrive in London. On weekends Clark joined Suzanne in Paris. Regardless of his generosity and consistency with her, he was not the easy-to-get guy who had to endure seven painful years after Carole's sudden death. Impulsiveness had cost him $150,000 (maybe more, depending on his salary, because Sylvia received a percentage) and one of the worst years of his life. Gable would not change his old habits of drinking, smoking, and going to bed with women, but he was more cautious than ever where a buck and a preacher were concerned.

He ordered a custom Jaguar, which arrived when he was doing an outdoor scene in the outskirts of London. With the camera still rolling, he grinned and rushed into the rain for a ride in his new car. It was a strict policy that the stars did not drive themselves to and from the studios, but the look on Clark's face convinced the director to go around the block a few times. "It was such a relief to see Gable truly happy again," he said. "It took me a while to recover from that short spin in his new Jaguar, but I knew he was more concerned about the car than my life."

When *Never Let Me Go* was finished, Gene Tierney apologized to Clark for turning down the part of Linda in *Mogambo*. "I can't bear to be away from my baby, as much as I'd like to see Africa," she explained. "Six months is too long." They talked about the newcomer who would do the part of Mary Astor in the first version. It was Grace Kelly, who had appeared in only two films, *Fourteen Hours* and *High Noon*.

Clark had dinner with Joan Harrison. Then he disappeared for a few days with Betty Chisholm, who was renting her Arizona house to spend time in Beverly Hills. "You can stay at the ranch," he suggested.

"I'd love to," she said.

• • •

On September 20, Gable flew his Jaguar to Paris, picked up Suzanne, and drove to the Villa d'Este on Lake Como, where they stayed for three weeks. He promised Suzanne to let her know when he was coming back, stored his beloved car in Rome, and flew to Nairobi on November 2, 1952.

Ava, who arrived with Frank Sinatra on their first wedding anniversary, insisted on a party in their suite. On this occasion, Clark Gable was introduced to his other co-star, twenty-four-year-old Grace Kelly, who was about to take on her first leading role. She wanted to do *Mogambo* very much, for three reasons—Clark Gable, Africa, and director John Ford. She flippantly said to a friend, "I'm going to do a picture in Africa with *old* Clark Gable and *old* Ava Gardner directed by *old* John Ford." Louella Parsons, however, wrote in her column that Gable was Hollywood's own king of hearts. "He's not always agreeable," she said. "He's not a fast man with a buck. He is frequently lazy and doesn't like to give interviews or dress up for parties. He often takes a snort too many. But his warmth, charm and simplicity make you forgive him anything. He's still the great lover on and off the screen."

Grace forgave Clark for being old the minute they were introduced. Sinatra didn't. He had accompanied Ava because he didn't trust her alone with Gable. John Ford didn't trust anyone. The Mau Mau guerrilla campaign against the white settlers was not as threatening as the stars he was going to direct.

Ava had never been married for one whole year before, and her anniversary blast set the pace for the next six months. It was more of a get-acquainted party than a happy first. The battling Sinatras were precisely that. Two weeks before arriving in Africa, it was a free-for-all in Palm Springs when Frank walked into his house and found Ava with Lana Turner. There are two undocumented versions of what happened. One is that Ava was in bed with Lana. The other was that Frank overheard them comparing bedtime stories about their mutual ex-husband, Artie Shaw. Frank went crazy and demanded that the two women leave the house. Their violent quarrel frightened neighbors who called police. They found Ava and Frank fighting in the driveway, and Lana screaming for help. Sinatra called off his trip to Africa, and Ava drove off alone in her car. Earl Wilson made a plea to Ava from Frank in his column and the couple reconciled . . . again.

In Nairobi, he gave her a mink coat for their anniversary. Ava tossed it aside. Gable's teeth almost fell out. "I'd never let a woman treat me like that," he whispered to a friend. The fact that Sinatra was flat broke, owed $100,000 in back taxes, and had no job prospects had everything to do with Ava's reaction to the fur coat. She had paid for his trip to Africa, a diamond ring from him to her, and the mink coat.

Gracie, as her family and friends called her, had never been away from home before without a chaperone. She prepared for this trip halfway around the world very carefully. This was apparent the first night at dinner, when she spoke to the waiter in Swahili. Clark pretended to be impressed, but he considered the performance rather juvenile—even trite. The English-speaking waiter sighed, and Gable puckered his lips quizzically. The tall, slim blonde had class underneath that Swahili act, he said to himself, but no way is she Philadelphia Main Line. If anyone could tell the difference between the bluebloods and the nouveaux riches, it was Gable. This gal was the latter.

The main topic of conversation was the Mau Mau infiltration. "Women carry pistols in their pocketbooks," he said. "The white residents can't trust their servants these days."

Kelly was blasé about all that. She wanted to know why he accepted the role of a man having an affair with a married woman.

"Because, my dear, the relationship between Linda and Victor does not go beyond infatuation."

"I didn't get that impression," she said, peeling a banana.

"Victor is a white hunter who plays by the rules on and off safari."

"Do you play by the rules, Mr. Gable?"

"Clark . . ."

"Do you play by the rules, Ba?"

He puckered up and grinned. "Did you call me 'Pa'?"

"B-A. Ba . . . Swahili for 'father.'"

"I'm old enough to be."

"Ba has nothing to do with age, necessarily," she explained. "It refers to one who is admired and respected . . . like *bwana* means . . ."

"Boss." He smiled.

"Yes," she said, studying his face. "Would you like my *ndizi*?"

"I've never turned down an offer like that in my life."

She handed him half of her banana.

"Thanks." He grinned.

"Do you plan any hunting while you're here?" she asked.
"I'm looking forward to it."
"May I join you?"
"This is very dangerous territory, my dear."
"I don't frighten easily."

Gable looked into her aqua eyes. She didn't blink. Interesting girl, he concluded . . . smooth tawny skin, sculptured nose with sensuous nostrils, perky lips, and thick yellow hair pulled back from her square jawline. She was very much like Carole. "Where did you learn to speak Swahili?" he asked, studying her face.

"On my own. Do you know what *mogambo* means in English?"
"I haven't the vaguest."
"It means passion."
"Does it!" He cheered, lifting his drink for a toast.

"So you see"—she smiled, avoiding his eyes—"there *is* more between Linda and Victor."
"That depends on one's interpretation of passion."
"You're rather old-fashioned about not making love to married women on the screen . . ."
"Maybe little girls from Philadelphia think it's old-fashioned, but I call it professional."
"Referring to your image?" She laughed. "Hollywood amuses me. Holier than thou for the public and unholier than the devil in reality."
"How many films have you done, Grace?"
"Two."
"That explains it. After a few more, you'll be as holy as I am."

Grace Patricia Kelly was born on November 12, 1929, in Philadelphia, Pennsylvania, of German and Irish descent. The Catholic Kellys were not Main Line or eligible for the *Social Register*. Grace's father was a bricklayer who borrowed $7,000 to go into his own brick contracting business. When he married, Jack Kelly was working on his first million.

After graduating from high school, Grace attended the American Academy of Dramatic Arts in New York City. She resided at the very proper Barbizon Hotel for women, did some modeling, and was the "Convention Girl for Old Gold Cigarettes," but refused to show her legs or pose for lingerie ads.

Grace was barely twenty when a family friend arranged a date with the Shah of Iran. They went to the smartest nightclubs in New York and were seen together every night. It all went swimmingly for Grace until word got out that she was collecting the jewels of a princess. Mother Kelly was furious. She told her daughter to return everything, but Grace retorted, "One does not insult royalty!"

Despite the pressure from her parents, she kept the diamonds, pearls, and gold jewelry from Van Cleef and Arpels, moved into a small apartment in Manhattan House at East Sixty-sixth Street and Third Avenue, and appeared in Denver summer stock theaters. Hollywood director Fred Zinneman thought she'd be perfect for Gary Cooper's Quaker wife in *High Noon*. Looking for a new face that radiated purity, Zinneman was convinced Grace was it when she wore white gloves to their interview. It is interesting that he would choose a twenty-one-year-old to play the bride of Gary Cooper, who was approaching his fiftieth birthday, but the contrast proved to be one of the human aspects of *High Noon*—the tired marshal who appeared much older than his years and the virginal Quaker bride whose religion forbade killing. Cooper won an Oscar, and Grace was barely noticed. After seeing herself on the screen, she was disillusioned. "I think I'll resume my acting classes in New York," she said.

Her first serious love affair had begun in Denver with actor Gene Lyons, who was trying desperately to get his marriage annulled so he could marry Grace in the Catholic Church. The Kellys did not think he was worthy of their daughter—a situation that would repeat itself often. One of Grace's friends said, "She was outgoing and very passionate. There was a lot brewing inside of Grace. She didn't bother with just anyone because she knew exactly what she wanted to do and no one was going to stand in her way. However, she did not take her affair with Gene lightly. They were a happy couple, but after six months in Europe and Africa, Grace came home a different person. Gene started to drink heavily and died an alcoholic. His one claim to fame was a supporting role on the 'Ironside' television series."

But in 1951, Grace was in love. She and Gene would become famous on the stage and settle down in Manhattan. Meanwhile, a well-known movie director was about to change all that. He was John Ford, the rough, gruff, and abrasive bull who told John Wayne what he could do with his horse. A veteran director of westerns whose rude and uncouth manner could not be ignored, Ford was not exactly tactful or softspoken. After looking at several screen tests of starlets, he ran Grace's again before calling her agent in New York. "I'm looking for Kelly's type," he bellowed. "You know, the frigid dame that's really a pip between the sheets. I'm referring to the role of Linda, not Honey Bear. Film's *Mogambo*, and Kelly will have to get her ass off to Africa soon if she tests well for the part. She's got potential as an actress, and what she doesn't have, I'll get out of her."

No one had told Grace she could act before. "Everything was so clear working with Gary Cooper," she said. "When I looked into his face, I could see everything he was thinking. But when I look into my own face, I see absolutely nothing. I know what I'm thinking, but it just doesn't show. I wonder if I'm ever going to be any good. I want to make my face show."

Gary Cooper was divorcing his wife for the love of actress Patricia Neal during *High Noon*. It was a confusing and depressing time for him, but his part of the marshal was just as disturbing—one reason he carried the part off so well. Known as "Studs" by Hollywood insiders, Cooper had a reputation similar to Gable's—falling in love or having an affair with his leading ladies. Grace was not one of his conquests. "She was a refreshing change from all those sexballs," Cooper said. "I thought she was pretty and... different, well educated, and came from a nice family. She was eager to learn, saw and heard everything. I think they chose her for *High Noon* because of her inexperience. They needed a woman in the background, if you know what I mean."

When *High Noon* was edited, most of Grace Kelly ended up on the cutting-room floor. It didn't matter, because the film went on to win four Academy Awards and she became part of this classic western.

"I'm not anxious to act in films," she said. "I prefer the reality of the stage and performing in front of an audience. Hollywood thrives on freaks. Beautiful stories are dissected... filmed out of sequence. Actors are trained robots who stand on markers and perform for the camera. Sometimes the end is filmed before the beginning. This is not feeling. It's strictly business. The stage is art. I have no intention of being imprisoned by a long-term studio contract. Once you sign your name, you're nothing but a puppet."

She agreed to test for *Mogambo*, but her agent warned Grace that if she got the part, it might involve a seven-year deal with MGM. "If you should do well and the movie clicks, the studio has every right to profit from your next film," he said.

"I've already given that horrible prospect some thought," she replied, looking down at her notes. "You'll tell them I'll sign providing I don't have to do more than three films a year, with the right to work on the stage."

"Is that all, Grace?" He laughed.

"I'd do just about anything to work with Clark Gable."

She got the part of Linda and a seven-year contract with MGM starting at $750 a week, with a limit of three films a year and the right to appear on the stage at reasonable intervals. She flew back to New York, got her shots for typhoid, paratyphoid, tetanus, cholera, smallpox, and the deadliest of all, yellow fever. With a touch of all six, she sweated it out in bed. It was worth it. This was the chance of a lifetime, and then the phone rang. It was her agent. "Bad news," he said. "Actors Equity won't grant you a permit to work in Africa."

"I don't understand."

"*Mogambo* is an MGM British production, and aside from John Ford and three principal stars, the entire cast and crew has to be British. Due to your lack of film credits, Grace, you're not a principal star."

She was crushed. "Isn't there anything you can do? What about John Ford? He knows everybody."

"And everybody knows him! Grace, this is the union. If they want an English actress, that's the way it will be."

"Clark Gable should be able to use his influence. He's in England right now doing a film."

"Let me tell you something about Gable. He got *Mogambo* because he's on his way out. If he doesn't impress his fans with this one, the guy's in trouble. Frankly, I think he is anyway, but there might be some demand for him if *Mogambo* succeeds. I'm really sorry about the permit, Grace, but we're working on both sides of the Atlantic to get it."

"I wish I'd known before I got those dreadful inoculations!"

Gene Lyons was nearby to cheer her up. He wanted the best for Grace and wasn't concerned about her attraction to "old" Clark Gable, but the strange African continent changed people. Some grew up, some grew old, and some went mad. Ernest Hemingway said there were no exceptions.

Meanwhile, Virginia McKenna, a well-known British actress, who had originally tested for the part of Linda and turned it down, was approached again. Within a week, however, Grace got her permit and boarded a plane for London—the beginning of a forty-eight-hour journey from England to Italy to Cairo and Khartoum, Africa.

When she finally arrived at the New Stanley Hotel in Nairobi, Grace soon forgot her jet lag when Ava's phonograph could be heard blasting from her suite. The door was open, so she looked in and said hello to everyone. Clark Gable asked her to sit down and relax. "Long trip." He smiled. "Bumpy?"

"Quite."

"Yeah, I flew into a storm. The hailstones were as big as my fist. The damn plane had dents all over. Scared the hell out of me."

"But you were in graver danger during the war. I would think you'd be immune by now."

"I don't like to fly anymore. Almost didn't accept this assignment because of it."

"I was so anxious to get here, nothing mattered. This is such a charming hotel."

"Yes, isn't it, but you'll only see it after dark, my dear. Every morning we all fly to the preserve at Mount Kenya, sixty miles from here, for shooting."

"Game?"

"No. *Mogambo.*"

She laughed and asked for another glass of wine. Gable made himself a double Scotch and swirled the ice cubes with his forefinger. "I didn't mean to frighten you, Grace. The compound is very impressive. It ain't the Stanley, but for us, it's pretty fancy camping."

"I must tell you that I fell in love with you in *Gone With the Wind.*"

He grinned sheepishly. "They all did, kid, but for all the love in this world, I don't get a dime."

"Not a percentage?" she gasped.

"Sad, but true." He scowled, to the tune of Sinatra's *All or Nothing at All* on the phonograph. "Never go for the quick money. You'll regret it for the rest of your life."

"Why didn't you insist before you agreed to play Rhett Butler?"

"Not that it's any of your business"—he winked—"but I wanted a fast divorce."

"To marry Carole?"

"Yes . . . but do me a favor and don't spread the word around about my not getting a piece of the action. I don't want anyone to think I'm dumber than I am already."

They had supper in the dining room with other members of the cast. Grace ordered for everyone in Swahili while Clark watched with amusement, knowing the waiter was British.

The next day they flew to the MGM location settlement near Mount Kenya. While the plane was making its descent, Gable told Grace, "This landing strip is eighteen hundred yards long. It was literally hacked out of the jungle."

"And what are all those tents?" she asked.

"Home, my dear. Home sweet home for the next few months, but those tents are upholstered and quite lavish. Thirteen of them are dining rooms. Over there is the movie theater, an entertainment section with pool tables, and a hospital with an x-ray unit."

He made sure she was comfortable in her tent, complete with hot and cold running water. "Around back are two large oil drums," he explained. "The one propped over a wood fire is the hot."

"A fire near my tent?"

He smiled. "The flames will keep the lions away at night."

"That's very amusing, Ba."

"Nothing to fear. Roaming around someplace are a hundred and seventy-five whites and three hundred and fifty natives, all part of the film unit. Then there's a great guy by the name of Bunny Allen, the great white hunter. You'll like him."

"And what is that?" she asked, pointing to a truck coming into camp.

"Native women."

"I thought you said we already had three hundred and fifty."

"We do, but they're all male." He laughed. "You see their wives stay home and do the menial work. This is quite a treat for them, Grace. They'd rather earn a few shillings by just standing around than working in the fields. They've come a long way."

"How?"

"In this film they're allowed to speak."

"Do you know what I think?" she asked.

"What's that?"

"You're a male chauvinist."

"I think you're right!"

John Ford's target on the first day of filming was Ava. He was setting the groundwork for what he expected from each of his stars. Since he and Ava spoke the same language, Ford treated her like dirt, criticized her unmercifully, and used vile language. When she had enough, Ava spun around and gave it all back to him, using a few blue words he hadn't heard. Then she stormed off the set. Those who had worked with Ford were very surprised when he followed her. "You're damned good," he said sternly. "Take it easy." In those few words Ford expressed his admiration for Ava. She understood him after that. He knew about her bitter bouts with Frank and was aware she might be pregnant, but he refused to pamper anyone. If she came to him for help, Ford would be the first to give it to her. In his opinion, no other actress could play Honey Bear, the stranded American showgirl who wanders into the white hunter's camp—and bed. To get the fire and gaiety out of Ava, Ford wanted her to know she could handle the part without trying so hard.

At the start Grace complained about the Sinatras. "They fight all the time," she told Gable. "I wish their tent weren't next to mine."

He grinned. "I bet they have a great time making up."

"I hear that, too."

"Frank's down on his luck, you know. I hope he gets that chance to test for Maggio. That's all he thinks about... besides Ava, of course."

"He's such a grand singer. Why would he want a part like that?"

"Because he *is* such a grand singer, Grace. All he needs is one small juicy part. That's all."

"I suppose it's none of our business"—she sighed—"but I hear everything and..."

"Look, if you want to tag along when I go on safari with Bunny, it's okay as long as he doesn't object."

"And Ava?"

"Ava hates killing of any kind. Besides, she loves to sleep until cocktails." Then he looked at Grace and asked, "Are you sure you want to go hunting with me? It's dangerous. Bunny and I have enough to do without worrying about a novice."

"I wouldn't want to be in the way."

"We'll see," he said thoughtfully.

"What more can I ask?" She smiled, taking his hand. They strolled along the banks of the Kagera River and did not try to hide their growing attraction to each other. If Sylvia hadn't soured Clark, he might have been more enthusiastic over Grace, who had already made up her mind she wanted Gable. Since Ava was the only other white woman for miles except for a few technicians' wives, he had no choice. Nor did he have anything to lose. Those in camp who knew him when Carole was alive, were reminded very much of their happiness whenever Grace called him "Ba," which sounded so much like Lombard's "Pa."

They flew back to the New Stanley Hotel for the weekend. Clark gave a surprise birthday party for Grace. She was deeply touched despite his casual remark, "Any excuse for a party!" Ava was all for that because Sinatra was flying home to test for *From Here to Eternity*. Ava paid for his round-trip ticket and watched him leave with mixed emotions. She had reached a stage of loving and hating Frank at the same time. Not long after his departure, Ava's health declined. She was nauseous every day and suffered from the heat. When she finally collapsed in a faint, Ford suggested that she fly to London. She checked into a clinic with a severe case of anemia, according to MGM officials. Ava told friends she had a miscarriage and was brokenhearted that she could not have Frank's baby, but there was every indication that she had an abortion. A cast member overheard her admit she had no intention of having Sinatra's child because their marriage was pure hell. Either way, it was a very difficult time for her. Ava was a time bomb and Ford knew it. When British officials put in a formal complaint about Ava's walking around nude in front of the native boys who prepared her bath, Ford tried to keep it from her, but Ava found out, took off her clothes, and ran through the camp in front of everybody. Grace glanced at Clark, who lit a cigarette. "Anything wrong?" he asked casually.

"No . . ."

He leaned back in his chair, put his feet up, and asked, "Do you remember that mama hippo charging our canoe in the river the other day?"

"How could I forget it?"

"Ava was alone in another boat. She might have been killed. And do you recall the rhinos that charged the truck? She didn't scream or panic or complain. Well, those are the things that are important. Ava's brave. Right now she's a bewildered girl having some harmless fun."

"I'm not sure I agree, Ba."

"I'm not so sure I care," he said sternly.

Grace found out that it was Ava, who was the sophisticate—the happy-go-lucky girl—who wept inwardly but never gave up. She was also Clark's pal and had been close to him for a few years. Alone and unchaperoned for the first time, Grace grew up fast in Africa. If

Gable did not respond to her femininity, she'd approach it differently. She got up early to be with him even when she wasn't filming. "Why do you do it?" he asked. "It's hell to bounce around in a tin wagon with nothing but mosquitoes and heat and God knows what. I have to do it, but you don't."

"I don't want to miss anything," she exclaimed. "I want to have stories to tell my grandchildren. That's why I want to go hunting with you and Bunny."

"Do I have a choice?"

"No."

"That's your answer."

It was as if they were playing scenes from *Mogambo*—he the white hunter and she the proper plain girl. She takes a walk into the jungle and he searches for her frantically. He finds her near a waterfall. She slips and he grabs her. They kiss. Unspoken love.

Maybe Grace thought she could reenact this scene. She stayed behind one day when he went on location. He returned and couldn't find her. She was not at the hotel. Told that she had gone for a walk toward the sea, he wanted to know why someone hadn't stopped her. "We were told not to wander off alone with the Mau Mau guerrillas everywhere!" he shouted, taking the path in the direction she had supposedly gone. He found her by the sea. She was sitting on a rock reading Hemingway's *Snows of Kilimanjaro*. He wanted to shake the life out of Grace, but he noticed tears in her eyes. "It's so beautiful," she sighed. ". . . Hemingway's leopard in the snow, and then I saw a lion walking along the seashore . . ."

"A lion!"

"Yes . . . a beautiful lion . . ."

"And you weren't afraid?" he asked, sitting down next to her.

"No. It was so moving. I had no fear at all."

"Neither did the lion, my dear. Promise me you won't go off alone again. Do I have your word?"

She didn't answer.

"Then you'll come along with me," he said, putting his arm around her. "I don't mind. I don't mind at all. As soon as my guns arrive, we'll go on safari, but for Christ's sake, Grace, don't go out alone . . ."

They sat by the sea together until dark. Observers said this was a common occurrence. She read to him from Hemingway's book and he recited poetry for her. They were like an old married couple. A member of the cast said, "Gracie was very plain. She wore frumpy clothes and her glasses and no makeup. She and Clark often had their meals alone or they'd sit in the lobby together. Grace kinda followed him around. He'd get up from his chair and she'd get up from hers. She was more attracted to him than he was to her. This was fairly obvious. I never saw Clark doing anything to impress her. He hugged Grace, but he kissed and hugged Ava, too. Clark was flattered, I think, that Grace was madly in love with him. He always held her hand when they took long walks and she'd lean against him. We all thought there was a chance they might get married. She resembled Carole, of course—blond hair and all—but she wasn't as easygoing and witty. Clark liked spunky women, and Grace was hardly that. She was smooth and intellectual."

It was taken for granted that they were "practically living together." Louella Parsons wired Clark about the romance, and he replied, "This is the greatest compliment I've ever had. I'm old enough to be her father. She's only a kid."

Grace had no comment.

Neither did John Ford. He couldn't care less who was sleeping together so long as they got to work on time. He was unsympathetic to the palsied trembling of Gable's head and hands, particularly apparent during love scenes. Clark knew when his timing was off, and Ford was blunt about the problem. Clark took it. He had to. But he did not have to socialize with the director, who wasn't tactful about his embarrassing affliction.

Ford referred to Grace as "Kelly." He bellowed when she acted according to the script. "Don't you have any instinct, Kelly? We're doing a movie, not a script!"

When he had a party for the British Governor of Uganda, Sir Andrew Cohan, and his wife, Ford's joke on Ava backfired. "Why don't you tell the Governor what you see in that hundred-twenty-pound runt you're married to?"

"Well," Ava replied, "there's ten pounds of Frank and there's one hundred and ten pounds of cock!"

Everybody, including the governor and his wife, thought it was hilarious. Ford was the only one who was shocked. He paled, in fact. Gable cherished Ava at times like this. He laughed the loudest at her description of him. "Clark?" she said. "He's the sort of guy if you say, 'Hiya, Clark, how are ya?', he's stuck for an answer."

Sinatra returned in time for the holidays. He had gotten the part of Maggio in *From Here to Eternity,* which eased the tension and was cause for celebration. He surprised Ava with noodles and all the ingredients for her homemade spaghetti sauce. She and Grace borrowed evening gowns from the wardrobe tent for Christmas Eve. The generator broke down, but there was only laughter in the darkness. "We ate by candlelight," Gable said. "I thought it was a very warm and romantic setting. Ava's sauce was the cause of the breakdown, but worth it. On Christmas Day I found one of my socks hanging on the tent. Grace had stuffed it. We trimmed the tree, sang Christmas carols with the natives, and had a holiday dinner flown in by MGM—turkey, Christmas puddings, champagne, and plenty of whiskey. Ford recited 'The Night Before Christmas'—something we never expected. We were family and it was a nice feeling. I'll never forget it..."

Soon after Christmas, they finished filming at Kagera. While the new location was being set up, Clark asked Grace if she'd like to spend a weekend at a beach resort on the Indian Ocean. "It's cooler at Malindi," he said, "and we can swim without crocodiles. I've been told it's a very beautiful spot."

"I'd love to," she replied. "Do you mind if Ava and Frank come along? I think they're on the verge of reconciling, and this just might do it."

Gable was noticing a gradual change in Grace. Was she actually giving up a rare opportunity to be alone with him for a few days? Had she developed compassion for those who had problems far beyond her comprehension? Not one to delve into women's psyches, Gable liked the new Grace and found himself getting involved more than he expected.

The two couples were forced to take an old plane to Malindi. "'Old' is a feeble word for it," Clark said. "The damn thing was held together by baling wire, but it was the only available transportation. The others didn't mind, but I had a long, long talk with the pilot, who assured me there was nothing to worry about. I kept thinking about the four of us—maybe the hottest properties in Hollywood—taking a chance like this. MGM would not have been happy."

Frank and Ava took advantage of the peaceful setting and kept to themselves. The hotel was small, cozy, and romantic, the view of the Indian Ocean soothing, and the cool breezes were a refreshing change from the heat and humidity of Tanganyika. Gable acknowledged Grace's love, which he assumed was only a crush. They had shared the harshness of Africa, been together under very unusual circumstances, most of them far from glamorous, and relied on each other's company almost exclusively. They swam together in the sea, walked along the soft beach, and watched the sun rise from their veranda. Grace was not a girl who fell in love easily. This was not an idle affair—a fact that Gable was forced to face and think over very seriously. She did not want it to end, and, to his surprise, neither did he.

Clark had made up his mind never to marry again, but if he did, his wife would not be twenty-seven years younger. He was growing tired of one-night stands, tired of hassling with MGM, and very tired of paying alimony. But there would always be the lingering loneliness that waited for him at the ranch when the good times were over. He knew only too well that the tender moments in Malindi were not real. The beautiful and sensual days with Grace were shared in another time and space. She was a passionate girl who gave of herself totally. Clark gave, too, but he had not seen many white girls for over two months. She was available. This was a record for a guy who had never been faithful to any woman for that length of time.

One of the crew said, "I think Gable was bored. He liked variety in women. Grace wasn't his type at all. If we had been in civilization, I don't think he would have given her a second glance after the first night. She had absolutely no personality when she arrived in Nairobi. John Ford made an actress out of her and Clark Gable made a woman out of her. Grace Kelly wasn't a star and she hadn't been around. Clark was used to gals who could get the best out of him. He wasn't pampered, but working in the jungles of Africa for such a long time was a new experience for everyone. It drew people close together—people who wouldn't bother with each other normally. I think it was a miracle we all remained friends when this movie safari was over."

Rumors about the Gable-Kelly affair were in the gossip columns almost daily now. Whether it was the intimate trip to Malindi or their constant togetherness on location, definite word leaked out that they were in love. MGM was giving Grace an enormous publicity campaign in preparation for *Mogambo*'s release. Her role in *High Noon* was built up, emphasizing her part as Gary Cooper's wife. They predicted she would be a major star after *Mogambo*. Movie fans recognized her picture in magazines and newspapers. Many were with Gable. MGM took advantage of the romantic gossip, and Clark did not protest or deny anything.

From the lovely beach resort, the cast settled into the desolate

Isoila desert country in Uganda. The waterholes were safe for swimming, and camel transportation was great fun. The last filming location was in Samburu country. It was almost time to leave the Dark Continent. Grace said she wanted to make the most of it.

"Not in Samburu territory," Clark exclaimed.

"Don't be silly."

"What do you know about these savages?" he asked.

"They're seven feet tall."

"Yeah, and they live on blood and milk."

"Not human blood, I hope..."

"I suppose they've had some of that, too, but their main diet is the blood of cattle. They shoot an arrow into the neck, drain some blood, plug the hole with mud, and go on to the next animal. Dracula is a saint compared to them."

"How interesting..."

"No long walks, Grace."

"I'll stay with you, of course. What I don't understand is why we're forced to go there."

"Because of the setting and regardless of their strange eating customs, Bunny says the Samburu won't bother us. Stay in camp. I don't want to lose you now after all we've been through."

She took his arm and put her head on his shoulder. "I don't want to lose you, either. Remember that, Ba."

"I'll call you when I get to London," he said.

"Aren't you flying back on the same plane?"

"I have to stop off in Rome for a few days."

"Why?"

"To make arrangements for my car to be shipped to England."

Ava, sitting nearby, apparently noticed tears welling in Grace's eyes. "Know what?" she chirped. "I think we should all stop off in the Holy City for a few days. That's what we'll do, Gracie—fly to Rome with Clarkie and Johnny Ford. While Frankie's in hulaland making *Eternity,* you and I'll have some fun. It's all set."

Gable scowled. "I'm not sure Grace wants to keep up with you, babe."

"Who asked you?" Ava teased. "Could it be you don't want her to keep up with me?"

He grinned. "Possible."

Grace beamed. "I'm looking forward to it. How long will it take us to finish filming in London? Any idea, Ba?"

"Ford's anxious to wrap things up by April, depending on the goddamn weather. I'm going to help him with the film editing, but at best we'll be in London for about three months."

The girls had a great time in Rome. Ava knew the right places to go—primarily out-of-the-way bars and cozy restaurants. Grace's eyes were opened a little wider, and by the time they got to London, she and Ava were very close friends. Clark decided to stay at the quaint Connaught Hotel to avoid reporters and the British MGM publicists, who booked Grace at the luxurious Savoy. Ava rented a house in Hyde Park Gate and kept open house day and night. Robert Taylor, her co-star in *Knights of the Round Table*, dropped by. At almost any hour someone was sitting on the floor having a drink, including Grace, of course, who was already beginning to hate being a studio contract player with an endless schedule of interviews and meetings. She clung to Ava and to Clark, who by this time was anxious to see Suzanne Dadolle in Paris. Because of his effort to help Ford with last-minute details, he had to cancel several engagements with her.

Gable resumed his heavy drinking in London, claiming that it was the only way to tolerate the damp and chilly weather. It was not unusual for him to finish a bottle of cognac before dinner and still walk straight. Robert Taylor said that the first time it happened, he was very concerned. "We had no idea he had that much to drink," Bob said. "When he left Ava's and drove off in his Jaguar, we noticed the empty bottle that no one else had touched. I called the hotel and he was just fine . . . didn't know what we were so concerned about."

Grace had seen Clark drink in Africa, but not like this, and she wondered if it had anything to do with the fact that *Mogambo* was almost finished. They dated frequently in London, and for her April came too quickly. "Can we fly back to New York together?" she asked.

"I'm sorry, Grace, but I want to see more of France and Switzerland. The studio's arranging for me to do a movie in Holland."

"Why didn't you tell me?" she asked, fighting back tears.

"Because I didn't think it was important, my dear."

"What a terrible thing to say!"

"Grace, this may be my last chance to see Europe. When I was your age I didn't know the Riviera existed. A strange-sounding place to me was Oregon. I didn't know what it was to live in a house, and now that I have one, it's meaningless. So you tell me, why should I rush back?"

"We've been together for six months, Ba."

"And now it's time for you to concentrate on becoming a good actress, because at the premiere of *Mogambo* you'll be a star. And remember the difference. And don't let any guy stand in your way. Keep your eyes open and your nose clean."

"I can stay in London for a while . . ."

"That wouldn't work out," he said, pouring himself a stiff drink.

"I've always wanted to see France . . ."

"What happened to the girl who knew exactly where she was going? The girl who told MGM what she wanted and got it? C'mon, babe, now's the time for those sacrifices and press conferences and mobs of people begging for your autograph."

"I read somewhere that you hated all that and refused to do it."

He laughed. "Yeah, because I couldn't speak the King's English, that's why! And I had two wives old enough to be my mother. You've got style, Grace, and getting through the preliminaries will be fun for you. As for me, I don't want it."

"But you're Clark Gable. People have the right to see you in person."

"They do," he said, taking out his false teeth. "And this is what I show them if they get overbearing!" He dropped them into his glass of Scotch, stirred the drink with two fingers, and put them back in his mouth. "That, my dear, is the King!"

On April 15, 1953, Gable drove Grace to Heathrow Airport to catch a plane for New York. Reporters were everywhere, but he ignored them as he led Grace to the gate and gave her a fond hug and kiss. She burst into tears and sobbed bitterly. He whispered something to her; she hesitated, kissed him again, and rushed to the plane. There were many accounts of this farewell, but they all agreed that Grace Kelly was very much in love with Clark Gable. She did not want to say good-bye, but he showed no emotion. Only kindness.

A few weeks later he was in Paris with Suzanne Dadolle, his traveling companion. In May he received word that his divorce from Sylvia was final, and friends held their breath. If he had sent Grace Kelly home and rushed into Suzanne's arms, was the French girl going to be wife number five? She told the press, "*Oui.*"

And that was the end of Clark's affair with Dadolle.

Grace went back to Gene Lyons, but dropped him for the debonair French actor Jean-Pierre Aumont, her co-star in a television special that summer. Conflicting acting commitments separated them, but only temporarily. Two years later they would resume the affair. Grace went to Hollywood, settled down in an apartment, and started work in Alfred Hitchcock's *Dial M for Murder* with Ray Milland. He was twice Grace's age and married, but he fell head over heels in love with her. Within a year, she became involved in her fourth affair, but this one was the scandal of Hollywood. Milland left his wife and MGM stepped in. Grace didn't care. She was nominated for best supporting actress in *Mogambo,* and Hitchcock wanted her for his next movie, *Rear Window.* The Kellys flew to California to talk to Grace, who listened with deaf ears. When Mrs. Milland filed for divorce, Grace fled to New York and Oleg Cassini. The Millands reconciled.

In October Gable was in Holland for *Betrayal* with Lana Turner, who was honeymooning with husband number four, Lex Barker. She felt bad about Clark because whenever they co-starred he was going through a major crisis. First it was Carole's death and then his sad homecoming from the war. Now it was a much older Gable, with his girth showing and his days numbered at MGM. Insiders knew the studio was not going to renew his contract. Turner did not discuss the delicate subject with him, but she knew it was just a matter of time for her too. "The studios could no longer afford us," she admitted. "We were all frightened."

Actually, Gable quit MGM when they would not agree to his terms. He demanded a salary increase and a percentage of the profits on each picture. They turned him down. The only deal was a separate contract for *Betrayal.* He returned to the ranch before Christmas 1953, a very unhappy and angry man. His last movie summed up his relationship with the studio he had been with for twenty-three years —betrayal. He fumed over not getting a share of the profits from *Gone With the Wind,* a $100 million grosser. He asked MGM for a copy of the film. They put a price of almost $4,000 on it. Gable was furious. He had the money, but it was the principle, and he refused to lower himself.

He had the tax advantage after twenty months in Europe. Money was not a problem and never would be again. Decoration of the ranch was finally completed. There was no evidence that Sylvia had ever lived there. The horrid pink bedroom was now a cool pale green, the living-room furniture was reupholstered with fabrics Carole had originally chosen, but whatever was left of Lombard was in good taste. There were no shrines any longer.

Betty Chisholm was one of the guests at the intimate welcome-home gathering at the ranch. Clark spent the holidays with her. He was still bubbling about Africa, and wore his safari outfits on hunting trips. His household staff remembers the day a rattlesnake was curled up and hissing on the grounds. Clark was summoned. He quickly changed into his African wardrobe, grabbed a rifle, and killed the rattler with one shot. He was quite proud of himself.

Gable was a fine hunter, and though he always was in Bunny Allen's company on African safaris, there was one occasion when a crocodile posed a threat to the crew and Clark took aim and killed it instantly. He surrounded himself with mementos from the Dark Continent. A jeep was upholstered in a zebra skin he had brought back with him. His friends got quite a chuckle when they saw him tearing up the roads and flying over bumps in his new toy.

Spending almost two years in Europe and Africa had been good for Gable. It helped him face the day he packed up his belongings at MGM, put them in the Jaguar, and drove through the studio gates for the last time. Howard Strickling and Dore Schary wanted to have the traditional farewell party, but Gable declined. He had lunch with a few studio friends (lower echelon) and laughed about things he had almost forgotten. Nothing heavy or important, and the drinks flowed. "Strange how it all happened," he said. "I never should have gotten this far. Here I am, though. *Mogambo's* a hit and I don't have a job." When someone reminded him that he was on the list of the top ten most popular movie stars he said, "Yeah, figure it out. I don't know how to begin again because I really can't say how it all started. But I feel free. This much I know. I'd like to produce my own stuff and want Grace Kelly for my leading lady. You know, Hitchcock saw her in *Mogambo* and that was it! I have good vibes about Grace. I'm proud of Ava, too. Who woulda thought she'd be nominated for best actress, huh? Two great gals—but they'll never know the Golden Era. The MGM family was like any other family—always bitching and complaining. It was tough, but looking back we were the exceptions... Lionel, the Baby, Joanie, Myrna. And how about Loretta on TV? She's got guts. No one really knows Loretta... all that prim-and-proper religious jazz isn't her. She has more balls than

Joanie. Well, it's over . . . nobody to tell me what to do, how to do it, and when to do it . . ."

Gable released the following statement to the press:

> I am discontinuing my long-term association with MGM after being with the company for more than twenty years, in order to avail myself of the opportunity of entering the free-lance field. I want to express my great appreciation to the many friends and associates of MGM whose help I have had and with whom I have had the pleasure of working. I wish also to pay tribute to my friends and associates who are no longer alive whose help and guidance over the years meant so much to me.

Clark went for the jugular with that last line—paying tribute to those at MGM *who were no longer alive.* His reference, of course, was to Irving Thalberg and maybe, in the deep recesses of his heart, Louis B. Mayer. But most certainly he did not want to express any gratitude to Dore Schary.

Instead of fishing the Rogue, Clark chose to play golf with Betty Chisholm in Phoenix for a few weeks until Grace returned to Hollywood. Clark saw Grace regularly at the Bel-Air Hotel, where they weighed the possibility of sharing the future. Beverly Hills was not Nairobi, however. The strong attraction was still there, but Clark wanted to retire in a few years, and Grace was on the brink of a brilliant career. They appeared at the Academy Awards together. The press went wild, even though Grace lost to Donna Reed in *From Here to Eternity,* which was also voted best picture. Grace was delighted when Frank Sinatra won an Oscar. She said this made up for her loss. Reporters described her as "cool" and unconcerned. Ava, who lost to Audrey Hepburn in *Roman Holiday,* did not attend the awards because the Sinatras were getting a divorce. After she completed *The Barefoot Contessa,* Ava established residence in Nevada, where Howard Hughes waited for her. He was unaware that the most distinguished bullfighter in Spain, handsome Luis Miguel Dominguin, was following on a later plane.

Ava was known for her love affairs and her three tumultuous marriages, but Grace Kelly was the symbol of virginal white when she met Gable—a romance that did not change her image. The danger to Ray Milland's marriage wasn't highly publicized. Nor did anyone know that she and Bill Holden had a "brief fling" during *Bridges at Toko-ri.* Holden was "wild about her." Then along came

Bing Crosby, who didn't want Grace as his co-star in *Country Girl* until he met her. "She's really something," he told Bill Holden.

"Yes, she's an exceptional actress."

"I'm referring to the girl herself. I'd go for it, but I understand you and she are—"

"Were," Holden interrupted. "There's not a guy breathing who wouldn't be attracted to Grace."

Bing asked her out, but she always brought along a girl friend. He considered Grace one of the women in his life who attracted him most, but the feeling was not reciprocated.

During Grace's flings, Gable was somewhere in the background, but a friend of hers said, "She couldn't take his false teeth." When asked by reporters why she and Gable did not consider marriage, Grace replied, "It might have worked out if it weren't for the difference in our ages."

Grace won the Oscar for *Country Girl*, and almost married Oleg Cassini and Jean-Pierre Aumont before becoming Her Serene Highness, Grace Patricia Grimaldi, Princess of Monaco, in April 1956.

Two years previously, she had given Clark a Mexican burro named "Ba."

Gable and Bob Taylor were both divorced and playing the field in the early fifties. Their hunting trips together usually included dames as well as game. Ralph C., a very close friend of Bob's, said they had great times. "Six or eight of us would pile into several cars and take off late in the afternoon," he related. "There was nothing fancy about these trips. We wore old clothes, drove station wagons, and didn't bother shaving. One of our favorite spots was high pheasant country in Idaho. Bob and Clark were fast drivers and always in the lead cars, sometimes an hour ahead of the rest of us. By the time I reached a town along the way, there were no girls or booze left. Picking up waitresses was an old habit. Sometimes these girls knew the boys were coming, but Gable likes variety. Most of them had no idea who he was. Taylor had a problem because he was exceptionally good-looking. He pulled his hat down to his eyebrows and had a five o'clock shadow. So did Gable. Since we traveled after dark to make better time, it was more conducive to picking up girls, too, without their being recognized.

"We were like a bunch of kids. The whole idea was to have fun, do a little hunting and fishing, lots of drinking, and have some harmless fun with girls. The only rule was no shop talk.

"One time we were driving through Idaho. There were four cars —Taylor on Gable's tail and the rest of us trying to keep up. I was alone and had a flat tire, which can be a lonely deal on a highway in Idaho. I got it fixed and then stopped at the first roadside inn I came to for some coffee. I asked the waitress if my hunting buddies had been there."

Ralph said she glared at him and replied, "Two bums with mustaches and one with a beard?"

"Yes," he replied. "What time did they leave?"

"About an hour ago."

He told her about his flat tire and asked if there was a gas station nearby where he could have it patched because he didn't want to continue on without a spare.

"Everything's closed," she said, "but I think your friends are still in town."

"Where?"

"There's a motel about ten miles from here . . ."

"A motel?" Ralph exclaimed. "But we're not spending the night here!"

"All I know is that they left the bar about an hour ago with three girls."

"What's the name of the motel?"

"There's only one," she said. "The sign says 'Motel.'"

Ralph followed her directions and found the broken-down place, which reminded him of the one in *It Happened One Night*—little cabins and a registration office the size of a small bathroom. He saw the station wagons and waited. Gable finally came out of one cabin with his arm around a woman.

"Hey, Ralph!" he yelled. "Mind taking this gal home while I get the others ready to roll?"

"I can't go without a spare."

"Leave the car here," Clark said. "We'll pick it up on the way back. Right, honey?"

The girl was delighted, nodded, and then got into Ralph's car. "She was a dirty blonde," he said, "and reminded me of Zasu Pitts. She was a real milkmaid. While I was driving her home, she promised to keep an eye on my car and have the tire fixed."

"Billie said you'd be back this way day after tomorrow," she told Ralph.

"Billie?"

"Your friend."

Ralph remembered that "Billie" had been Gable's nickname when he was a boy.

"Are you a movie stunt man too?" she asked.

"No, just a friend..."

"Billie must live an exciting life in Hollywood, meeting all those stars..."

"Stunt men take too many chances. Dangerous job, you know."

Ralph listened to the girl, who had no idea she had just spent an hour with Clark Gable.

By the time Ralph got back to the motel, the others had returned to the roadhouse and were having a few drinks. "Taylor was sitting at a corner table taking a nap," he said. "He could sleep anywhere anytime, snooze for a little while, and get up completely refreshed. Gable was having a good time with the local crowd and another dame that could have been my mother. She wasn't bad-looking, but I wouldn't have touched her with a ten-foot pole. I stood next to him at the bar and he introduced me to her. 'This is Constance,' he said. 'She's from up Oregon way. We were just discussing how beautiful the country is up there. Have a drink, Ralph, and then we'll be goin'.' He gave Constance the same line. His name was 'Billie' and he was a stunt man."

She asked him questions about Hollywood, and though Ralph had heard conversations like this before, it made him nervous. Gable could have claimed he was an accountant or a doctor or a dentist. "That would be asking for trouble," he explained. "People always have an angle. They don't mean to, but it's only natural. If I were a dentist, she'd ask about an aching tooth. An accountant brings up the subject of taxes. The doctor bit is the worst. Everybody likes a free diagnosis. I tried the old salesman routine once. What did I sell? I said that I sold insurance. Forget it! It took me hours to get that girl into the hay. A stunt man doesn't take much explaining, and if I should make a slip about somethin', I'm pretty much covered."

He told Constance, "No one sees my puss in a movie. I do long shots, kid. I'm supposed to resemble lots of people... same weight, and height, hair coloring. That's important for realism."

"What big stars have you worked with?" Constance asked.

"...Cooper, Bill Boyd, John Wayne..."

"How exciting!" she said, swigging beer and chewing on a wad of gum.

"Not really."

"What about Van Johnson or Peter Lawford or Clark Gable?"

"They never do any rough stuff," he said, adjusting his old hat.

"You're too tall to double for them anyhow," she said. "I hear most of the movie guys are short."

"Not like Mickey Rooney." Clark smiled. "He's only five feet tall, you know."

When she went to the ladies' room, he looked at Ralph and laughed. "They always think we're short."

"You taking her to the motel?" Ralph asked.

"It's getting late. If we're gonna get to the lodge before daybreak, guess I'll have to skip this one."

Clark told Constance he'd see her on the way home. Ralph wanted to know what he intended to do with two girls. "You can be nice to the other one." He laughed. "After all, she's doing you a big favor by looking after your car."

"She's not my type."

"What the hell does that mean?" he asked.

"I couldn't make love to her."

"Goddamn it, Ralph, get with it! What's the difference? She wasn't bad and she didn't ask any questions. I'm tellin' ya, country girls are great. Just great."

"So I hear, but I tell Bob that someday he'll be recognized and get into a lot of trouble."

"Not likely. Look at us. We're a motley group, for Christ's sake. I looked at myself in the mirror back there at the motel and almost threw up. If anyone recognized me, Ralph, I wouldn't let them. I swear to God, I wouldn't let them know who I was."

They got to the lodge in time to do some pheasant hunting, went to sleep for a few hours, had lunch, and played poker, and then Clark suggested that they take a drive to a bar and grill. "It was a nice place," Ralph said. "They had a pool table, a dance floor, jukebox, and plenty of action."

Gable watched two girls come in and sit down at a table. One was a blonde with blue eyes and a magnificent figure. He went over and asked if he could buy them a drink.

"Get lost!" the blonde said.

"My dear, we're just a couple of hicks trying to be friendly."

"Who the hell do you think you are?"

"Nice girls don't talk like that."

"Nice boys take off their hat!" she exclaimed.

He smiled. "Apparently you haven't spent much time with hunters."

"I know what you're hunting for, and I'm not interested."

"If you change your mind, babe, I'll be at the bar."

Clark was amused, but she was a challenge and didn't take his eyes off her and she knew it. He waged a bet that if she stayed for any length of time, he'd win her over. Taylor laughed. "She's got class, Clark, and your fingernails are dirty."

They made their bets and waited. Clark tilted his hat back, and that was when she noticed him. He turned on the grin and charm. All he needed was a glimmer of encouragement, and she gave it to him when she went the long way to the powder room.

Ralph said he'd never forget that night. "We were always doing something crazy—always making bets on something. I knew damn well Clark would win this one if he had to reveal his true identity."

The girls ended up at the bar. He apologized for not shaving. "How was I to know someone like you would show up in this joint?" he said.

"Don't you ever take off your hat?" she asked.

He winked. "I didn't bring a comb."

Gable was so anxious to win the bet, he kept buying one more round of drinks. When they were all feeling no pain, he made his pitch. The gorgeous blonde smiled and said, "You must be kidding!" and left. Taylor was laughing so hard, Clark slammed his fist on the bar. "I'm not paying the whole goddamn bar tab!" he said.

"You were the generous one," Bob teased. "Pay up your bets and settle with the bartender."

"It's too early to go back to the lodge."

Ralph said it was unlikely he'd find a girl like the one who had walked out on him.

"Who cares?" Gable laughed. "Just as long as she's breathing."

Ralph got the impression that Clark wasn't overly concerned about being recognized. "What he feared most was a woman making fun of him behind his back. He could never live up to his reputation as a lover. Knowing Taylor so well, I can verify it's hard for a virile male idol not to prove himself with the ladies. They're supposed to fool around. It's expected of them. They didn't believe the studio buildup, but it was difficult to ignore. They tried to be themselves, but after a while some of it rubs off. Bob was framed by a girl in

Rome. He was having an innocent affair with her and his wife, Barbara Stanwyck, flew to Italy for a showdown. She went home and filed for divorce. Bob tried to keep a low profile, but the girl was waiting for him when he was leaving for the airport. She brought the press and threw herself in his arms for the big farewell. He was helpless. Their picture appeared in all the newspapers and that sealed his fate. This was the kind of thing Gable dreaded, but he was a very lucky man.

"I didn't envy Bob and Clark . . . one reason why these hunting and fishing trips were good for them. They could be themselves, or try to, anyway."

Clark saw a good deal of Betty Chisholm. She stayed with him at the Encino ranch and he enjoyed visiting her in Phoenix. The weather influenced him—the hotter the better. He hinted that one of the reasons he did not follow Dolly O'Brien or Anita Colby was due to the cold weather in the East. It depressed him. The dry heat of Arizona appealed to Gable and was in Betty's favor.

Virginia Grey never forgave him for marrying "Lady Ashcan," but allowed Clark back into her life. Adela Rogers St. Johns remained close to him, too. Joan Crawford's door was open, but she was dating the vice-president of Pepsi-Cola, became Mrs. Alfred Steele in May 1955, and relocated in New York City.

Gable's stable was thinning out and there were no champions in the running for wife number five. The loneliness waned with age and so many disappointments. Time and money weren't important. If he couldn't find a good script (in the fifties they were rare), he had many hobbies to keep him busy, and there was always Europe. Booze was still a big part of his life, day and night. It would be until his death. Hunting, fishing, and golfing took up much of his time, but the greatest accomplishment was Dore Schary's desire to have him back. Every time Clark turned them down, MGM raised the ante. "Rub it in and see how high you can get those sons of bitches," he told his agent. "And when you get their very best offer, tell them to shove it up their ass."

Schary came through with a $500,000 offer that was flatly and colorfully refused.

Twentieth Century–Fox wanted Clark to read *Soldier of Fortune*, and he liked it. He signed a contract for two films, $400,000 up front and 10 percent of the profits. Clark wanted Grace for his leading lady in *Soldier of Fortune*, on location in Hong Kong.

"I have a prior commitment," she said on the telephone.

"Cancel it. Hong Kong's worth it."

"Oh, I wish I could, Ba. We were meant to share exotic places together."

"Do what you can," he said.

"I would never tangle with Hitch."

"You'd better watch yourself, babe. He's a genius, and that makes him the sickest of all."

"I know he's strange, but . . ."

"Strange? Grace, he hates women. He uses them."

"Would you have me turn down *To Catch a Thief*? It's marvelous, and I'll be on the French Riviera. Do you remember the Riviera, Ba? You refused to take me there."

"Grace, *Soldier of Fortune* is just as good. You can go to France anytime, but Hong Kong?"

"Sorry, darling. And please don't worry about Hitch. I can handle him!"

"I don't doubt that, babe!"

Twentieth Century–Fox signed Susan Hayward as Clark's leading lady.

"Who?" he asked.

When he met Hayward, Clark remembered her well. He scowled. "I used to stare you down at parties and never got a nod."

"Not me!" she exclaimed.

"Yes, you!"

"I'm as blind as a bat," she said. "Why didn't you come over to me and say something?"

"Not without some kinda look. Know what I mean?"

"You bastard!" She laughed. "Friends said you couldn't keep your eyes off me and I didn't believe them."

"I just never got around to finding out who you were," he said.

"From what I understand, names are unimportant to you." She winked.

Several witnesses claim that whenever the two stars were at the same party, Clark did indeed notice Susan the minute she entered a room. He couldn't remember why he never followed up, but considered her a rare beauty. When they finally did get together, she was involved in a custody battle with her estranged husband, Jess Barker, and could not leave the country. Clark filmed *Soldier of Fortune* in Hong Kong. Scenes with Susan were shot in Hollywood. "I guess we met too late," he told a friend. "We've both been stung many times, and I understand she has the hottest temper in Hollywood. I'm too old for that."

When Gable heard that Kay Williams was divorced from her last husband, sugar heir Adolph Spreckels II, and living in Bel-Air, he called her up. Knowing his passion for golf and hot sun, she invited him to her Palm Springs home. Kay and Clark were old friends. The lady, with sparkling blue eyes and shining blond hair, was very wealthy in her own right. Her two children, Adolph III, age five, and Joanie, age three, had million-dollar trust funds. Kay's divorce settlement included half a million dollars. Her oil well wasn't doing badly, either.

Kay's third marriage, to Adolph Spreckels, did not make sense to those who knew her as a well-adjusted, witty lady. Spreckels had a reputation that rivaled Bluebeard's. He had been accused of beating his first wife and arrested for possessing dope. Each consecutive wife (Kay was his fifth) took him to court for maiming her. Kay had her share of pain during the three years she was married to Spreckels, until he beat her unconscious with her own shoe.

Kay was thirty-nine when she came back into Gable's life. They began to date before his trip to the Orient, and she was waiting for him at the airport when he returned just before Christmas 1954. He was satisfied to see only one or two women, and especially comfortable with Kay, whom he had known for ten years.

It is doubtful that Betty Chisholm was a contender, though she seems to have gone out of her way to be with him. Virginia Grey had built her own wall of defense in his company. Robert Taylor remarried, and his wife, Ursula, was expecting their first child. So he no longer saw Virginia. Much like Gable, he had been seeing Ava Gardner and Eleanor Parker not long before he eloped. Unlike Gable, however, Taylor had signed another contract with MGM and would stay on until 1958 as the longest-lasting contract player in Hollywood history—twenty-five years.

In an interview, Taylor was asked what he thought of himself as an actor. "There are two types of stars in Hollywood—actors and personalities. Well, I'm a personality," he said.

"What about Gable, Bob? What do you consider him?"

"A friend who likes to hunt as much as I do."

"Professionally..."

"Professionally what?"

"Do you think Gable is a personality or an actor?"

"Both!"

"Is there any reason why you consider yourself a personality rather than an actor, Bob?"

"Hell, if you've seen any of my movies you'd know the answer to that. People come to the theater to see Robert Taylor, not a good piece of acting. The critics still refer to me as pretty, handsome, and beautiful—a freak. I learned a long time ago to accept myself for what I am. That doesn't mean I'm not tryin' to do better, but I'm also tryin' to catch a bigger fish, just like Gable. That's the way it goes in Hollywood these days."

Taylor lived on a ranch in Mandeville Canyon and had his own plane, which made it possible for Gable to go along on one-day fishing and hunting jaunts. Howard Strickling remained a close friend to both actors and described them as symbols of small-town America. They were unassuming and straightforward, and hated anything phony. A 1954 press interview with Gable echoes Taylor's attitude toward stardom. "I'm no actor," Clark told a reporter, "and I never have been. What people see on the screen is me. I've spent a lot of time learning this business. I don't know how to go about learning to be a personality. No matter what I was, I'd work at being as close to the best as I could get. Not that I am the best, but I try."

Taylor's wife, Ursula, said, "Clark always made a woman feel beautiful."

At the age of fifty-three, he still had the rare ability to tantalize the ladies with his mere presence.

Judy Garland swore it was his blue bedroom eyes and dimpled grin, which age could not diminish. "He was born with it," she said. "Nothing about him was acquired. He drove women nuts on the screen before they knew who he was. When he realized it, he used it to his best advantage. I was only sixteen years old when L. B. Mayer asked me to sing 'You Made Me Love You' for Clark at his MGM birthday party in 1937. Looking at him close up, my knees almost caved in. About ten years later we met at a banquet and Clark told everyone at the table, 'She ruined all my birthday parties. Just when I was startin' to have a good time, in comes this rotten kid with that song. She was a real pain in the ass!' We all laughed, of course, but when I looked at him—and he was almost fifty—my knees almost caved in again. When Clark teased, this was an expression of how much he liked you. I, for one, never got used to seeing him around the studio. It was always a thrill."

There were no more studio parties or serenades by movie brats or well-planned publicity campaigns. A more relaxed Gable was not as shy with the press, but he talked with only those reporters and columnists who had proven themselves trustworthy over the years. More than once he laughed off his reputation as a womanizer. "There are many disappointed ladies who will verify that I'm a lousy lay."

No one could keep *Confidential* magazine in the fifties, however, from digging into the dark pasts of famous people. Clark was no exception, but his former girl friends refused to discuss him. There was Josephine, of course, the impoverished woman who supposedly "created" Clark Gable. The *Confidential* article described him as an opportunist with no heart or guilt or gratitude. Hedda Hopper's version was that Clark hadn't seen his first wife in twenty-five years and wasn't aware of her living conditions. Hedda said she convinced him to "do something about it" and he did. This is doubtful, because Josephine broke their agreement in 1932 by talking to reporters. He did, however, retire the mortgage on her property in his will.

Josephine would always be featured in articles about Gable showing the vivid contrast between the tanned, robust, and rich King of Hollywood and the old wrinkled face of his poor drama coach, approaching seventy. The younger generation found it impossible to believe that this was the first Mrs. Gable.

Josephine might have taught him good posture and the art of walking, but she was all wrong about "I think you should begin to present the man in the story and not Gable. You're trying to take over the whole show instead of giving a show. Think of the character and not of Gable." He did the reverse and became a star. When asked if he regretted leaving the stage, Clark replied, "Yes and no. Life is a series of changes. After the stage came movies, and now television is killing both. I'm not keen on TV and hope to avoid it. As for the stage, there's nothing like it, but I don't think I could face a live audience again. The movies made me what I am, and I'll stay with it as long as the fans still want to see me."

Gable prepared for *The Tall Men* with Jane Russell, Robert Ryan, and Cameron Mitchell—the story of a post–Civil War drive of Texas longhorns from San Antonio to Montana. Clark practiced his riding and roping with Kay in Palm Springs until March, when the cast left for Durango, Mexico. They were greeted by a company of seventy-five people, three thousand head of cattle, and three hundred horses. Clark liked Jane Russell immensely. In the film he called her "Grandma," and the name stuck. *The Tall Men* was a cordial undertaking. Jane had reconciled with her husband, and though she was under contract to Howard Hughes, he allowed her to free-lance with his approval. Maybe Clark doubted her acting, but after a few scenes he told everyone she was "damn good." Jane wanted him for her next movie, *The King and Four Queens.* He read the script in Mexico and said, "I'll do it, Grandma!"

Gable said, "On our first day here, the Mexicans stopped what they were doing and concentrated on Jane. Nothing unusual about that, because the lady is endowed, to put it mildly. She was used to attention, but when the world stopped, Jane got a little uneasy. I asked one of the English-speaking actors how we could get things back to normal. I mean, we couldn't have the whole village making our leading lady feel self-conscious. I found out they were amazed to see a woman wearing trousers. Jane was wearing pedal pushers. She got a big laugh out of it. I don't think many people knew Jane very well. She was a religious girl with psychic abilities, but kept it to herself. There were a lot of pranks we played on each other. The one that stands out is in the scene where I had to carry her out to a carriage. She put a forty-pound weight underneath her petticoats. Jane was a lot of woman. That's what I figured. When I got her to the carriage, she asked, 'Was I heavy?' I told her I knew I had a real gal in my arms, and then she reached underneath her dress and showed me the weights. Jane reminded me of Ava. They had potential, but never the opportunity to prove it because of their enormous sex appeal."

Knowing that Jane had reconciled with her husband during *The Tall Men*, Clark teased her about John Payne, whom she was dating when Clark first saw her at the Hollywood merry-go-round of parties. "Clark was a big kidder," she said. "He'd wait until Robert was nearby and then he'd talk about John. It was all in fun, but if Clark thought he was gettin' to ya, he kept it up. I'm glad we worked together when he was finally at peace with himself. Kay Spreckels came to Mexico to visit him and they were so happy together. He told me they were engaged."

IV
FADE-OUT

CHAPTER TEN

Kathleen (Kay) Williams was born in Erie, Pennsylvania, on August 7, 1916, on her parents' farm. After her marriage to a local boy, she wanted to try modeling in New York City, and with her husband's encouragement, Kay became moderately successful. She enjoyed the company of the fashionable supper-club set and soon outgrew Erie and her husband. Kay married Argentine playboy Alzago (Macoco) Unzue and left him ten days later. She moved to Hollywood and took up acting. Clark dated Kay until she married Adolph Spreckels, heir to a San Francisco sugar fortune. They separated and reconciled many times. Spreckels accused Kay of adultery with Clark Gable. That suit was dropped when the couple got back together. Though undoubtedly Kay had been around, there was a softness about her. She knew how to get what she wanted. If Kay reminded Clark of Carole, there was good reason. When he was in Hong Kong he was asked about his relationship with her and he replied, "Just a friend." She called him long distance and gave him some of his own medicine. "Listen to me, you son of a bitch. Don't do me any favors. It will be a long, long time before I'll marry you!" Carole did not let him get away with anything, and neither did Kay. If Clark was cautious after the disastrous Sylvia, Kay was even more leery. Spreckels tried to beat her to death—an incident not easily forgotten. Then there were her two children, who needed love and guidance following the bitter divorce. Clark spent as much time as possible with them in Palm Springs and told friends he was very fond of Joanie and "Bunker."

On July 11, 1955, Clark and Kay drove across the California line to Minden, Nevada, and were married by a justice of the peace. The bride wore a navy blue suit. Clark did, too, as usual. He called her Kathleen and occasionally "Ma." She called him "Pa." The children and their governess stayed in the guesthouse. Otherwise nothing was changed. Kay did not mind Carole's ghost. She forgot the past and

concentrated on Clark's happiness. "He offered to buy a new house,"
she said, "but I liked the ranch very much. I had my fill of mansions
and palatial homes. Maybe at one time they were what I wanted, but
not anymore."

Because of the children, Clark put his rifles away and converted
the gun room into a den. The Gables settled down to a routine life
that he loved—planting, plowing, and painting fences. Late in the
afternoon he and Kay spent time with the children, but they dined
alone after cocktails. Their social life was as active as he wanted it to
be. There were industry parties he felt obligated to attend, but he
kept them to a minimum. Shortly after his marriage to Kay, there
were many invitations from friends to celebrate the occasion. The
newlyweds made an appearance, left early, and spent the rest of the
evenings alone with a bottle of champagne. Clark's drinking subsided, but he needed more liquor than the average guy. His days of
finishing a bottle of whiskey were over, though friends said he might
revert back to his old habits occasionally. Robert Taylor said, "A man
doesn't change overnight. He might level off. Gable was still adjusting to life without MGM. For example, he wasn't even sure how to
plan a secret wedding. The studio did all those things with plenty of
protection. I had my plane, so eloping was easy for me. Clark complained about being a 'piece of property,' but that had its advantages
and it was very, very difficult to adjust. We were always surrounded
by people. The studio kept us busy with photo sessions, interviews,
meetings, premieres, dinners, publicity tours, fan magazine stuff,
polls, learnin' how to play golf, polo, tennis, ride horseback, handle a
pistol, square dance—you name it. Then there were the star-status
dressing rooms. The bigger you got, the more space you got. Gable
used to say it was for kids, but when it was all over, he missed it. I
did. There was an emptiness inside that would be there forever. I
had the same feeling when I graduated from college, but kids are
supposed to start all over again. When you're in your fifties, it's very
hard. If Clark didn't have someone like Kay, I don't think he would
have lasted as long as he did."

Taylor was right about Kay. She tried to make up for what she
considered "lack of attention and care" that MGM provided for her
husband. It was a joyous day when she told Clark she was going to
have a baby, three months after they were married. Several weeks
later, however, Kay became ill with a viral infection and she had a

miscarriage. Clark was disappointed, but finding out he could father a child was a revelation that meant another chance was very possible. Doctors said Kay, despite a minor heart ailment, was able to have another baby.

The holidays made them forget the loss they suffered. Clark discovered what a difference children could make at Christmas. He told Joanie and Bunker how he went searching for a tree, chopped it down, and lugged it home. No fancy trimmings, however. A string of popcorn and real candles and maybe some homemade paper decorations. His stocking was filled with fruit and candy, and he received only one gift each year. "If it hadn't been for my stepmother, I doubt that I would have received anything," he said.

It had been almost a year since Gable had worked, but he was in the process of forming a production company with Jane Russell and her husband, Bob Waterfield, for A *King and Four Queens*. While details were being worked out, Clark and Kay accepted an invitation to take a cruise on the magnificent yacht owned by shipping magnate D. K. Ludwig. At the end of January they sailed down the West Coast to Acapulco. The weather was bad, however. "All I did was eat and sleep," Clark said. He knew the excess weight would have to come off before starting another picture. Putting on and losing weight was taking its toll on Gable. Though he told everybody how great he felt, Kay knew better. Twice he had such severe chest pains, he had to stop his car and lie on the grass until the pressure subsided. This cured him of speeding. He thought it was a big joke when the police gave him a ticket for driving too slowly. Joan Crawford, who hadn't seen Clark in a while, did comment after his death that she couldn't understand why Clark usually got a clean bill of health after a physical examination. "I heard that he was trembling something fierce," she said. "His complexion was gray, and when he didn't have to stand, he sat down. Clark did not want to give in. That was it. And one reason why he continued to drink and no one can tell me he cut down more than just a little bit. He wasn't a closet drinker, but he'd slug down a few if no one was around. I also heard he had Parkinson's disease, but I never really got any confirmation on that one. Everyone I talked to said he didn't look good, but he was happy as hell. Who said attitude wasn't important?"

In the spring of 1956, Gable, Russell, and Waterfield formed Gabco-Russfield Productions. Clark was disappointed that Jane was not able to co-star with him in A *King and Four Queens*, but he was delighted with Eleanor Parker, who might have been Mrs. Robert Taylor. In fact, she was planning on it and waiting for him on the set of *Many Rivers to Cross* when he suddenly eloped with Ursula Theiss. Parker was Taylor's favorite leading lady, and she complemented him on the screen more than any other actress. Gable was pleased with her too, though Eleanor did not have the spunk he appreciated. Taylor had been in love with her at one time but said, "She makes me nervous."

The production crew who worked on A *King and Four Queens* knew Gable well. One said, "He was a mess. It's a terrible thing to say, but he was puffy and flabby and his eyes were dull. There was no kidding around. In fact, he worked after five because, as he put it, his money was involved. We all hoped he'd give up the idea of trying to produce his own movies, and he did when A *King and Four Queens* left a lot to be desired. He looked much better on film than he did in person. He had a reputation of being a heavy drinker. We assumed he was still hitting the bottle."

When the Gables returned home from the movie's filming location, Kay went into the hospital with chest pains. Clark stayed in an adjoining room for three weeks. The doctor permitted her to rest at the ranch providing she did not climb any stairs. A bedroom was set up for her on the main floor until she was well enough to send Clark off on one of his long-overdue hunting and fishing trips.

Gone With the Wind was released again, and Gable was voted the most popular actor in the United States. "If it hadn't been for that damn picture," he said, "nobody would want me anymore. In fact, they wouldn't even remember who I was." Having his face before the public and his name on marquees across the country didn't hurt his next film for Warner Brothers, *Band of Angels*, opposite his former girl friend Yvonne de Carlo. They barely conversed off-camera until she blurted out a four-letter word. "I purposely acted like a saint in his company," she said, "but lost my composure when some fans got out of hand and I told him how I felt. That eased the tension and we were friends again. His wife, Kay, was fun. She'd be very quiet and ladylike and then come out with something raw. She loved to tell Clark to get off his ass and he'd grin and do it. He loved dirty jokes. That was one way of getting his attention."

• • •

In January 1957 Representative Wayne L. Hayes of Ohio paid tribute to Gable's twenty-fifth anniversary as a screen star, calling him a "hometown boy who made good in Hollywood." The tribute was read into the *Congressional Record*: "Mr. Gable still reigns unchallenged as one of the world's most popular and best-known movie personalities. Time cannot wither nor custom stale his infinite appeal."

The congressman cited Gable's rise from obscurity as an example of "how a young American can advance himself and become famous."

Clark found out that one sure way *not* to advance himself was working for himself. He gave up the idea of producing his own films. The unspoken truth was that he was not a fast study and had all he could do to learn his lines. Worrying about production costs and film distribution and profits and losses was almost as tiresome as balancing his checkbook, and he couldn't do that. When this decision was made, Gable felt and looked better. He told Kay, "Hell, I'm an actor, not a businessman."

"That's not true," she said.

"Are you kiddin'?"

"I think you do very well figuring ten percent of the profits, Pa."

Paramount Pictures wanted Gable for *Teacher's Pet*, a comedy with Doris Day. Clark was cast as a cynical newspaperman, and Doris as a small-town teacher of journalism who mistakes him for an older student. Doris was at the height of her popularity, but unassuming, energetic, and professional. Clark apparently liked her well enough to attend an outdoor barbecue she gave for the cast, without the benefit of liquor. He brought a flask of bourbon. Kay was so impressed with Day's house that she hired the same decorator to "brighten up the ranch." While the work was being done, the Gables went to Del Monte Lodge at Pebble Beach near Carmel, California, where they celebrated their second wedding anniversary. Close friends joined them at a French restaurant in Carmel. Clark's taste in food had changed. He preferred rich gourmet food instead of spareribs and dumplings these days, and his waistline showed it.

Despite twenty-five pounds of excess weight, Gable had a healthy glow. He felt good about life and told a reporter, "I'm a very happy man." When asked about his wife, Clark said, "What can I say about Kay? She's a wonderful woman and the perfect companion. I worry about her health, though. She has angina pectoris. It's not serious, but very painful. Naturally, she has to watch herself. Sometimes it's indigestion, but I worry anyway."

Kay walked into the room as he was talking. She laughed. "When I do the cooking, it's indigestion."

The reporter wanted to know if she cooked often.

"When we're on location," she replied. "We usually rent a house, and it's more relaxing to stay home and have a cozy dinner after a hard day's work. We love to camp out, too, and I always cook then. It's more fun to rough it than get all dressed up and go to a restaurant."

Did she hunt and fish with her husband?

"Yes. At least I try. Clark is a good teacher," she said. "Very patient. We've taken to golf. He plays very well and I'm not bad. We don't get a chance to do all the things we'd like to. Clark is busier now than he ever was. After he makes a movie, we travel across country to promote it. We had a marvelous time during *A King and Four Queens*, filmed in Louisiana. Southern hospitality is very much alive. Clark was mobbed wherever we went. It was fun and very gratifying, but we cherish our vacations."

The interview did not reveal anything personal. They were happy. They were busy. The children adored Clark and he made sure to find time for them. They often talked about selling the ranch and went house-hunting. On his penny-pinching days, Clark reminded Kay that he had bought the property with the idea that it would pay for itself. That didn't happen. "He'd bitch and moan," Kay told friends. "Ursula said that Bob [Taylor] was the same way. Something was always breaking down on the ranch. Clark would grab a hammer and fix whatever it was. The place was too big, the fruit trees blossomed and didn't bear fruit, sometimes the chickens laid eggs and more often they didn't. Then he'd take me house-hunting and we'd discuss putting the ranch up for sale. Even after we had the house all fixed up again, Clark complained that the ranch was too expensive to run. And I knew he didn't have the heart to move. If he didn't have something to worry about, he'd go out and find something."

Gable bought a new Mercedes-Benz 300 SC two-door coupe and ordered custom luggage to match the car's light tan upholstery. Now he had one favorite car instead of many, and the same applied to women. He had an eye for both, however.

In September 1957, Clark co-starred with Burt Lancaster in *Run Silent, Run Deep* for United Artists. On location in San Diego, he

insisted on a submarine ride so he'd know what it was like, since this
he-man picture dealt with underwater warfare. It received very good
reviews, as opposed to *But Not for Me* with Lilli Palmer. Critics were
unanimous about anything Gable did. "He still has it," they said.
"Even if the story's bad, Gable's everlasting charm will keep you in
your seat."

The question often asked was when did he plan to retire. His 10
percent deal was paying off handsomely. He had nothing to worry
about financially. "I'd like to make two or three more films," he said.
"By then I'll be sixty and ready to settle down. When a man has a
family to support, though, it's hard to say. . ."

Gable cut down on his drinking when he got married, but gradually went back to his old habits. He joked about doctors' orders to
slow down, give up excessive drinking and cigarettes, but he drank
more and chain-smoked. "What's the point of living if you can't do it
to the hilt?" was his philosophy.

"I'm a lucky bastard," he told a friend. "They fired Tracy when
he was on location in Colorado. He sat on a rock and cried like a
baby. Can you imagine that? He's the greatest actor in this town.
Everyone in Hollywood will tell you that. He was fired because he
wanted to change directors. Twenty years ago I did the same thing.
Don't know how I got away with it, but I wasn't gonna have that fag
Cukor calling me 'Dear' in front of everybody. Carole thought it was
funny, but she liked gays, you know. I asked her once why she didn't
have any girl friends and she said, 'I do—Billy Haines!' That was
suppose to get to me, of course. Carole could say anything and get
away with it, but not Cukor, so I had him fired. They couldn't very
well fire me. Even Gary Cooper turned down the part of Rhett
Butler because he thought *Gone With the Wind* was going to be a flop!
But MGM kept the faith. Yes, sir! L. B. Mayer died not long ago,
and do you know what he said on his deathbed? He said to Howard
Strickling, 'Don't let them worry you. Nothing matters. Nothing
matters.' I hated his guts, but they kicked him out too, as if yesterday
never existed. So why am I still here? Doesn't figure. I did all the
wrong things . . . the worst was not getting a percentage of *Gone With
the Wind*, but that's how much I wanted to pay off Ria and marry
Carole. It was worth it. What burns the hell out of me is that the
studio didn't offer it to me anyway. I console myself because Carole
was worth it—the millions I lost, I mean. After we got married, I
asked her what she wanted more than anything. We were lookin'

over the property, and she said, "I'd like more manure for the bottom thirty.' She meant it, too. Sometimes I wonder how she'd take things the way they are today, and I always come up with the same answer —with a laugh. She'd get through it better than me. That's what's so strange about life. The brave ones don't make it . . ."

The big question these days was television. Joan Crawford asked everyone in the movie colony to ban the tube. Loretta Young was very successful, and Barbara Stanwyck was waiting for an action-filled western series. Robert Taylor told Clark, "I'm going for it. ABC-TV has offered me "The Detectives." The money's too good to turn down. My bucks are tied up in property. I need the cash, and you know goddamn well there's not a decent script around, not for me, anyway. My days as the knight in shining armor are over, and I know it."

"A weekly show's tough to do," Clark said, "but you've got ten years on me. I don't think I'm cut out for it."

"I don't even own a television set."

"I do because of the kids."

"I'm waiting for Crawford to picket my ranch."

Gable laughed. "She'll back off. She always does. Remember the *Photoplay* awards dinner when she was queen of the ball until that delicious Marilyn what's-her-name . . ."

"Monroe."

"Yeah, until Marilyn Monroe walked in and Joan was left alone with her vodka? That blond dame's dress was so tight, I'm sure she was sewn into it. Her tits popped out like two watermelons, and you know how Joan feels about that! She worries about her falsies showing. Boy, was she mad. She told the press it was the most shocking display of bad taste she'd ever seen. Joanie said, 'There's nothin' wrong with my tits, but I don't go around throwing them in people's faces!'" Gable chuckled. "Methinks Miss Crawford forgot the good ol' days. She knows better than anyone what a gal has to do in this damn town for attention. Anyway, when she found out how the big-titted dame cried all night after reading the interview, Joanie backed off, saying she should have taken 'the poor young thing' aside and taught her good manners. You wait, Bob, she'll give in to the tube, also, and if I had an offer like yours, I'd grab it. What can I say except 'Good luck'!"

"What about you? Any plans?" Bob asked.

"Thought you'd never ask, baby! I'm goin' to Italy and make a film with Sophia Loren."

Taylor shook his head. "I could never do it."

"What?"

"Play opposite a woman half my age. I turn down scripts every day for that reason."

"I think you're wrong, pal, but seems you're doin' okay without my advice."

"Sophia Loren, eh?"

"Times like this I wish I were ten years younger." Gable grinned. "Takes a little gettin' used to."

"You'll be working in Rome, I guess."

"One of the reasons I'm doing *It Started in Naples*. Kay and I would like to see Europe again with the kids."

"I was in Rome for six months with *Quo Vadis*," Taylor said.

"Hell, everyone knows that, babe. Barbara divorced you for bein' a bad boy over there. I can't afford another one..."

"Another what?" Taylor asked.

"Divorce. What didja think I meant?"

"After-hours stuff. Forget it."

"I can't forget it. I just don't do anything about it. These days it's gratifying holdin' and kissin' them and gettin' paid for it. Take Jane Russell. She was there. All of her. Whatever I held, she was *all* there. Like the old man said, 'I get my thrills that way.' Christ, no more divorces. This is it for me. When Kay gets ill, I panic inside. She's the best thing besides Carole that ever happened to me. The thought of losing... well, I don't want to talk like this."

"When you get back from Rome, we'll do some trout fishin'."

"I'm with you, pal."

Gable surprised the world when he agreed to appear with Doris Day at the annual Academy Awards to present an Oscar. They were introduced by Bob Hope as "two of the most popular stars in Hollywood." Gable's dignity and carriage were beyond description. Any rumors that he was ill were dispelled that night. Except for the gray hair and more weight, he looked the same. Or as everyone said, "Gable will always be Gable." His peers were in awe. As for Clark, he was "nervous as hell."

• • •

In June 1959, Clark and Kay sailed for Europe with the children. After a vacation in Austria, he began filming in Rome. *It Started in Naples* was a romantic comedy that did very well. As one critic wrote, "With Gable and Loren on the marquee, who cared?" The two stars got along extremely well. He called her earthy, honest, and very sexy—"All woman!" Reporters were hoping for a romance, but they were out of luck again. It didn't matter if Kay was around or not, Clark adored her and was faithful.

He arrived back in the United States weighing 230 pounds. "It was the delicious pasta," he said. "I ate it every day—sometimes three times a day." Several scripts were waiting for Clark, but he put them aside to look for another house in Palm Springs. "This place will be our home away from home," he said cheerfully. "Golf is good exercise for Kay, and I'm takin' it up seriously myself."

He had put on so much weight, Gable had no intention of working for a while. The manila envelopes remained unopened until he got a call from his agent. "Have you read the Arthur Miller script yet?"

"Since when is he doing screenplays?" Clark asked.

"What difference does that make?"

"I'd like to know before I get involved, that's all."

"I think he wrote it for his wife."

"Who's that?"

"You don't know who Miller's wife is?"

"I get them all confused. Who is she?"

"Marilyn Monroe."

"Come on, pal, I'm not doin' any picture written for a dame. Besides, she's too young. What kinda script is it, anyway?"

"A western . . . sort of . . ."

"What's that supposed to mean?" Clark bellowed. "Sort of!"

"Please do me a favor and read *The Misfits*. If Miller wrote it for Marilyn, he sure as hell patterned the part of Gay Langland after you. Arthur's in town and wants to talk to you about it."

"I'm goin' to Palm Springs for the holidays."

"Clark, read it before you go. Do it as a favor to me, because if you're interested, I want you to talk to Miller while he's in town."

Gable didn't like *The Misfits*. He failed to understand what Miller was trying to get across. He liked the part of the aging drifting cowboy who makes a few bucks rounding up mustangs for a dog-food factory, but Gay Langland was a complicated man. His character had depth and meaning underneath the rugged exterior.

"Just like you," Kay said.

"A little too heavy for me." Clark scowled. "I'm not kiddin' myself, Ma. I haven't for years. The public comes to the movies to see Gable as Gable. They don't want me pulling any tricks and getting serious on 'em. Besides, I'm too old to change."

Those whose opinion he respected, including Howard Strickling, were opposed to Clark's doing *The Misfits*, too. It wasn't only the complicated and soul-searching role of Langland. John Huston, the director, was tougher and more temperamental than John Ford. Then there was the moody method actor Montgomery Clift, who popped pills with his spiked orange juice. No one had to remind him about the reputation of Marilyn Monroe, who was also hooked on drugs and known to lose control. The consensus was that Clark should forget the project. It wasn't for him. If he were going to do two more films and retire, *The Misfits* would be a terrible mistake. If he wanted to end his career in movies on top, there was no point in proving to the world he couldn't act.

While Clark was pondering the pros and cons of *The Misfits*, Marilyn Monroe was falling in love with French actor Yves Montand, who was married to Simone Signoret. This affair would affect Gable indirectly. Marilyn's life with Arthur Miller was coming to an end. They would remain together for the sake of *The Misfits* before getting a divorce. Marilyn, who suffered from insomnia when she was depressed or lonely, did not need sleeping pills during her affair with Montand, whom she wanted to marry. After they completed *Let's Make Love* in Hollywood, she returned to New York first. He followed in a few days. Marilyn reserved a hotel room filled with flowers, hired a limousine, and met Yves at the airport with two glasses and a bottle of champagne. Montand was surprised to see Marilyn. He was in a hurry to catch a plane to France. She tried to convince him to stay. "What about us?" she asked.

"It was wonderful," he said with a kiss. "But that's all it was, Marilyn. Just wonderful."

"I thought it was more than that."

"I'm in love with Simone. Surely you knew that."

It was a tearful scene and, sadly, the press was nearby to see and hear Marilyn being rejected as she held a bottle of Piper-Heidsieck and two empty glasses. Humiliated and shocked, she began a ritual of overeating, overdrinking, and oversleeping. She could never get through *The Misfits*. She'd refuse to do it, that's all. Arthur's story was strange, anyway. If she couldn't comprehend what his message was, how could she memorize her lines... say them with any meaning? She argued with Miller's decision to do the film in black-and-white instead of color. She argued about the depressing theme. She resented her husband's writing such a drab and stupid script for her. "I hate everything about it," she cried.

Then Miller telephoned her about Gable, and Marilyn forgot the heartbreaking affair with Montand, the hatred she had for her husband and the morbid *Misfits*. All she thought about was Clark Gable. "My mother gave me a picture of him when I was a kid. She told me to pretend he was my father and I did. I became very close to that face. Gable became my fantasy. I dreamed of seeing him on the street, but now I'll have him all to myself."

She would play Roslyn, a divorced woman who moves in with the old-timer Gay Langland.

What Marilyn didn't know was that her idol was undecided.

What her idol didn't know was that for *The Misfits* he would be offered more money than any other performer in history.

What neither of them knew was that they would both be dead within two years.

While Marilyn was fighting bitterly with Miller about "that dreadful movie that belongs to you, not me!", Gable was asking for the impossible and getting it—10 percent of the gross, a guarantee of three-quarters of a million dollars, $48,000 a week for overtime, and complete control over the script.

Taylor said, "I did television for one reason—M-O-N-E-Y—and Clark signed to do the Miller movie for the same reason. He could not turn down so much money. That's all I wanted and that's all he wanted. We were movie freaks and it was tough finding work, but Clark was going to show them he was the guy who got more money than anyone else—his way of retiring with great dignity."

The picture was scheduled to begin in March 1960, but Marilyn wasn't ready. Clark went on a crash diet in the meantime, and got down to 195 pounds. He was used to starting a project on time and resented waiting for the call from Reno. There was another factor, also. He liked hot weather, but he knew how unbearable it could get in Nevada during the summer. The original plans were to finish *The Misfits* before August, but the new starting date was July 18. Clark drove his beloved Mercedes to Minden, where he and Kay celebrated their fifth wedding anniversary before settling into their living quarters on location in Nevada. The one-story house had a pool and adjoined the golf course.

Producer Frank Taylor gave a dinner party for the cast. Clark wasn't anxious to attend. "I know it's going to bug the hell out of me to work with those method actors," he told Kay, "but socializing with them is even worse."

She convinced him to go anyway. "Did it ever occur to you they might think you're a snob, Pa?"

"No, it didn't. They should know better."

"They have their world and you have yours. Don't you think it would ease the situation if you met them on common ground instead of in front of the camera?"

"Yeah, I suppose so . . ."

Montgomery Clift and Kevin McCarthy assumed Gable was over the hill. They had little respect for his acting which "had no range." He had made millions by always playing himself. Not much to look up to. Instead of meditating before doing a scene, old man Gable looked at himself in the mirror and played his part without believing he was the character. He was one of the reasons movies were dying.

When Clark and Kay walked into the Taylors' living room, however, the group, including Clift and McCarthy, stood up instinctively. They had no idea he was such a powerful man, in more ways than one. When he sat down, they gathered around him on the floor to discuss Miller's play. He listened to Clift's adaptation of his part of a rodeo cowboy . . . how he got into the mood and how he believed that he was Perce Howland. Gable listened, and when he was asked how he planned to approach his role, he said casually, "I gather up everything I was, everything I am and hope to be. That's about it . . ."

Clark's stand-in, Lew Smith, had known Gable for many years. "He didn't have to explain a damn thing to those kids," Smith said. "He won the battle the minute those amateurs saw him. Clark never lost that magical presence. He was taller than most people thought he was, too. Hollywood always publicized their leading men as being six feet tall, but most of them were much shorter. Gable was over the mark and he had broad shoulders. He never slouched, either. I know

Kay was glad he went to the party, because if there was any doubt who the King was, he proved he was that night by just being himself."

Gable and Clift had one thing in common, however. Neither could pass the insurance physical for The Misfits. Clark had to remain in bed for a week before the doctor signed the necessary papers. Clift was mixing booze and pills but leveled off in order to pass the examination.

Marilyn had nothing wrong with her physically, but her tortured mind bordered on insanity, or so she thought. Knowing her mother had been in a mental institution was frightening for the former bit player, whose new role as sex goddess did nothing for her morale. The Montand affair nearly killed Marilyn. She would never have done The Misfits had it not been for Gable, and now that she was safely entrenched at the Mapes Hotel in Reno with her husband in silent torture, she was terrified at the thought of meeting the King. She might have attended Taylor's get-acquainted party had Arthur gone with her, but he was busy at the typewriter and she was afraid to go alone. On the night before her first scene with Gable, she tossed and turned alone in bed, gulping down Nembutals until an overabundance finally put her into a sound sleep. In the morning, no one could get her out of bed. For two hours Miller, her masseur, and her secretary tried to rouse Marilyn. When she could open her eyes, and after taking several uppers, she could not face Gable alone, knowing she was two hours late. "What will he say?" she cried. "How could I have done this to him?"

Shaking, nauseous, and weak, Marilyn reported for work with an entourage of fourteen. She took one look at Gable and rushed to the honey wagon to throw up. When, at last, she pulled herself together and another hour passed, Marilyn Monroe met Clark Gable.

"I'm so sorry for being late," she purred.

"You're not late, honey." He smiled, putting his arm around her. They walked away from the others. He talked to her softly, and she laughed. "I was in heaven," she told Clift. "He told me I was worth the wait . . . that I was beautiful, sexy, and all he thought I'd be. It would be fun working together . . . if only he were younger, you know . . . that kind of thing. I wanted to tell him he was perfect just the way he was. I adored him. I loved him at first sight."

Clift had switched to grape juice laced with liquor. He seemed interested only in his own well-being. Unsure of himself, bothered by the heat and the sick perfection of director Huston, he wasn't interested in Marilyn's fatal crushes. She found only the little boy in Monty, and the pathetic show began. Gable looking after Monroe and Monroe looking after Clift. Gable trying to resist Monroe and Clift yearning for his boyfriend back in New York. Marilyn knew he was a homosexual, one reason she was comfortable with him. Who else did she have?

Lew Smith said *The Misfits* was a circus, but the cast made up a pretty fair sideshow. "Maybe Monroe idolized Gable like a father," he said, "but she was in there pitching for more. She wanted him, if you know what I mean, and he was a big flirt and tease. He loved to pat her plump fanny, knowing she never wore anything underneath. Or he'd pinch her and whisper something in her ear."

Carefully selected reporters were allowed on the set. Though their primary interest was Marilyn Monroe, she avoided them, much to the distress of United Artists and producer Taylor. Gable offered to fill in for her. "I'm a poor substitute, I know," he said, "but maybe it will pacify them."

The articles described the fifty-nine-year-old King of Hollywood as "robust, weather-beaten, a heavy smoker who never puts a Kent in his mouth without a Dunhill filter. He also likes Cuban cigars with his own labels. He inhales over ten of these a day. He wears a size 40 suit, 44 inches long, has a 36-inch waist and 45-inch chest."

Reporters described Kay Gable as remarkably beautiful with a clear complexion, blue eyes, 5 feet 4 inches tall and richly blond. She looks at her husband as if to say, "Let's go to bed." And he grins back as if to say, "That's what I was thinkin'!"

Gable defends Marilyn to the press, but he won't talk about her. "She's a sensitive girl," he said. "And it's awfully hot here . . ."

She asked him one day, "How can you take it? The mobs of people? The press? I hate it."

"When things get tough, I take out my false teeth, like this"—he took them out—"and do my Gabby Hayes impersonation."

She laughed but looked at him lovingly. Teeth or no teeth, he was the best thing that had ever happened to her. He was known to have affairs with his leading ladies, but not since his marriage to Kay. Maybe this time it would be different. He had to drive sixty miles to and from location every day, and his wife wasn't always around. If she couldn't seduce Clark Gable, and that was all she wanted out of life right now, she'd never sleep again. Her first move was the scene in which she was in the bedroom the morning after she and Gable spent their first night together. He comes in and finds her wrapped only in a sheet. Underneath was a completely nude Marilyn. The scene was repeated several times, with Gable kissing her good morning. "I was so thrilled when his lips touched mine, I wanted to do it over and over," she told her staff. "Then the sheets dropped and he put his hand on my breast. It was an accident, but I got goose bumps all over. Everything he did made me shiver—the kiss, the touch, his eyes. That night I didn't need a sleeping pill, but I dreamed that we did it. God, I was in heaven. When I woke up, I knew I had to have him. Whenever he was near me, I wanted to grab him around the neck and hold him forever. I wanted him to kiss me, kiss me, kiss me. There were times I thought he'd give in—ask to meet me later —but he never did. We did a lot of touching and kissing and feeling. I never tried harder in my life to seduce any man. He was my dream come true. His wife caught us smooching once. I don't think she likes me, but I don't really care. She's got him. I don't."

If Gable was frustrated over not having Marilyn, he was upset about many things. Reno was a wild town, and everyone seemed to be having more fun than he was—picking up girls, gambling, and staying up late until the bars closed. He saw himself a few years ago and wanted to go back in time, do some carousing, spend one wild night with Marilyn, be the envy of the other men, wake up with blurred memories of the empty bottles and the blonde who went back to her own room.

He envied John Huston's wild binges and orgies. He resented the stories in vivid detail every morning. He had done all those things with style a few years ago, but didn't brag about it. Clark Gable didn't have to. "In my day," he grumbled, "I used to take off on Fridays and show up Monday morning for work in my tux. That told the whole lovely story. . ."

Marilyn, when she showed up at all, raved about "Rhett Butler." "Doesn't he look marvelous!" she said. "The other day we were doing a scene and he started to tremble just a little bit. I can't begin to tell you how endearing that was to me. To find my idol was human!"

While she raved about Gable, she ranted at Miller in front of the entire cast. The couple came and went in separate cars and slept in separate suites. And the tension mounted.

On August 26, seated with Marilyn in a station wagon, Gable delivered his lines: "Honey, we all got to go sometime, reason or no reason. Dyin's as natural as livin'. Man who's afraid to die is too afraid to live, far as I've ever seen. So, there's nothing to do but forget it, that's all. Seems to me . . ."

That night Marilyn took an overdose of sleeping pills. After her stomach was pumped, she was wrapped in a wet sheet, carried to a plane, and flown to the Westside Hospital in Los Angeles for ten days. She tried to reach Yves Montand, who was back in Hollywood, but he refused to return her calls.

Bored and restless, Gable began to drink heavily in the 115-degree heat. He sat and waited, waited and sat with his script open, dressed in western garb and smoking one cigarette after another, sipping whatever was around—bourbon, Scotch, or brandy. He watched the men work with the wild horses. It made him sick to watch them limp home at the end of the day. One man was seriously hurt. But he had so much time to observe the cowboys, Clark was convinced he could do most of his own stunts, and no one tried to stop him, including Huston. While his stand-in and the other stunt men stayed helplessly on the sidelines, Clark balanced himself on the hood of a car, rolled across it, and fell to the pavement. In another scene, he was dragged by a truck traveling twenty-five miles per hour. He wrestled with a wild stallion, got snarled in a lariat, and was dragged face down until a wrangler could stop the horse.

Kay knew nothing about this until one night she saw him coming out of the shower. "He was bruised and bloody on one side. When I asked him what happened he said he was dragged on a rope 'by accident.' I told him he was out of his mind."

Whatever pain he suffered was soon forgotten when Kay told him she was pregnant. They wanted to keep it a secret until she had carried beyond the three-month danger period. His attitude changed when he knew he was going to be a father. It made everything more bearable. He called Joan Crawford, who found the news "exhilarating" but noticed his voice was despondent. "Spit it out," she said. "What's wrong?"

"This fuckin' film," he replied. "They're all nuts. Monroe's never on time if she shows up at all, so no one else gets here on time. We don't start shootin' until afternoon, but goddamn it, I leave at five and that's it! The title pretty much sums this group up!"

Marilyn returned to work and Clark greeted her with "Get to work, beautiful." Her tardiness continued, but he quipped, "Why are sexy women always late?" When she did not forget her lines, he kissed her on the lips and whispered, "Thanks." To get a smile out of her, he called her "Chubby" or "Fatso," with a pinch on the fanny.

Marilyn got flustered easily and ran to the honey wagon to throw up. This meant more delays until she changed her clothes and had her hair and makeup redone. Clark recognized the signs, and when he knew she was upset, he took Marilyn away from the others and talked to her. "Just take it easy, honey."

"I have problems," she said. "I'm so sorry..."

"You don't have to apologize to me."

"I could never have gotten through this without you."

"Nonsense."

"It's true. Even on the days I was late, the only reason I came at all was to work with you."

"An honor, honey."

"Did you know I've carried a picture of you with me everywhere since I was a kid?"

He grinned. "With or without a mustache?"

"As Rhett Butler."

"Oh..."

"Do you remember meeting me six years ago?"

He shook his head.

"At the premiere of *The Seven Year Itch*. It was the first time I ever saw you in person. We talked about doing a movie together."

"My dear, after seeing you wiggle both ends in that film, I recall little else. However, I'm sorry we didn't get around to working together sooner."

"Me too, but my dream came true. Here we are."

"I've seen some of the rushes, honey, and we work well together. When this is over—"

She interrupted, "Everything is over except the endless nights and blinding days..."

"Don't talk like that." He smiled. "I really would like to do another movie with you."

"Are you serious?"

"Yes, I am. After *Diamondhead*, let's get together and discuss it. Deal?"

Marilyn threw her arms around him. "Deal..." She sighed. "You won't forget?"

"I'm the kind of guy who keeps his promises," he said, giving her a hug.

Kay was upset about two things—Marilyn's chasing after her husband and finding out Clark was doing his own stunt work. She did not mention Marilyn, but she ripped him apart for exerting himself. He explained to her, "I thought it would be easy. Day after day I watched the same stunts. The horses were so tired I figured by the time it was my turn, they'd be too tired to give me any trouble. What surprised me is that no one gave a damn if I got killed or not. You know we were never allowed to take chances when the studio had us under contract. We were protected on and off the set. I was curious if Huston would try to stop me. Hell, no. He was delighted!"

"And the others?" she asked.

"Monty did his own thing and is one bloody young man, but he's self-destructive like Marilyn. They don't care if they live or die. I don't understand this generation."

"You'd better understand the next one, Pa. Our son will be part of it."

"It's going to be a good life from now on. This *Diamondhead* deal is for the same money I'm gettin' now—good cnough for me to retire. So, Kathleen, while I'm finishing up here in Reno, why don't you make a sketch of the nursery?"

"I've already done that, Pa. There's plenty of room for another wing, and I thought it would be nice if the children were all together. What do you think of the idea?"

"As soon as we get home, the job's done, Ma."

On October 18, 1960, the entire cast flew back to Los Angeles. Clark argued with Miller about script revisions. "As far as I'm concerned, we're finished!" he said. "All I'm interested in now is seeing what's on film."

He viewed *The Misfits* with producer Frank Taylor. When it was over, Clark said, "I want to shake your hand, Frank. I now have two things to be proud of in my career—*Gone With the Wind* and this."

On November 4, he said good-bye to the cast, but did not stay for the farewell party. He wasn't feeling well. The next day while working around the ranch, Clark got a pain in his chest so severe he had to lie down. He said nothing to Kay. He didn't have to. "Clark was ashen and sweating," she said. "We had an early dinner and retired, but in the middle of the night he woke with a headache and what he described as indigestion. In the morning, he tried to get dressed and almost collapsed. I called the doctor despite Clark's protesting over and over that he was all right. The ambulance came. He was so embarrassed, but we made him get in. Through it all, he was concerned because I was pregnant. We had a terrible time trying to convince him he must go to the hospital. I went with him in the ambulance, and was stunned when he apologized to me for what happened."

Gable had suffered a coronary thrombosis and was in critical condition. Kay sat by his bedside during the day and slept on a cot next to him at night. Doctors told her that the back of Clark's heart muscle was badly damaged, and if he recovered he would not be out of danger for two weeks. In forty-eight hours Clark was sitting up in bed, and the pacemaker was removed from his room a week later. Kay thought it would be safe for her to spend an hour or two at the ranch. When she returned to the hospital, Clark asked her never to leave him again.

On the morning of November 16, he asked for some good books to read. Adela Rogers St. Johns knew his preferences and promised to stop by the following day. Since he had not been allowed visitors other than Kay and Howard Strickling, Clark looked forward to seeing his friends.

That night at ten Kay kissed him good night and went to her adjoining room to lie down. The doctor said, "Around eleven, Clark turned the page of a magazine he was reading, put his head back, took a deep sigh, and died."

Kay held her husband in her arms for two hours.

The King of Hollywood was buried with full military honors by the United States Air Force. Services were held at the Church of the Recessional at Forest Lawn Memorial Park in Glendale, California. Among the pallbearers were Spencer Tracy, Jimmy Stewart, and Robert Taylor.

Clark Gable was laid to rest in a crypt next to Carole Lombard, who believed in life after death and that she would be waiting at the other end of the dark tunnel. "Did you have to bring the armed forces with you, Pa? What a ham!"

THE AFTERMATH

In November 1960, Arthur Miller packed his bags and moved out of 444 East 57th Street in New York. He said nothing to Marilyn and took nothing that reminded him of their marriage.

On the seventeenth, she heard the news that Clark Gable was dead.

"I loved him," she told the press. "He wanted to do another movie with me."

Kay Gable didn't think that was true. In an interview days after her husband's death she said, "It wasn't the physical exertion that did it. It was the horrible tension, that eternal waiting, waiting, waiting. He waited around forever, for everybody. He'd get so angry waiting that he'd just go ahead and do anything to keep occupied. That's why he did those awful horse scenes where they dragged him behind a truck. He had a stand-in and a stunt man, but he did them himself. I told him he was crazy, but he wouldn't listen."

Reporters embellished whatever Gable's widow said. It did not take much imagination or ingenuity to blame his death on Marilyn's tardiness and absence during *The Misfits*. The newspapers were brimming over with Clark's patience, kindness, and self-control, which eventually erupted in the heart and took his life. It was the talk of Hollywood. There were witnesses who spoke candidly about Monroe's lack of concern for those working on *The Misfits*. Gable, in particular.

She denied the terrible accusations, but was not mentally equipped to deal with them. She told her close acquaintances, "Why didn't he tell me? Why didn't he say something? I'd have done anything for him. Anything! All he had to do was ask me to be on time. That's all. He always said, 'It's all right, honey'—like he understood.

If he asked me to be ready before dawn, that's what I would have done."

Marilyn locked herself in her lonely apartment, pulled down the shades in her bedroom, and remained in the dark for days until she was convinced that if it hadn't been for her problems, Gable might still be alive. She had killed him—the man she adored and respected above all others. The guilt mounted until there was nothing else to do but end her own life. In mid-December her maid found Marilyn about to jump out of the bedroom window, but pulled her back. A few weeks later she was admitted to the Payne Whitney Clinic by her psychiatrists.

The Misfits received mixed reviews. Critics were not pleased with Marilyn's serious role. "Miss Monroe is a comedienne. *Some Like It Hot* proved that."

Gable's reviews were overwhelmingly the best of his career. The *New York Times* said, "Clark Gable was as certain as the sunrise. He was consistently and stubbornly all man."

Movie fans had lost their male legends who were "stubbornly all man" in rapid succession: Humphrey Bogart in 1957, age fifty-eight; Tyrone Power in 1958, age forty-five; Errol Flynn in 1959, age fifty; Clark Gable in 1960, age fifty-nine; Gary Cooper in 1961, age sixty; Dick Powell in 1963, age fifty-nine; Alan Ladd in 1964, age fifty-one; Spencer Tracy in 1967, age sixty-seven; and Robert Taylor in 1969, age fifty-seven.

The sixties featured the method actors, Montgomery Clift, Sal Mineo, and Marlon Brando. (James Dean was killed in 1955.) John Wayne was still reciting "That'll be the day!" when threatened in his perennial westerns. Paul Newman, Burt Lancaster, Kirk Douglas, Steve McQueen, William Holden, Henry Fonda, and Jimmy Stewart dominated the screen while Elvis Presley wiggled on and off during the birth of the Beatles.

Robert Taylor, who did two television series and whatever movies were "suitable for Grandma to watch, too," including one with his former wife, Barbara Stanwyck, was approached in a restaurant by a young girl who asked, "Haven't I seen you on television?"

He scowled. "More off than on."

"You'll have to get with it," she giggled.

"An old book is better than a blank page," he said, walking away.

One of those old books is *Gone With the Wind*.

Though John Clark Gable, born on March 20, 1961, will not benefit from a percentage of the profits, his father died a rich man. In the last five years of his life, the King made more than $7 million. The common stock he held amounted to very little, but there was his twenty-acre ranch in Encino, the house in Palm Springs, and a building site in Palm Desert given to him by Marion Davies, who had hoped Clark would be her neighbor one day.

Gable liked his money where he could see and touch it. He said he picked up this habit from Wallace Beery, who put money in a safe deposit box only when his pockets overflowed. "I remember him carrying over a million once," Clark said.

Adela Rogers St. Johns, who met Gable when he was taking riding lessons in preparation for *The Painted Desert*, knew him as well as anyone else. In her first article about him she said he never sent flowers to a woman in his life. Clark was so angry, he sent her a carload, but admitted she told the truth. St. Johns said that women came far down on Gable's list of life's "summum bonum."

First, his men friends, and man pursuits, hunting and fishing and poker and drinking.

Second, his work.

Third, women and children.

He told Adela, "Men don't get sore if their womenfolks like me on the screen. I'm one of them, they know it, so it's a compliment to them. If I can do it, they can do it, and they figure it might be fun to go home and make love to their wives. They see life with a high price tag on it, but they get an idea that no price is too high if it's life. I'm not going to make any motion pictures that don't keep right on telling them that about a man. The things a man has to have are hope and confidence in himself against odds, and sometimes he needs somebody, his pal or his mother or his wife, to give him that confidence. He's got to have some inner standards worth fighting for or there won't be any way to bring him into conflict. And he must be ready to choose death before dishonor without making too much song and dance about it. That's all there is to it."

After Gable's death, Adela wrote, "The King is dead. Long live the King. There has been no successor, nor will be. The title died with him. Is it strange that from the man who was an 'exaggeration of life,' I learned that death is a door life opens?"

• • •

Kay Gable died from heart failure in 1983.

The once isolated and small farmhouse that Clark bought for Lombard with her $50,000 still stands in the now fashionable and overcrowded San Fernando Valley. The property has been subdivided into an expensive housing development called Clark Gable Estates. Some tracts have been sold for more than a million dollars each. The new streets bear such names as Tara Drive and Ashley Oaks.

John Clark Gable, who resembles his mother, settled in Malibu. Though proud of his name, the twenty-six-year-old race-car driver prefers anonymity. In a rare interview, he said he inherited the love of fast driving from his famous father.

In 1986 John's wife, Tracy, gave birth to a baby girl, Kayley.

CHRONOLOGY OF
CLARK GABLE'S FILMS

FORBIDDEN PARADISE
(Paramount, 1924)

Director: Ernest Lubitsch. *Cast:* Pola Negri, Rod La Rocque, Adolphe Menjou (Gable was an extra).

THE PACEMAKERS
(F.B.O., 1925)

Director: Wesley Ruggles. *Cast:* William Haines, Alberta Vaughn, George O'Hara (Gable was an extra).

THE MERRY WIDOW
(MGM, 1925)

Director: Eric Von Stroheim. *Cast:* Mae Murray, John Gilbert, Tully Marshall (Gable was an extra).

THE PLASTIC AGE
(F.B.O., 1925)

Director: Wesley Ruggles. *Cast:* Clara Bow, Donald Keith, Gilbert Roland (Gable was an extra).

NORTH STAR
(Associated Exhibitors, 1926)

Director: Paul Powell. *Cast:* Strongheart, Virginia Lee, Stuart Holmes (Gable was an extra).

THE PAINTED DESERT
(Pathé, 1931)

Director: Howard Higgin. *Cast:* William Boyd, Helen Twelvetrees, William Farnum, Jr., Farrell MacDonald, Clark Gable. *80 minutes.*

THE EASIEST WAY
(MGM, 1931)

Director: Jack Conway. *Cast:* Constance Bennett, Adolphe Menjou, Robert Montgomery, Anita Page, Clara Blandick, Clark Gable. *Review: Motion Picture Herald:* "Newcomer Gable shines briefly in this mildly entertaining adaptation of a slightly dated screen play." *86 minutes.*

DANCE, FOOLS, DANCE
(MGM, 1931)

Director: Harry Beaumont. *Cast:* Joan Crawford, Lester Vail, William Bakewell, William Holden, Clark Gable. *Review: Variety:* "Clark Gable's characterization of the gang chieftain is a vivid and authentic bit of acting." *82 minutes.*

THE SECRET SIX
(MGM, 1931)

Director: George Hill. *Screenplay:* Frances Marion. *Cast:* Wallace Beery, Lewis Stone, John Mack Brown, Jean Harlow, Clark Gable, Ralph Bellamy. *Review: New York Times:* "Clark Gable, who has been seen mostly as a gangster, undertakes the part of a newspaper writer named Carl, does valiant work." *83 minutes.*

THE FINGER POINTS
(First National, 1931)

Director: John Francis Dillon. *Screenplay:* Robert Lord. *Cast:* Richard Barthelmess, Fay Wray, Regis Toomey, Robert Elliott, Clark Gable. *Review: Variety:* ". . . Clark Gable again scores with his fine voice and magnetic personality." *90 minutes.*

LAUGHING SINNERS
(MGM, 1931)

Director: Harry Beaumont. *Screenplay:* Bess Meredyth, from *Torch Song,* a play by Martin Flavis. *Cast:* Joan Crawford, Neil Hamilton, Clark Gable, Marjorie Rambeau, Guy Kibbee. *Review: New York Times:* "New leading man Clark Gable, as a Salvation Army worker, is rather unconvincing as the saviour of the fallen Joan Crawford." *71 minutes.*

A FREE SOUL
(MGM, 1931)

Director: Clarence Brown. *Screenplay:* John Meehan, based on a novel by Adela Rogers St. Johns. *Cast:* Norma Shearer, Leslie Howard, Lionel Barrymore, Clark Gable, James Gleason, Lucy Beaumont. *Review: New York Herald Tribune:* "Clark Gable is a fascinating villian who will convince the female customers that he is naughty but nice. His acting, however, is nowhere on the same level as the superb Lionel Barrymore. Mr. Gable would do well to sit back and take a lesson." *91 minutes.*

NIGHT NURSE
(Warner Brothers, 1931)

Director: William Wellman. *Screenplay:* Oliver H. P. Garrett, based on the novel by Dora Macy. *Cast:* Barbara Stanwyck, Ben Lyon, Joan Blondell, Clark Gable, Charles Winninger, Vera Lewis. *Review: Variety:* "Clark Gable goes around socking everybody, including Barbara Stanwyck, and is finally done away with by inference." *72 minutes.*

SPORTING BLOOD
(MGM, 1931)

Director: Charles Brabin. *Screenplay:* Willard Mack and Wanda Tuchock, from the novel *Horseflesh* by Frederick Hazlitt. *Photography:* Harold Rosson. *Film Editor:* William Gray. *Cast:* Clark Gable, Ernest Torrance, Madge Evans, Marie Prevost. *Review: Time:* "This one is indubitably not Mr. Gable's best work, though far from his worst." *82 minutes.*

SUSAN LENNOX—HER FALL AND RISE
(MGM, 1931)

Director: Robert Leonard. *Screenplay:* Wanda Tuchock, from the novel by David G. Philips. *Photography:* William Daniels. *Film Editor:* Margaret Booth. *Cast:* Greta Garbo, Clark Gable, Jean Hersholt, Alan Hale. *Reviews: Variety:* "Teaming with the great Garbo marks the peak of Gable's vogue." *Motion Picture Herald:* "Gable is excellent." *London Film Weekly:* "Clark Gable gives a strong, if straightforward performance as Garbo's lover." 76 *minutes.*

POSSESSED
(MGM, 1931)

Director: Clarence Brown. *Screenplay:* Lenore Coffee, from the play *The Mirage* by Edgar Selwyn. *Photography:* Oliver T. Marsh. *Cast:* Joan Crawford, Clark Gable, Wallace Ford, Skeets Gallagher. *Reviews: Film Daily:* "This man Gable that we've been watching for little over a year has come a long way from his villain roles. His performance suggests that he may become a solid actor. A personality he already is; but so much talent will take him a good deal farther than his good looks." *Variety:* "Gable again is the stiff, cold-blooded manly leading man. Since graduating from gangster parts he has failed to register any strong emotion. Happy or sad, it's always the same Gable." *76 minutes.*

HELL DIVERS
(MGM, 1931)

Director: George Hill. *Screenplay:* Harvey Gates and Malcolm S. Boylan, based on a story by Frank Wead. *Photography:* Harold Wenstrom. *Film Editor:* Blanche Sewell. *Cast:* Wallace Beery, Clark Gable, Conrad Nagel, Dorothy Jordan, Marjorie Rambeau, Marie Prevost. *Review: Variety:* "Gable is not placed to advantage in this assignment." *100 minutes.*

POLLY OF THE CIRCUS
(MGM, 1932)

Director: Alfred Santell. *Screenplay:* Carey Wilson, based on the play by Margaret Mayo. *Photography:* George Barnes. *Film Editor:* George Hively.

Cast: Marion Davies, Clark Gable, C. Aubrey Smith, Raymond Hatton, Ray Milland. *Review: Motion Picture Herald:* "Sell Miss Davies all you want to: she'll need it in this one. But don't try to foist Mr. Gable as a preacher. This because of past roles, which he has so admirably filled, and because he simply doesn't register as a member of the clergy." *72 minutes.*

RED DUST
(MGM, 1932)

Director: Victor Fleming. *Screenplay:* John Lee Mahin. *Photography:* Harold Rosson. *Film Editor:* Blanche Sewell. *Cast:* Clark Gable, Jean Harlow, Gene Raymond, Mary Astor, Donald Crisp, Tully Marshall, Willie Fung. *Review: London Film Daily:* "Gable is perhaps more gruffly virile than ever before. He and Harlow make an excellent team." *83 minutes.*

STRANGE INTERLUDE
(MGM, 1932)

Director: Robert Z. Leonard. *Screenplay:* Bess Meredyth and C. Gardner Sullivan, based on the play by Eugene O'Neill. *Photography:* Lee Garmes. *Film Editor:* Margaret Booth. *Cast:* Norma Shearer, Clark Gable, Alexander Kirkland, Ralph Morgan, Robert Young, May Robson, Maureen O'Sullivan. *Review: London Film Weekly:* "Clark Gable's powerful personality shines steadfastly through the misty atmosphere of mixed psychology." *110 minutes.*

NO MAN OF HER OWN
(Paramount, 1932)

Director: Wesley Ruggles. *Screenplay:* Maurine Watkins and Milton H. Gropper, based on a story by Edmund Goulding and Benjamin Glazer. *Photography:* Leo Tover. *Cast:* Clark Gable, Carole Lombard, Dorothy Mackaill, Grant Mitchell, George Barbier, Elizabeth Paterson. *Reviews: Variety:* "Gable is close to the whole picture himself as a swank card-gyp who hits the trail heavy for the women." *Motion Picture Herald:* "Lots of prolonged howls of laughter and loads of action that presents Gable at his present best, sophisticated comedy. Luscious Carole Lombard is appropriately the object of his tomfoolery and frustrations." *London Film Daily:* "Gable's imprudently confident love-making exactly fits the character he is playing. Carole Lombard, cool, sincere and intelligent, makes the perfect heroine." *85 minutes.*

THE WHITE SISTER
(MGM, 1933)

Director: Victor Fleming. *Screenplay:* Donald Ogden Stewart, based on the novel by F. Marion Crawford and Walter Hackett. *Photography:* William Daniels. *Film Editor:* Margaret Booth. *Cast:* Helen Hayes, Clark Gable, Lewis Stone, May Robson, Edward Arnold. *Reviews: Motion Picture Herald:* "Mr. Gable is forceful in a story that isn't." *Hollywood Reporter:* "White Sister is a great picture. Hayes and Gable are already stars of the first magnitude. Their performances now equal anything of their brilliant past." *110 minutes.*

HOLD YOUR MAN
(MGM, 1933)

Producer and director: Sam Wood. *Screenplay:* Anita Loos and Howard Emmett Rogers, from Loos's original story. *Photography:* Harold Rosson. *Film Editor:* Frank Sullivan. *Cast:* Jean Harlow, Clark Gable, Stuart Erwin, Dorothy Burgess, Muriel Kirkland, Gary Owen. *Review: London Film Weekly:* "Being themselves is the job at which Harlow and Gable have made good. It may be that in real life the one is the essence of retirement and the other shy and introspective, but it is as a pair of charming toughs, hard as nails, and superbly imprudent, that we have come to know them on the screen. The film is hardboiled, cheekily smart stuff, just right for these two." *89 minutes.*

NIGHT FLIGHT
(MGM, 1933)

Director: Clarence Brown. *Screenplay:* Oliver Garrett, based on the story by Antoine de Saint-Exupéry. *Photography:* Oliver T. Marsh, Elmar Dyer, and Charles Marshall. *Cast:* John Barrymore, Helen Hayes, Clark Gable, Lionel Barrymore, Robert Montgomery, Myrna Loy, William Gargan. *Review: London Film Weekly:* ". . . there are too many stars in little parts. Gable, for example, sits in a plane throughout his performance." *84 minutes.*

DANCING LADY
(MGM, 1933)

Producer: David O. Selznick. *Director:* Robert Z. Leonard. *Screenplay:* Allen Rivkin and P. J. Wolfson, based on the novel by James Warner Bellah. *Photography:* Oliver T. Marsh. *Film Editor:* Margaret Booth. *Cast:* Joan Crawford, Clark Gable, Franchot Tone, May Robson, Fred Astaire, Robert Benchley, Ted Healy. *Review: Time:* "The versatile Mr. Gable is cast surprisingly as a stage director instead of a gangster, and might make hoofing the rage. Perhaps the film should have been called 'Dancing Man' to introduce the new Clark Gable." *94 minutes.*

IT HAPPENED ONE NIGHT
(Columbia, 1934)

Director: Frank Capra. *Screenplay:* Robert Riskin, based on a story by Samuel H. Adams. *Photography:* Joe Walker. *Film Editor:* Gene Havlick. *Cast:* Clark Gable, Claudette Colbert, Walter Connolly, Roscoe Karns, Alan Hale, Ward Bond. *Reviews: New York Times:* "Clark Gable's at his best." *London Film Weekly:* "Gable is brilliantly impudent without being in the least unlikeable." *Film Daily:* "Mr. Gable and Miss Colbert reach new heights." *105 minutes.*

284 GABLE'S WOMEN

MEN IN WHITE
(MGM, 1934)

Director: Richard Boleslavsky. *Screenplay:* Waldemar Young, based on the play by Sidney Kingsley. *Photographer:* George Folsey. *Film Editor:* Frank Sullivan. *Cast:* Clark Gable, Myrna Loy, Jean Hersholt, Elizabeth Allan, Otto Kruger, Wallace Ford. *Reviews: Film Daily:* "Gable as a struggling doctor is very real and warm and unlike anything we've seen him doing before. It is unusual, yet very natural, not to see him battling the ladies around in a rough moment. This may be the beginning of a new Clark Gable." *Motion Picture Herald:* "Gable does a remarkable acting job." *80 minutes.*

MANHATTAN MELODRAMA
(MGM, 1934)

Director: W. S. Van Dyke. *Screenplay:* Oliver T. Marsh, H. P. Garrett, Joseph Mankiewicz, based on the original story by Arthur Caesar. *Photographer:* James Wong Howe. *Film Editor:* Ben Lewis. *Cast:* Clark Gable, William Powell, Myrna Loy, Leo Carillo, Nat Pendleton, Mickey Rooney. *Reviews: Film Daily:* "Gable manages his exacting role with power and appeal." *Hollywood Reporter:* "Gable's back in the type of role he does best: a do-gooder gangster. And he comes off great." *London Film Weekly:* "William Powell steals the picture from Clark Gable." *93 minutes.*

CHAINED
(MGM, 1934)

Producer: Hunt Stromberg. *Director:* Clarence Brown. *Screenplay:* John Mahin, based on an original story by Edgar Selwyn. *Photographer:* George Folsey. *Film Editor:* Robert Kern. *Cast:* Joan Crawford, Clark Gable, Otto Kruger, Stuart Erwin, Una O'Connor, Akim Tamiroff. *Reviews: Photoplay:* "Joan Crawford in the moonlight on the open sea appears quite seductive and Clark Gable seems to agree. In his role as the spurned lover we are shown a new dimension of his ever surprising acting skills. *London Film Weekly:* "Gable adopts the particularly Gable-ish attitude of regarding himself as a sap for letting Joan play around with him the way she does." *74 minutes.*

FORSAKING ALL OTHERS
(MGM, 1934)

Producer: Bernard Hyman. *Director:* W. S. Van Dyke. *Screenplay:* Joseph L. Mankiewicz, based on the play by Edward Barry Roberts and Frank Morgan Cavett. *Photography:* Gregg Toland and George Folsey. *Film Editor:* Tom Held. *Cast:* Joan Crawford, Clark Gable, Robert Montgomery, Charles Butterworth, Billie Burke, Rosalind Russell, Ted Healy. *Review: London Film*

Weekly: "Clark Gable forgets all the he-man stuff, and clowns and wise-cracks his way through the picture with an unbridled sense of humor." *82 minutes.*

AFTER OFFICE HOURS
(MGM, 1935)

Producer: Bernard H. Hyman. *Director:* Robert Z. Leonard. *Screenplay:* Herman J. Mankiewicz, based on the story by Laurence Stallings and Dale Van Every. *Photography:* Charles Rosher. *Film Editor:* Tom Held. *Cast:* Constance Bennett, Clark Gable, Stuart Erwin, Billie Burke, Harvey Stephens. *Review: London Film Weekly:* "Because we laughed at Clark Gable in *It Happened One Night* and *Forsaking All Others,* the idea now seems to be that he should clown as much as he possibly can. Which is really a pity. This could have been a better picture if Gable had been allowed to do some more straight acting." *75 minutes.*

CALL OF THE WILD
(Twentieth Century–Fox, 1935)

Producer: Darryl F. Zanuck. *Director:* William Wellman. *Screenplay:* Gene Fowler and Leonard Praskins, based on a novel by Jack London. *Photographer:* Charles Rosher. *Film Editor:* Hanson Fritch. *Cast:* Clark Gable, Loretta Young, Jack Oakie, Reginald Owen, Frank Conroy, Katherine DeMille, Sidney Toler, James Burke. *Review: Time:* "Gable is no stranger to the rugged life that Jack London depicted in his work. His characterization in this picture is appropriate and all that we have learned to expect from him." *95 minutes.*

CHINA SEAS
(MGM, 1935)

Producer: Albert Lewin. *Director:* Tay Garnett. *Screenplay:* Jules Furthman and James K. McGuiness, based on the novel by Crosbie Garstin. *Photography:* Ray June. *Film Editor:* William Levanway. *Cast:* Clark Gable, Jean Harlow, Wallace Beery, Lewis Stone, Rosalind Russell, C. Aubrey Smith, Robert Benchley, Donald Meek, Akim Tamiroff. *Reviews: New York Times:* "If any member of the cast were to be singled out as outstanding it would be Clark Gable." *Hollywood Reporter:* "Clark Gable plays the captain of the ship with ease and assurance that will win him many new admirers." *90 minutes.*

MUTINY ON THE BOUNTY
(MGM, 1935)

Producer: Irving Thalberg. *Director:* Frank Lloyd. *Screenplay:* Talbot Jennings, Jules Furthman, and Carey Wilson, based on the book by Charles Nordhoff and James N. Hall. *Photography:* Arthur Edeson. *Film Editor:*

Margaret Booth. *Cast:* Charles Laughton, Clark Gable, Franchot Tone, Herbert Mundin, Eddie Quillan, Dudley Digges, Spring Byington, Movita. *Review: London Film Weekly:* "Gable's Fletcher Christian is a brilliant characterization. A fine natural performance, full of those small touches that make a character live." *132 minutes.*

WIFE VERSUS SECRETARY
(MGM, 1936)

Producer: Hunt Stromberg. *Director:* Clarence Brown. *Screenplay:* Norman Krasna, Alice D. Miller, and John L. Mahin, based on the novel by Faith Baldwin. *Photography:* Ray June. *Film Editor:* Frank E. Hull. *Cast:* Clark Gable, Jean Harlow, Myrna Loy, May Robson, James Stewart, Hobart Cavanaugh. *Review: New Yorker:* "For the lead man Gable, the part is nearly as cliché-conceived as the plot, and is rescued, perhaps, only by the feeling he projects that he is not just any businessman who has come up against those odds, but reacts like he could be." *88 minutes.*

SAN FRANCISCO
(MGM, 1936)

Producers: John Emerson, Bernard Hyman. *Director:* W. S. Van Dyke. *Screenplay:* Anita Loos, based on a story by Robert Hopkins. *Photography:* Oliver T. Marsh. *Film Editor:* Tom Held. *Cast:* Clark Gable, Jeanette MacDonald, Spencer Tracy, Jack Holt, Ted Healy, Shirley Ross, Margaret Irving, Al Shean. *Review: New York Sun:* "With those earthquake scenes, with Miss MacDonald's golden voice and beauty, with the dimpled Mr. Gable in the he-man role, and with Mr. Tracy quietly humorous as the understanding priest, *San Francisco* does not have to worry about length or anything else." *115 minutes.*

CAIN AND MABEL
(Warner Brothers, 1936)

A *Cosmopolitan Production. Director:* Lloyd Bacon. *Screenplay:* Laird Doyle, based on a short story by H. C. Witwer. *Photography:* George Barnes. *Film Editor:* William Holmes. *Cast:* Marion Davies, Clark Gable, Allen Jenkins, Roscoe Karns, Ruth Donnelly. *Reviews: Newsweek:* "Clark Gable and Marion Davies fit in this picture like a fat hand squeezed into a small glove. Too much talent for such a skimpy, thinly woven plot." *New York Times:* "Mr. Gable's roles are becoming routine matters." *Time:* "It's the end of some very fine feelings about Mr. Gable and Miss Davies and musical comedy. See it at your own risk." *90 minutes.*

LOVE ON THE RUN
(MGM, 1936)

Producer: Joseph L. Mankiewicz. *Director:* W. S. Van Dyke. *Screenplay:* John L. Mahin, Manual Seff, and Gladys Hurlbut, from the story by Alan Green and Julian Brodie. *Photography:* Oliver T. Marsh. *Film Editor:* Frank Sullivan. *Cast:* Joan Crawford, Clark Gable, Franchot Tone, Reginald Owen, Mona Barrie, William Demarest. *Reviews: Hollywood Spectator:* "Such a finished trio as Joan Crawford, Clark Gable and Franchot Tone can make us believe the unbelievable and entertain us with it." *Box Office:* "Clark Gable contributes his best comedy role since *It Happened One Night.*" *81 minutes.*

PARNELL
(MGM, 1937)

Director: John Stahl. *Screenplay:* John Van Druten and S. N. Behrman, based on the play by Elsie T. Schauffler. *Photographer:* Karl Freund. *Film Editor:* Frederick Y. Smith. *Cast:* Clark Gable, Myrna Loy, Edna May Oliver, Edmund Gwenn, Alan Marshall, Donald Crisp, Billie Burke, Donald Meek. *Review: Script:* "Clark Gable in his worst miscasting." *96 minutes.*

SARATOGA
(MGM, 1937)

Producer: Bernard Hyman. *Director:* John Conway. *Original screenplay:* Anita Loos and Robert Hopkins. *Photography:* Ray June. *Film Editor:* Elmo Vernon *Cast:* Clark Gable, Jean Harlow, Lionel Barrymore, Frank Morgan, Walter Pidgeon, Una Merkel, Hattie McDaniel. *Review: New York Herald Tribune:* "Jean Harlow's last picture made this particular individual feel sad. Partly because of a still fresh memory of the gifted young actress's untimely death, but almost a premonition of disaster. Her few brief glimpses of natural brilliance as a comedienne, such as when Mr. Gable hides her under the bed, only seem to intensify the shadow hovering over her spirit and subduing it." *102 minutes.*

TEST PILOT
(MGM, 1938)

Producer: Louis D. Lighton. *Director:* Victor Fleming. *Screenplay:* Vincent Lawrence and Waldemar Young, based on a story by Frank Wead. *Photography:* Ray June. *Film Editor:* Tom Held. *Cast:* Clark Gable, Myrna Loy, Spencer Tracy, Lionel Barrymore, Samuel S. Hinds, Marjorie Main, Virginia Grey. *Review: Cue:* "As the trio, Clark Gable, Spencer Tracy and Myrna Loy turn in probably the best performances of their careers." *118 minutes.*

TOO HOT TO HANDLE
(MGM, 1938)

Producer: Lawrence Weingarten. *Director:* Jack Conway. *Screenplay:* Laurence Stallings and John L. Mahin, based on a story by Len Hammond. *Photography:* Harold Rosson. *Film Editor:* Frank Sullivan. *Cast:* Clark Gable, Myrna Loy, Walter Connolly, Walter Pidgeon, Leo Carrillo, Johnny Hines, Marjorie Main, Willie Fung. *Review: New York Times:* "Mr. Gable plays the annoying Chris Hunter with his customary blend of bluster and blubber." *105 minutes.*

IDIOT'S DELIGHT
(MGM, 1939)

Producer: Hunt Stromberg. *Director:* Clarence Brown. *Screenplay:* Robert Sherwood, based on his own play. *Photography:* William Daniels. *Film Editor:* Robert J. Kern. *Cast:* Norma Shearer, Clark Gable, Edward Arnold, Charles Coburn, Joseph Schildkraut, Burgess Meredith, Skeets Gallegher, Virginia Grey. *Review: Hollywood Reporter:* "Gable and Shearer give their brightest performance to date." *105 minutes.*

GONE WITH THE WIND
(MGM, 1939)

Producer: David Selznick. *Director:* Victor Fleming. *Screenplay:* Sidney Howard, based on a novel by Margaret Mitchell. *Photography:* Ernest Haller. *Film Editors:* Hal Kern and James Newcom. *Cast:* Clark Gable, Leslie Howard, Olivia de Havilland, Vivien Leigh, George Reeves, Hattie McDaniel, Thomas Mitchell, Evelyn Keyes, Ann Rutherford, Butterfly McQueen. *Reviews: Film Daily:* "Clark Gable and Vivien Leigh are certain for this year's top awards." *Photoplay:* "Clark Gable has only to be himself, so perfectly cast he is as Rhett Butler." *Hollywood Reporter:* "No actor and a role were ever so perfectly wed as Clark Gable and Rhett Butler." *Variety:* "Gable gives the performance of the year and Vivien Leigh is not far behind." *225 minutes.*

STRANGE CARGO
(MGM, 1940)

Producer: Joseph L. Mankiewicz. *Director:* Frank Borzage. *Screenplay:* Lawrence Hazard, based on the book *Not Too Narrow, Not Too Deep* by Richard Sale. *Photography:* Robert Plank. *Film Editor:* Robert J. Kern. *Cast:* Clark Gable, Joan Crawford, Ian Hunter, Peter Lorre, Paul Lucas, Albert Dekker. *Reviews: Variety:* "Clark Gable plays the toughest of the convicts. Joan Crawford, a brothel gal. Their performances complemented by the mystical Ian Hunter." *Film Daily:* "Clark Gable fits his role admirably." *105 minutes.*

BOOM TOWN
(MGM, 1940)

Producer: Sam Zimbalist. *Director:* Jack Conway. *Screenplay:* John Mahin, based on a short story by James Grant. *Photography:* Harold Rosson. *Film Editor:* Blanche Sewell. *Cast:* Clark Gable, Spencer Tracy, Claudette Colbert, Hedy Lamarr, Frank Morgan, Chill Wills. *Reviews: New York Times:* "Mr. Gable and Mr. Tracy have the most to do and are the best. The former looks and acts like an oil man." *New York Herald Tribune:* "Tracy and Gable come across tough and alive in their kind of movie." *116 minutes.*

COMRADE X
(MGM, 1940)

Producer: Gottfried Reinhardt. *Director:* King Vidor. *Screenplay:* Ben Hecht and Charles Lederer, based on a story by Walter Reisch. *Photography:* Joseph Ruttenberg. *Film Editor:* Harold F. Kress. *Cast:* Clark Gable, Hedy Lamarr, Oscar Homolka, Felix Bressart, Eve Arden, Sig Rumann. *Reviews: Film Daily:* "Clark Gable is perfection in this part." *Newsweek:* "Gable handles his role splendidly." *90 minutes.*

THEY MET IN BOMBAY
(MGM, 1941)

Producer: Hunt Stromberg. *Director:* Clarence Brown. *Screenplay:* Edwin Justus Mayer, Anita Loos, and Leon Gordon, based on the story by John Kafka. *Photography:* William Daniels. *Film Editor:* Blanche Sewell. *Cast:* Clark Gable, Rosalind Russell, Peter Lorre, Reginald Owen, Jessie Ralph. *Reviews: Film Daily:* "The teaming of Gable and Russell is most advantageous." *Time:* "Gable is grand." *86 minutes.*

HONKY TONK
(MGM, 1941)

Producer: Pandro Berman. *Director:* Jack Conway. *Screenplay:* Marguerite Roberts and John Sanford. *Photography:* Harold Rosson. *Film Editor:* Blanche Sewell. *Cast:* Clark Gable, Lana Turner, Frank Morgan, Claire Trevor, Marjorie Main, Albert Dekker, Chill Wills. *Review: Variety:* "Gable is in top form in the picture. He gives out with enough masculine charm to make the femme fans flutter plenty. Miss Turner, who is graced by a tremendous sex appeal, proves she also can act as well as turn the boys on. They click together in a lively, lusty Western that makes to wish you had been there." *105 minutes.*

SOMEWHERE I'LL FIND YOU
(MGM, 1942)

Producer: Pandro S. Berman. *Director:* Wesley Ruggles. *Screenplay:* Marguerite Roberts, based on a story by Charles Hoffman. *Photography:* Harold

Rosson. *Cast:* Clark Gable, Lana Turner, Robert Sterling, Patricia Dane, Reginald Owen, Lee Patrick. *Review: Photoplay:* "The first picture made by Clark Gable since his tragic bereavement comes out a honey with Mr. Gable proving himself a true hero in his adherence to duty: a duty that must have caused him suffering, what with the pertinent lines and situations all reminiscent of his sorrow." *108 minutes.*

ADVENTURE
(MGM, 1945)

Producer: Sam Zimbalist. *Director:* Victor Fleming. *Screenplay:* Frederick Hazlitt Brennan and Vincent Lawrence, based on the novel by Clyde Brion Davis. *Photography:* Joseph Ruttenberg. *Film Editor:* Frank Sullivan. *Cast:* Clark Gable, Greer Garson, Joan Blondell, Thomas Mitchell, Tom Tully, Harry Davenport. *Reviews: Time:* "*Adventure* was clearly carpentered to fit the old Gable formula; and ex-aerial-gunner-photographer Gable himself fits the formula as smoothly and as agreeably as ever. If he is a little chubbier around the jowls, he is still able to sling his weight around—and in his bright eye is the same old wicked fire." *Photoplay:* "What use for us to cite the flaws and bemoan the story, for it's Gable's first postwar picture and movie fans, if for no other reason than that, will send its rating sky high." *125 minutes.*

THE HUCKSTERS
(MGM, 1947)

Producer: Arthur Hornblow, Jr. *Director:* Jack Conway. *Screenplay:* Luther Davis, based on the novel by Frederic Wakeman. *Photography:* Harold Rosson. *Film Editor:* Frank Sullivan. *Cast:* Clark Gable, Deborah Kerr, Sidney Greenstreet, Adolphe Menjou, Ava Gardner, Keenan Wynn, Edward Arnold. *Review: Hollywood Reporter:* "Clark Gable zooms back to the pre-eminent place he long held in Hollywood with this smash performance." *115 minutes.*

HOMECOMING
(MGM, 1948)

Producer: Sidney Franklin. *Director:* Mervyn LeRoy. *Screenplay:* Paul Osborn, based on the original story by Sidney Kingsley. *Photography:* Harold Rosson. *Film Editor:* John Dunning. *Cast:* Clark Gable, Lana Turner, Anne Baxter, John Hodiak, Cameron Mitchell, Marshall Thompson. *Review: Hollywood Reporter:* "This is what audiences have been waiting for; reteaming of the two hottest romantic figures on the screen, Clark Gable and Lana Turner." *113 minutes.*

COMMAND DECISION
(MGM, 1948)

Producer: Sidney Franklin. *Director:* Sam Wood. *Screenplay:* William Laidlaw and George Froeschel, based on the play by William Wister Haines. *Photography:* Harold Rosson. *Film Editor:* Harold Kress. *Cast:* Clark Gable, Walter Pidgeon, Van Johnson, Brian Donlevy, Charles Bickford, John Hodiak, Edward Arnold, Marshall Thompson, Cameron Mitchell. *Reviews: New Yorker:* "Mr. Gable is properly severe and glum." *Theatre Arts:* "The only disappointment is Clark Gable, who in every way fails to match the stage performance." *Time:* "Gable cannot always hold the center of the stage." *112 minutes.*

ANY NUMBER CAN PLAY
(MGM, 1949)

Producer: Arthur Freed. *Director:* Mervyn LeRoy. *Screenplay:* Richard Brooks, based on the book by Edward H. Heth. *Photography:* Harold Rosson. *Film Editor:* Ralph Winters. *Cast:* Clark Gable, Alexis Smith, Wendell Corey, Audrey Totter, Frank Morgan, Mary Astor, Lewis Stone, Barry Sullivan. *Review: Box Office:* "Gable walks comfortably through his assignment. The part is a natural for Clark Gable and he plays it with all the debonair authority that has kept him at the top of the ladder." *112 minutes.*

KEY TO THE CITY
(MGM, 1950)

Producer: Z. Wayne Griffin. *Director:* George Sidney. *Screenplay:* Robert Riley Crutcher, based on the story by Albert Beich. *Photography:* Harold Rosson. *Film Editor:* James E. Newcom. *Cast:* Clark Gable, Loretta Young, Frank Morgan, James Gleason, Marilyn Maxwell, Raymond Burr, Lewis Stone. *Reviews: Variety:* "A comedy made to measure for Gable and Miss Young." *Film Daily:* "*Key to the City* puts the mighty Gable right back where he belongs—on the top of the heap with a story geared particularly to his virile talents and the preference of his fans." *Hollywood Reporter:* "The part is tailor-made Gable, and to it he brings the full impact of his personality." *99 minutes.*

TO PLEASE A LADY
(MGM, 1950)

Producer and director: Clarence Brown. *Original screenplay:* Barre Lyndon and Marge Decker. *Photography:* Harold Rosson. *Film Editor:* Robert J. Kern. *Cast:* Clark Gable, Barbara Stanwyck, Adolphe Menjou, Will Greer, Roland Winters, William McGraw. *Reviews: Film Daily:* "Clark Gable in the rugged, hard-boiled type of role that originally brought him his immense popularity." *Motion Picture Exhibitor:* "Gable at his charming best! Miss

Stanwyck in a flip characterization which counts. In their first love scene, Gable slaps her face and she comes back for more. Gable is still the romantic figure of old." *91 minutes.*

ACROSS THE WIDE MISSOURI
(MGM, 1951)

Producer: Robert Sisk. *Director:* William Wellman. *Screenplay:* Talbot Jennings, based on a story by Talbot Jennings and Frank Cavett. *Photography:* William Mellor. *Film Editor:* John Dunn. *Cast:* Clark Gable, Ricardo Montalban, John Hodiak, Adolphe Menjou, Maria Elena Marques, J. Carroll Naish, Jack Holt. *Reviews: Hollywood Reporter:* "Clark does a first-class job as the two-fisted trapper." *Newsweek:* "With Gable and color on deck to supply marquee draw, *Across the Wide Missouri* should get along in the action runs. It is, however, a long way from top Gable." *78 minutes.*

CALLAWAY WENT THATAWAY
(MGM, 1951)

Producers, directors, and screenwriters: Norman Panama and Melvin Frank. *Photography:* Ray June. *Film Editor:* Cotton Warburton. *Cast:* Fred MacMurray, Dorothy McGuire, Howard Keel, Jesse White. *Guest Stars:* Clark Gable, Elizabeth Taylor, Esther Williams. *Review: Hollywood Reporter:* "Surprise appearances by Esther Willliams, Clark Gable and other Metro headliners lend zip to the nitery Hollywood atmosphere." *81 minutes.*

LONE STAR
(MGM, 1952)

Producer: Z. Wayne Griffin. *Director:* Vincent Sherman. *Screenplay:* Borden Chase and Howard Estabrook, based on the magazine story by Borden Chase. *Photography:* Harold Rosson. *Film Editor:* Ferris Webster. *Cast:* Clark Gable, Ava Gardner, Broderick Crawford, Lionel Barrymore, Beulah Bondi, Ed Begley, James Burke. *Review: Film Daily:* "A second Western in a row appears to agree with Clark Gable, who shines rough and brutal as a Texas cattle baron who straddles a not-too-neutral fence. He brings the role to life on the screen as though there were nothing more to it than walking heavily, speaking firmly with adequate facial grimacing, and smiling smoothly to charm the ladies, Ava Gardner in this instance. This is Gable's virile best." *94 minutes.*

NEVER LET ME GO
(MGM, 1953)

Producer: Clarence Brown. *Director:* Delmer Daves. *Screenplay:* Roland Millar and George Froeschel, based on the novel *Came the Dawn* by Roger Bax. *Photography:* Robert Krasker. *Film Editor:* Frank Clarke. *Cast:* Clark Gable, Gene Tierney, Richard Haydn, Bernard Miles, Belita, Kenneth More. *Re-*

views: New York Times: "A little older, a little fatter, a little shrewder, and a little more cynical, perhaps Clark Gable is nonetheless pervious to feminine beauty." *New Yorker:* "Mr. Gable, at this point in his career, is grizzled, not withered. And there can be little doubt that as long as he is able to get around, he will represent all that is wholesome, brave, kind and regular in the American male." *69 minutes.*

MOGAMBO
(MGM, 1953)

Producer: Sam Zimbalist. *Director:* John Ford. *Screenplay:* John Mahin, based on the play by Wilson Collison. *Photography:* Robert Surtees and F. A. Young. *Film Editor:* Frank Clarke. *Cast:* Clark Gable, Ava Gardner, Grace Kelly, Donald Sinden, Philip Stainton, Eric Pohnmann. *Review: Time:* "Gable plays his he-man part with the bemused ease to be expected of a man who has done the same thing many times before." *115 minutes.*

BETRAYED
(MGM, 1954)

Director: Gottfried Reinhardt. *Screenplay:* Ronald Miller and George Froeschel. *Photographer:* F. A. Young. *Film Editors:* John Dunning and Raymond Poulton. *Cast:* Clark Gable, Lana Turner, Victor Mature, Louis Calhern, O. E. Hasse, Wilfred Hyde White, Ian Carmichael, Nora Swinburne. *Review: Time:* "At 53, Gable (who was recently called by one half-crushed actress 'the Pudge Heffelfinger of osculation') still has the he-manliest hug in the business." *108 minutes.*

SOLDIER OF FORTUNE
(Twentieth Century–Fox, 1955)

Producer: Buddy Adler. *Director:* Edward Dmytryk. *Screenplay:* Ernest K. Gann, based on his novel of the same title. *Photographer:* Leo Tover. *Film Editor:* Dorothy Spencer. *Cast:* Clark Gable, Susan Hayward, Michael Rennie, Gene Barry, Alex D'Arcy, Tom Tully, Anna Sten. *Review: Hollywood Reporter:* "Miss Hayward, sultry and reluctantly fascinating, is far better than she has been in most of her recent pictures and seems potentially to be a perfect running mate for the dynamic and ruggedly handsome Gable." *96 minutes.*

THE TALL MEN
(Twentieth Century–Fox, 1955)

Producers: William A. Bacher and William B. Hawks. *Director:* Raoul Walsh. *Screenplay:* Sydney Boehm and Frank Nugent, based on the novel by Clay Fisher. *Photography:* Leo Tover. *Film Editor:* Louis Loeffler. *Cast:* Clark Gable, Jane Russell, Robert Ryan, Cameron Mitchell, Juan Garcia, Harry Shannon. *Reviews: Variety:* "The earthiness of Miss Russell's character and the masculine virility of Gable's makes for plenty of sizzle in their love scenes together. Gable can count this among one of his best in a long time." *Time:* "Come Sioux or stampede, jawhawker or dust devil, nothing bothers Clark—except, of course, the fact that he has to act. But like most of his parts, this one requires nothing much but his anxious little smirk." *122 minutes.*

THE KING AND FOUR QUEENS
(United Artists, 1956)

A *Russ-Field-Gabco Production. Producer:* David Hempstead. *Director:* Raoul Walsh. *Screenplay:* Margaret Fitts and Richard A. Simmons, from an original screen story by Margaret Fitts. *Photography:* Lucien Ballard. *Film Editor:* David Brotherton. *Cast:* Clark Gable, Eleanor Parker, Jo Van Fleet, Jean Willes, Barbara Nichols, Sara Shane. *Reviews: Film Daily:* "Clark Gable shows again why he is now and apparently ever shall be one of the screen's few great personalities. It is his best role in some time." *Hollywood Reporter:* "Gable is at his most romantic and dashing." *New York Times:* "Clark Gable may still be regarded as the 'King' of Hollywood, but he won't be for long if he continues to appear in pictures such as *The King and Four Queens.* It certainly represents a dreary comedown for Hollywood royalty." *86 minutes.*

BAND OF ANGELS
(Warner Brothers, 1957)

Director: Raoul Walsh. *Screenplay:* John Twist, Ivan Goff, and Ben Roberts, based on the novel by Robert Penn Warren. *Photography:* Lucien Ballard. *Film Editor:* Folmar Blangsted. *Cast:* Clark Gable, Yvonne de Carlo, Sidney Poitier, Efrem Zimbalist, Jr., Patric Knowles, Rex Reason. *Reviews: Variety:* "Gable's characterization is reminiscent of his Rhett Butler in *Gone With the Wind,* although there is no paralleling of plot. It is too bad, however, that Gable is allowed to look so unusually and unfairly worn. It makes his romance with Miss de Carlo, convincingly presented as a young woman in her early twenties, seem somewhat incredible." *New Yorker:* "Mr. Gable's dimples look tired." *Newsweek:* "Here is a movie so bad that it must be seen to be disbelieved. Performances, including Gable's, make summer TV seem as dramatically powerful as the Old Vic." *127 minutes.*

RUN SILENT, RUN DEEP
(United Artists, 1958)

Producer: Harold Hecht. *Directors:* Robert Wise and Edward L. Beach. *Screenplay:* John Gay. *Photography:* Russ Harlen. *Cast:* Clark Gable, Burt Lancaster, Jack Warden, Brad Dexter, Nick Cravat. *Reviews: Life:* "The film is good Gable." *New York Times:* "Superior acting on the part of Mr. Gable." *93 minutes.*

TEACHER'S PET
(Paramount, 1958)

Producer: William Perlberg. *Director:* George Seaton. *Screenplay:* Fay and Michael Kanin. *Photography:* Haskell Boggs. *Film Editor:* Alma Macrorie. *Cast:* Clark Gable, Doris Day, Gig Young, Mamie Van Doren, Nick Adams. *Reviews: Saturday Review:* "Miss Day looks too businesslike, and Mr. Gable looks and sounds a little too much like President Eisenhower." *Films in Review:* "Clark Gable is feeling and showing his age. The masculine self-confidence he has projected for 30 years has gone. Gable himself seems to know it has gone, but he resorts to this film. And film historians can perceive the beginning of the end of Gable's great career." *120 minutes.*

BUT NOT FOR ME
(Paramount, 1959)

Producers: William Perlberg and George Seaton. *Director:* Walter Lang. *Screenplay:* John Michael Hayes, based on the play *Accent on Youth* by Samuel Raphaelson. *Photography:* Robert Burks. *Film Editor:* Alma Macrorie. *Cast:* Clark Gable, Carroll Baker, Lilli Palmer, Lee J. Cobb, Barry Coe, Wendell Holmes. *Reviews: New York Times:* "The quaint but refreshing thing about Clark Gable is that he is willing to act his age. What's more, he's willing to make jokes about it and let his script writers make jokes about it, too." *Life:* "For more than a quarter of a century Clark Gable's persuasive charm has drawn movie-lovers by the millions. Radiating good-humored masculine appeal, he had something for everybody. For ladies he was the great lover; for men he was the hard-fighting man's man; for both he was the fun-loving comedian. Now he proves despite his 57 years, he is still the indestructible all-around charmer." *Time:* ". . . then too there is Clark Gable. No director has ever asked 'The King' to act, but his presence alone gives any film the atmosphere of Hollywood's glorious pre-Method past. Gable's voice may croak a little, but he still has the confidence of a man who knows that so long as he goes on playing the King, no one will dare play the Ace." *105 minutes.*

IT STARTED IN NAPLES
(Paramount, 1960)

Producer: Jack Rose. *Director:* Melville Shavelson. *Screenplay:* Melville Shavelson, Jack Rose, and Suso Cecchi d'Amico, based on the story by Michael Pertwee and Jack Davies. *Photographer:* Robert Surtees. *Cast:* Clark Gable, Sophia Loren, Vittorio De Sica, Marietto, Paolo Carlini. *Reviews: New York Times:* "Clark Gable, who isn't precisely an inconspicuous sort, lets himself be exposed throughout the picture as a sort of sourpuss in the shadow of the girl (Loren). He glowers, Gable-wise, and makes crude noises, betokening the superior male." *Variety:* "Gable and Loren are a surprisingly effective and compatible pair." *New Yorker:* "The picture gains an adventitious interest from the fact that Clark Gable often sounds exactly like President Eisenhower." *100 minutes.*

THE MISFITS
(United Artists, 1961)

Producer: Frank E. Taylor. *Director:* John Huston. *Original screenplay:* Arthur Miller. *Photography:* Russell Metty. *Film Editor:* George Tomasini. *Cast:* Clark Gable, Marilyn Monroe, Montgomery Clift, Thelma Ritter, Eli Wallach, James Barton, Estelle Winwood, Kevin McCarthy. *Reviews: New York Daily News:* "Gable has never done anything better on the screen, nor has Miss Monroe. Gable's acting is vibrant and lusty, hers true to the character as written by Miller. The screen vibrates with emotion during the latter part of the film as Marilyn and Gable engage in one of those battles of the sexes that seem eternal in their constant eruption. It is the poignant conflict between a man and a woman in love with each other trying to maintain individual characteristics and preserve a fundamental way of life." *Saturday Review:* "Gable finally became the actor he might have been all along, if a part had come along to test him to this degree." *Films in Review:* "Gable's role is so illy-conceived and written, he could do little more than smile his way through it." *New York Herald Tribune:* "Gable's performance is little less than great." *124 minutes.*

INDEX

But Not for Me, 261, 295
Butterfield Eight, 171

Café de Paris, 122
Cain and Mabel, 124, 286
Callaway Went Thataway, 292
Call of the Wild, 19, 110, 112–13, 115, 116, 285
Capra, Frank, 105, 108, 125, 185
best director Oscar (1935), 111
Carpentier, Harlean (Jean Harlow), 22, 93
Carroll, Nancy, 51
Cassini, Oleg, 220, 239, 242
Casting Couch, The, 116
Cat on a Hot Tin Roof, 171
Chained, 109, 284
Chaney, Lon, 112
Chaplin, Charlie, 88, 149, 153, 158, 196
Chauchoin, Lily (Claudette Colbert), 22
Chevalier, Maurice, 121
Chicago, 51
Childhood, Gable's, 23–25
China Seas, 114, 285
Chisholm, Betty, 195, 196, 203, 221, 240, 241, 247, 249
Christian, Linda, 196
Cleopatra, 110
Clift, Montgomery, 265, 267, 268, 269, 273, 276
Cobb, Irwin S., 111
Cohan, George M., 57
Cohan, Sir Andrew, 233
Cohn, Harry, 104, 111
Colbert, Claudette, 16, 17, 22, 105
best actress nomination (1935), 110–11
Colby, Anita, 187, 190, 196, 199–200, 217, 247
Cole, Jack, 176
Collier, Constance, 58
Colmans, Ronald, 209
Columbia Pictures, 104–5, 108
Columbo, Russ, 129–30
Command Decision, 196, 291
Comrade X, 171, 289
Confidential magazine, 251
Connaught Hotel, 237
Conway, Jack, 174, 175
Cooper, Gary, 153, 154, 225, 226, 235, 261, 276
Copperhead, The, 50
Cornell, Katharine, 58
Country Girl, 242
Cowl, Jane, 46–47, 49, 155
Crawford, Joan, 17, 18–19, 21, 22, 64–65, 69–72, 77, 78–80, 81, 82, 91–93, 94, 97, 98, 99, 106, 108, 109, 116,

122, 123–24, 133–34, 137, 147–48, 153–56, 160, 166, 175, 181, 182, 183, 185, 186, 191, 200, 217, 218, 247, 257, 262, 271
divorce from Fairbanks, 101
divorce from Tone, 134
and Jean Harlow, 100–101
L. B. Mayer's attitude toward relationship with Gable, 81–87, 92
origin of name, 69
Oscar for Mildred Pierce, 188
pornographic movies of, 116
and Spencer Tracy, 18
Crosby, Bing, 127, 188, 242
Crowther, Bosley, 112
Cukor, George, 20, 156, 158–60, 163, 168, 261

Dadolle, Suzanne, 219–20, 221, 222, 237, 238
Dance, Fools, Dance, 70, 71, 279
Dancing Lady, 101, 102, 104, 283
Danielovitch, Issur (Kirk Douglas), 22
Daughter, rumor of Gable's with Loretta Young, 19, 114
Davies, Marion, 16, 77, 87–89, 91, 97, 106, 123, 124, 277
Davis, Bette, 153
Davis, Luther, 193
Day, Doris, 22, 259, 263
Dean, James, 276
Death, circumstances of Gable's, 273–74
aftermath of, 275–78
burial, 274
de Carlo, Yvonne, 203, 258
Dees, Mary, 139
de Havilland, Olivia, 197
Del Monte Lodge, 259
De Mille, Cecil B., 135
Depression, Great, 16, 73, 187
and It Happened One Night, 108
and movies, 74
"Detectives, The," 262
Dial M for Murder, 239
Diamondhead, 272, 273
Dietrich, Marlene, 99
Dillon, Josephine, 33–52, 53, 58–59, 63, 64, 75–76, 78, 96–97, 106, 187, 251
alimony, attempted blackmail for, 76
divorce from, 57–58
marriage to, reasons for, 43, 44
"open letters" to Gable by, 102–4
separation from, 53–54
Dishonored Lady, 58
Dominguin, Luis Miguel, 241
Donat, Robert, 170